"When Neil Johnson says this book is for teachers on the go, he means it."
Richard Paul Evans, *#1 New York Times* bestselling author

Language Arts
Mini Lessons
for Teachers *on the Go!*
Over 300 Mini Lessons
Color Version

NEIL K. JOHNSON

Language Arts Mini Lessons
for Teachers on the Go!
Color Version
Over 300 Mini Lessons
Neil K. Johnson Copyright 2023
All Rights Reserved.

Teachers may copy material for their own students. Otherwise, information may not be reproduced, copied, cited, or circulated in any printed or electronic form without written permission from Book-Wise Publishing and the author. This book is based on the knowledge, ideas, personal research, and experience of the author.

Editing and Producing: K Christoffersen
Cover and Interior Design: Fran Platt and K Christoffersen

BookWise Publishing, Riverton, Utah
bookwisepublishing.com

ISBN: 978-1-60645-266-0 eBook
ISBN: 978-1-60645-265-3 Paperback
ISBN: 978-1-60645-267-7 Paperback Color Version

Library of Congress Number 2021909248

LanguageArtsMiniLessons.com

Language Arts Mini Lessons for Teachers on the Go!
Nonfiction

6/20//2023

For Educators: How to Use This Book

Each lesson and skill is designed and taught independently from the others. Use this book in a variety of ways—whether as self-directed student work or through direct instruction. Regularly review essential language arts skills *with* your pupils, and you will build stronger, more enthusiastic language arts students.

Lessons are divided into sections. Use them as a teacher's guide or student worksheet.

Choose to use the book using one of the following methods:

As a teacher's guide for direct instruction, spend a few minutes explicitly teaching the single skill outlined in the Mini Lesson. Use the Check Understanding or Student Activity to engage in metacognition through repetition.

At the beginning or end of class, write the questions on the board, then work through the Mini Lesson as a class.

Make a copy of the Mini Lesson for the class and use it as a warm-up and follow up with a class discussion or class review.

Utilize *your* method of using this book. I encourage you to get creative!

THIS TEXT IS NOT MEANT TO REPLACE YOUR INSTRUCTION—IT IS MEANT TO ENHANCE IT!

Thank you for choosing *Language Arts Mini Lessons for Teachers on the Go!*

Neil K. Johnson

About the Author

Neil K. Johnson taught school for 44 years—first drama, and then English—and he loves kids. He was able to teach over 7,000 students, and he awoke almost every morning excited to work with them. Many of them won awards for their writing and drama. He was chosen as the 2010 Utah English Teacher of the Year, and he was president of the Utah Council of Teachers of English. He was also president of two state drama and speech teacher associations.

Neil received his bachelor's degree from Brigham Young University and his master's degree from the University of Wisconsin at Superior. He also did doctoral work at the University of Utah and the University of Northern Colorado.

In 1989 Neil wrote The Drama Sourcebook, and it was purchased by one-third of the high schools in America. He also compiled and published three books containing 30 plays from various authors. This current book, Language Arts Mini Lessons, contains over 300 Mini Lessons and is mostly based on the knowledge and experience Neil gained from his many years in the classroom.

Neil and his current wife Sharee both lost their first spouses to cancer. They married and blended their families, resulting in a wonderfully large and fulfilling posterity.

Acknowledgments

You. This book is dedicated to *you*, the teachers and homeschool parents who teach our children language arts. How do you write a book about language arts for language arts experts? It's very intimidating.

Teachers and Students. This book is especially dedicated to the many wonderful teachers with whom I've worked or from whom I've received ideas and the approximately 7,000 students I've taught and learned from during my 44 years of teaching. I wish I could give credit to all whose ideas helped my students and me.

Outstanding Presenters. Among others, here are some of the many dedicated teachers who imparted their knowledge to me: Vicki Spandel, Lois Lowry, Kelly Downs, and Tina Howard. Last and certainly not least is my ninth-grade English teacher, Juanita Rogers, who helped me to learn grammar structure, which eventually opened the gates to many kinds of writing.

Editing and Production. Karen K. Christoffersen, BookWise Publishing, for her expertise in editing and production, as well as her countless hours and patience. She went far beyond her necessary duties as editor, also Kris Anne Gottfredson, Bryan Ellingford, Nik Rice, Mo Tanner, and Robin Rhoton for their editing and proofreading.

Design and Layout: Fran Platt of Eden Design.

Assistant Editor: Joshua Brothers used his vast knowledge and skills in language arts to make the lessons more substantive and applicable.

Cover and interior design elements. Fran Platt, Eden Design and Karen K. Christoffersen who used their talents well in designing this book.

Advisor. Brad Gurney for his expertise, vision, and insights.

I would also like to thank the following people for their hard work on this book: Sharee Johnson, my wife, for her patience and counseling, and Kelly Johnson and Greg Johnson for their help in marketing.

Each of these people added immensely to the quality of the book.

Gratefully,

Neil K. Johnson

Table of Contents

For Educators: *How to Use This Book* iii
About the *Author* iv
Acknowledgments v
Chapter One: *Study Skills* 1
    Mini Lesson *1: Note-Taking* 2
    Mini Lesson *2: Verbal and Non-Verbal Signs* 3
    Mini Lesson *3: Textbooks and Other Study Material* 4
    Mini Lesson *4: Test-Taking* 5
    Mini Lesson *5: Lowering Test Anxiety* 6
    Mini Lesson *6: Library Reference Skills* 7
    Mini Lesson *7: Reference Materials* 8
    Mini Lesson *8: Media* 9
    Mini Lesson *9: Media Reference Skills* 10
    Mini Lesson *10: Summary of Reference Skills* 11
Chapter Two: *Speed Reading* 12
    Mini Lesson *11: Speed Reading* 13
    Mini Lesson *12: Speed Reading Skills* 14
    Mini Lesson *13: Practice Speed Reading* 15
    Mini Lesson *14: Speed Reading Drills Part 1* 16
    Mini Lesson *15: Speed Reading Drills Part 2* 17
    Mini Lesson *16: Speed Read an Entire Passage* 18
    Mini Lesson *17: Pushing the Limits Speed Reading* 20
    Mini Lesson *18: Pacing* 21
    Mini Lesson *19: Chunking* 22
    Mini Lesson *20: Conquering Sub-Vocalization* 23
Chapter Three: *Writing Process / Pre-Writing* 24
    Mini Lesson *21: Writing Process / Pre-Writing* 25
    Mini Lesson *22: Interesting Your Readers* 26
    Mini Lesson *23: Brainstorming for Nonfiction Sources* 27
    Mini Lesson *24: Brainstorming for Narrative Sources* 28
    Mini Lesson *25: Nonfiction or Expository Outline* 29
    Mini Lesson *26: Narrative Outline* 30
    Mini Lesson *27: Narrative Outline / Characters and Setting* 32
    Mini Lesson *28: Narrative Outline / Plot* 33
    Mini Lesson *29: Creating a Web* 34
    Mini Lesson *30: Drafting / Stream-of-Consciousness* 35
    Mini Lesson *31: Point of View / Person* 36
    Mini Lesson *32: Preparing to Draft Your Narrative* 37
    Mini Lesson *33: Draft Your Narrative* 38

Mini Lesson *34: Revise a Draft* *39*
Mini Lesson *35: Revise Your Own Writing* *41*
Mini Lesson *36: Do Not Edit Yet*... *42*
Mini Lesson *37: Revise, But Don't Edit* *43*
Mini Lesson *38: Prepare to Edit* *45*
Mini Lesson *39: Edit* *46*
Mini Lesson *40: Proofreading* *47*
Mini Lesson *41: What Proofreaders Do*... *48*
Mini Lesson *42: Proofreading Symbols* *50*
Mini Lesson *43: Analyzing Your Proofreading* *51*
Mini Lesson *44: Practice!* *52*

Chapter Four: *Six Traits of Writing*.. *53*
    Mini Lesson *45: Six Traits of Writing* *54*
    Mini Lesson *46: Trait 1 Idea Development* *55*
    Mini Lesson *47: Choose an Idea to Develop* *56*
    Mini Lesson *48: Creating Ideas for Narrative Writing* *57*
    Mini Lesson *49: Improving Idea Development* *58*
    Mini Lesson *50: Trait 2 Organization / Expository Writing*.. *59*
    Mini Lesson *51: Trait 2 Organization / Narrative Writing* *60*
    Mini Lesson *52: Improve Organization* *61*
    Mini Lesson *53: Write and Compare* *62*
    Mini Lesson *54: Rough Outline* *63*
    Mini Lesson *55: Trait 3 Voice and Enthusiasm*.. *64*
    Mini Lesson *56: Trait 3 Voice / Improvement Suggestions* *65*
    Mini Lesson *57: Voice in Expository Writing*.. *66*
    Mini Lesson *58: Voice in Argumentative Writing* *67*
    Mini Lesson *59: Voice in Narrative Writing* *68*
    Mini Lesson *60: Voice in a Story*.. *69*
    Mini Lesson *61: Write a Description* *72*
    Mini Lesson *62: Write a Short Fairy Tale* *73*
    Mini Lesson *63: Word Choice Using Accurate and Vivid Words*... *74*
    Mini Lesson *64: Show, Don't Tell* *76*
    Mini Lesson *65: Improve Voice and Imagery* *77*
    Mini Lesson *66: Expository and Argumentative Word Choice* *78*
    Mini Lesson *67: Narrative Word Choice* *79*
    Mini Lesson *68: Trait 5 Sentence Fluency* *80*
    Mini Lesson *69: Improve Sentence Fluency* *81*
    Mini Lesson *70: Sentence Length* *82*
    Mini Lesson *71: Trait 6 Writing Conventions* *83*

Chapter Five: *Modes and Genres*.. *84*
    Mini Lesson *72: Modes and Genres*... *86*
    Mini Lesson *73: Experience with Modes and Genres* *87*
    Mini Lesson *74: The Descriptive Mode* *88*
    Mini Lesson *75: The Importance of Description*... *89*
    Mini Lesson *76: Creating Description*... *90*
    Mini Lesson *77: Prose* *91*
    Mini Lesson *78: Imagery in Poetry* *92*
    Mini Lesson *79: Describing / Images* *95*
    Mini Lesson *80: Create a Free Verse Poem* *96*

Mini Lesson 81: *Expository Mode* 97
Mini Lesson 82: *Expository / Functional Genre* 99
Mini Lesson 83: *Expository / Informational Genres* 100
Mini Lesson 84: *Argumentative Mode* 101
Mini Lesson 85: *Argumentative Mode Genres* 102
Mini Lesson 86: *Essay Outline* 103
Mini Lesson 87: *Three Parts of an Essay* 104
Mini Lesson 88: *Create an Essay Draft* 105
Mini Lesson 89: *See All Sides of an Issue* 106
Mini Lesson 90: *Narrative Mode* 107
Mini Lesson 91: *Genres in the Narrative Mode* 108
Mini Lesson 92: *Drama* 109
Mini Lesson 93: *Fantasy* 110
Mini Lesson 94: *Folklore* 111
Mini Lesson 95: *Horror* 112
Mini Lesson 96: *Mystery* 113
Mini Lesson 97: *Personal Narrative* 114
Mini Lesson 98: *Poetry* 115
Mini Lesson 99: *Poetry Terms* 117
Mini Lesson 100: *Science Fiction* 118
Mini Lesson 101: *Young Adult Literature* 119
Mini Lesson 102: *Reviewing Narrative Writing Genres* 120
Mini Lesson 103: *Business Mode* 121
Mini Lesson 104: *Block Business Letter Format* 122
Mini Lesson 105: *Business Email Format* 124
Mini Lesson 106: *Friendly Letter Format* 125
Chapter Six: *Contest Writing* 126
Mini Lesson 107: *Why Enter a Contest?* 128
Mini Lesson 108: *Writing Process for a Contest* 129
Mini Lesson 109: *Pre-Writing Introduction* 131
Mini Lesson 110: *Three Main Categories of Contests* 132
Mini Lesson 111: *Essay Outline* 133
Mini Lesson 112: *Trait 1 Ideas* 135
Mini Lesson 113: *Trait 2–Organization / Outline* 136
Mini Lesson 114: *Trait 2 Organization / Plot* 139
Mini Lesson 115: *Poetry Organization* 143
Mini Lesson 116: *Rough Draft* 145
Mini Lesson 117: *Stream-of-Consciousness Writing* 146
Mini Lesson 118: *Rough Draft Review* 147
Mini Lesson 119: *Trait 3 Voice* 148
Mini Lesson 120: *Revising Overall Content* 151
Mini Lesson 121: *Trait 4 Word Choice* 154
Mini Lesson 122: *Editing Paragraphs and Sentences* 156
Mini Lesson 123: *Editing Usage and Punctuation* 158
Mini Lesson 124: *Editing Spelling and Capitalization* 159
Mini Lesson 125: *Editing Rhyme and Rhythm* 160
Mini Lesson 126: *Proofreading* 161
Mini Lesson 127: *Proofreading Each Other's Papers* 162

Mini Lesson *128: Proofreading Ideas and Organization* 163
Mini Lesson *129: Proofreading–Voice and Word Choice* 164
Mini Lesson *130: Proofreading Paragraphs and Sentences* 166
Mini Lesson *131: Proofreading Usage and Punctuation* 167
Mini Lesson *132: Proofreading Spelling and Capitalization* 168
Mini Lesson *133: Trait 5 Sentence Fluency* 169
Mini Lesson *134: Proofreading Rhyme and Rhythm* 171
Mini Lesson *135: Word Choice in Poetry* 172
Mini Lesson *136 Some of the Best Writing Contests* 173

Chapter Seven: *From Phrases to Paragraphs* 174
Mini Lesson *137: Sentences and the Sentence Backbone* 176
Mini Lesson *138: Practice Using the Sentence Backbone* 179
Mini Lesson *139: Phrases and Clauses* 180
Mini Lesson *140: Prepositional Phrases* 181
Mini Lesson *141: Identifying Prepositional Phrases* 183
Mini Lesson *142: Creating Prepositional Phrases* 184
Mini Lesson *143: Prepositional Phrases* 185
Mini Lesson *144: Verbal Phrases* 186
Mini Lesson *145: Understanding Clauses* 188
Mini Lesson *146: Dependent Clauses with Commas* 190
Mini Lesson *147: FANBOYS Conjunctions* 191
Mini Lesson *148: Types of Complements* 192
Mini Lesson *149: Reviewing Sentence Parts* 194
Mini Lesson *150: Practice Sentence Parts* 196
Mini Lesson *151: Sentences with Errors* 197
Mini Lesson *152: Sentence Fragments* 198
Mini Lesson *153: Run-On Sentences* 199
Mini Lesson *154: Types of Sentences* 200
Mini Lesson *155: Complex Sentences* 201
Mini Lesson *156: Compound Sentences* 202
Mini Lesson *157: Sentence Combining* 203
Mini Lesson *158: Review Different Sentence Types* 204
Mini Lesson *159: Subject/Verb Agreement* 206
Mini Lesson *160: Paragraphs* 208
Mini Lesson *161: Topic Sentences in Paragraphs* 209
Mini Lesson *162: Practice Paragraphs* 210
Mini Lesson *163: Supporting Sentences in Paragraphs* 211
Mini Lesson *164: Paragraph Principles* 212
Mini Lesson *165: Sentences in Paragraphs* 213
Mini Lesson *166: Summary Review for Paragraphs* 214
Mini Lesson *167: Dialogue Paragraphs* 216
Mini Lesson *168: Punctuation in Dialogue Paragraphs* 217
Mini Lesson *169: Focus on Layout* 219
Mini Lesson *170: Improve Your Writing and Layout* 220

Chapter Eight: *Parts of Speech* 221
Mini Lesson *171: Identifying Parts of Speech* 222
Mini Lesson *172: Using Parts of Speech in Sentences* 223
Mini Lesson *173: Nouns* 224
Mini Lesson *174: Pronouns* 226

Mini Lesson *175: Pronoun Contractions* 228
Mini Lesson *176: Indefinite Pronouns* 229
Mini Lesson *177: Plural Indefinite Pronouns* 230
Mini Lesson *178: Vague Indefinite Pronouns* 231
Mini Lesson *179: Proper Adjectives* 232
Mini Lesson *180: Verbs and Auxiliary Verbs* 233
Mini Lesson *181: Verb Tenses* 235
Mini Lesson *182: Adverbs* 237
Mini Lesson *183: Adverbs and Adverb Contractions* 238
Mini Lesson *184: Conjunctive Adverbs* 240
Mini Lesson *185: Adjectives and Adverbs* 241
Mini Lesson *186: Synonyms and Substitutes for Said* 242
Mini Lesson *187: Prepositions* 243
Mini Lesson *188: Preposition or Adverb* 245
Mini Lesson *189: Coordinating and Correlative Conjunctions* 246
Mini Lesson *190: Interjections* 248
Mini Lesson *191: Identifying the Parts of Speech* 249
Mini Lesson *192: Review the Parts of Speech* 250
Mini Lesson *193: Review Pronouns, Nouns, Adjectives, Interjections* 251
Mini Lesson *194: Review Verbs, Adverbs, Prepositions, Conjunctions* 252

Chapter Nine: *Writing Mechanics* 253
Mini Lesson *195: Capitalization* 254
Mini Lesson *196: Capitalizing Titles* 255
Mini Lesson *197: Do Not Capitalize* 256
Mini Lesson *198: Practice Capitalization* 257
Mini Lesson *199: Punctuation Introduction* 258
Mini Lesson *200: Commas* 259
Mini Lesson *201: Practice with Commas* 261
Mini Lesson *202: Comma Splices* 262
Mini Lesson *203: Semicolons* 264
Mini Lesson *204: Colons* 266
Mini Lesson *205: End Marks* 267
Mini Lesson *206: Apostrophes–Singular, Plural, or Possessive* 268
Mini Lesson *207: Apostrophes/Contractions vs Possessive Pronouns* 270
Mini Lesson *208: Dashes, Commas, and Parentheses* 271
Mini Lesson *209: Hyphens* 272
Mini Lesson *210: Quotation Marks in Dialogue* 273
Mini Lesson *211: Quotation Marks / Underlining / Italics* 274
Mini Lesson *212: Commas and Periods Review* 275
Mini Lesson *213: Punctuation Review* 276
Mini Lesson *214: Making Errors on Purpose* 277

Chapter Ten: *Literary Elements* 278
Mini Lesson *215: Characterization* 279
Mini Lesson *216: Conflict* 280
Mini Lesson *217: Plot Exposition* 281
Mini Lesson *218: Plot Rising Action* 282
Mini Lesson *219: Plot Crises* 283
Mini Lesson *220: Plot Climax and Resolution* 284
Mini Lesson *221: Dialogue and Point of View* 285

Mini Lesson *222: Setting and Imagery* 287
Mini Lesson *223: Finding Story Elements* 288

Chapter Eleven: *PAIR and KWL Compared* 293
    Mini Lesson *224: Compare PAIR with KWL* 294
    Mini Lesson *225: PAIR Prior Understanding / General Comprehension* 295
    Mini Lesson *226: PAIR Anticipating / General Comprehension* 296
    Mini Lesson *227: Inputting / General Comprehension* 298
    Mini Lesson *228: Relating / General Comprehension* 299
    Mini Lesson *229: Prior Understanding in Expository Text* 300
    Mini Lesson *230: Anticipating in Expository Text* 302
    Mini Lesson *231: Inputting in Expository Text* 303
    Mini Lesson *232: Relating in Expository Text* 304
    Mini Lesson *233: Prior Understanding in Argumentative Text* 305
    Mini Lesson *234: Anticipating in Argumentative Text* 307
    Mini Lesson *235: Inputting in Argumentative Text* 308
    Mini Lesson *236: Relating in Argumentative Text* 309
    Mini Lesson *237: Prior Understanding in Narrative Text* 310
    Mini Lesson *238: Anticipating in Narrative Text* 312
    Mini Lesson *239: Inputting in Narrative Text* 313
    Mini Lesson *240: Relating in Narrative Text* 315
    Mini Lesson *241: Comprehension Application* 316
    Mini Lesson *242: Text Organization Patterns* 319

Chapter Twelve: *Expanding Your Vocabulary* 320
    Mini Lesson *243: Introduction to Spelling* 321
    Mini Lesson *244: Spelling Rules and Patterns* 322
    Mini Lesson *245: Misspelled Words Due to Schwa* 323
    Mini Lesson *246: Identify the Schwa (ise/ize) Sound* 324
    Mini Lesson *247: Spelling Review* 325
    Mini Lesson *248: Spelling Rules Review* 326
    Mini Lesson *249: Reading Vocabulary / Context* 328
    Mini Lesson *250: Using Context Clues* 329
    Mini Lesson *251: Prefixes* 330
    Mini Lesson *252: Prefixes and Suffixes* 331
    Mini Lesson *253: Suffixes* 332
    Mini Lesson *254: Word Relationships* 334

Chapter Thirteen: *MLA Research Citations* 335
    Mini Lesson *255: MLA* 336
    Mini Lesson *256: Why You Should Use Citations–MLA* 337
    Mini Lesson *257: Works Cited–MLA* 339
    Mini Lesson *258: Documentation for Works Cited–MLA* 341
    Mini Lesson *259: Plagiarism–MLA* 342
    Mini Lesson *260: Quotes–MLA* 343
    Mini Lesson *261: Ellipses–MLA* 344
    Mini Lesson *262: Citing Common Electronic Sources–MLA* 345
    Mini Lesson *263: End-of-Paper Citations–MLA* 346

Chapter Fourteen: *APA Research Citations* 347
    Mini Lesson *264: Research and Citations–APA* 348
    Mini Lesson *265: Pre-Writing–APA* 349
    Mini Lesson *266: Elements Needed for a Title Page–APA* 350

Mini Lesson 267: Proper Format for a Manuscript–APA 351
Mini Lesson 268: Outline–APA 352
Mini Lesson 269: Case Rules in Titles–APA 353
Mini Lesson 270: Author / Date Citations–APA 354
Mini Lesson 271: Direct Short and Block Quotations–APA 355
Mini Lesson 272: Reference List Entries–APA 357
Mini Lesson 273: Reference Author Elements–APA 358
Mini Lesson 274: Reference, Date, Title, and Source–APA 359
Mini Lesson 275: Ellipses–APA 360

Chapter Fifteen: *SAT and ACT Tips* 361
Mini Lesson 276: SAT/ACT 362
Mini Lesson 277: Types of Reading Questions SAT/ACT 363
Mini Lesson 278: Types of Writing Questions SAT/ACT 364
Mini Lesson 279: Theme, Conventions, Audience, Organization 365
Mini Lesson 280: Guess Questions to Pass the SAT/ACT 366
Mini Lesson 281: Review Writing Materials to Pass SAT/ACT 368
Mini Lesson 282: SAT and ACT Essay Writing 369
Mini Lesson 283: Pre-Writing Your Essay 371
Mini Lesson 284: Write Your Rough Draft 373
Mini Lesson 285: Revise Using the Writer's Checklist 374

Chapter Sixteen: *Speaking and Listening* 375
Mini Lesson 286: Speaking Principles 376
Mini Lesson 287: Facial Expressions, Gestures, and Posture 377
Mini Lesson 288: Speaking and Presenting Techniques 378
Mini Lesson 289: Vocal Techniques 379
Mini Lesson 290: Vocal Techniques with the Alphabet 380
Mini Lesson 291: Pause for Effect 382
Mini Lesson 292: Pausing and Eye Contact 383
Mini Lesson 293: Physical Characteristics 384
Mini Lesson 294: Voice and Physical Characteristics 385
Mini Lesson 295: Mood 386
Mini Lesson 296: Poise 387
Mini Lesson 297: Involvement and Energy 388
Mini Lesson 298: Imagery 389
Mini Lesson 299: Presenting Literature Aloud 390
Mini Lesson 300: Practice Voice and Character Placement 391
Mini Lesson 301: Vary Posture, Character Placement, and Gestures 392
Mini Lesson 302: PAIR Listening–Prior Understanding 393
Mini Lesson 303: PAIR Listening–Anticipating 394
Mini Lesson 304: PAIR Listening–Inputting 396
Mini Lesson 305: PAIR Listening–Relating 397

Chapter Seventeen: *Citizenship* 398
Mini Lesson 306: Citizenship and Behavior 399
Mini Lesson 307: The Golden Rule 400
Mini Lesson 308: The Three R's 401
Mini Lesson 309: Combine the Golden Rule and Three R's 402
Mini Lesson 310: Participating in Groups 403
Mini Lesson 311: Outline a Fictitious Situation 404

Appendix 405
Works Cited 420

Chapter One: Study Skills

Why is this chapter important for you? Just as learning to defend, rebound, dribble, and shoot help a basketball player, study skills help students to play the game of academics! Strong fundamental study skills will help you succeed in language arts and other academic subjects.

The Lessons

Chapter One: Study Skills 1
    Mini Lesson 1: Note-Taking 2
    Mini Lesson 2: Verbal and Non-Verbal Signs 3
    Mini Lesson 3: Textbooks and Other Study Material 4
    Mini Lesson 4: Test-Taking 5
    Mini Lesson 5: Lowering Test Anxiety 6
    Mini Lesson 6: Library Reference Skills 7
    Mini Lesson 7: Reference Materials 8
    Mini Lesson 8: Media 9
    Mini Lesson 9: Media Reference Skills 10
    Mini Lesson 10: Summary of Reference Skills 11

NAME _____   Language Arts Mini Lessons

Mini Lesson 1: Note-Taking

How can learning this help you? Note-taking enables the student to identify, organize, comprehend, and remember the material, which allows future references to remind them of what they have *already* studied.

NOTE-TAKING HELPS IN THREE WAYS

Actively listen and keep on-task.

Remember information needed for the future.

Transfer information from short-term memory to long-term memory and have the ability to access much more of the information later.

NOTE-TAKING IS EASY

Write the most important things. *Connect* it to your understanding.

Write legibly to be able to read it later.

Abbreviate common words and phrases. Make sure you are able to understand them.

Examples: write is *wr*, reading is *rdg*.

Follow what the teacher emphasizes to catch important information.

Connect your notes to your own life.

ML 1 Check Understanding: Note-Taking

What are the three benefits of taking notes?

1. _____

2. _____

3. _____

4. How do you connect the notes to your own life. _____
_____

5. Why is it important to write legibly? _____

Mini Lesson 2: Verbal and Non-Verbal Signs

How can learning this help you? Verbal and non-verbal signs are helpful as they indicate when the teacher wants something written down.

VERBAL SIGNS FROM THE TEACHER TO WRITE THIS DOWN

The teacher repeats something.

The teacher's voice gets louder or softer.

The teacher gives key hints.

> Example: "The important point here is . . ."
> Example: "As you read the chart on page . . ."
> Example: "This will be on your exam!"

NON-VERBAL SIGNS FROM THE TEACHER TO WRITE THIS DOWN

The teacher writes on the board.

The teacher points to something already written.

The teacher pauses.

The teacher paces around.

ML 2 Check Understanding: Verbal and Non-Verbal Signs

What are three verbal signs teachers give that suggest writing something down?

1. _____

2. _____

3. _____

What are two of the four non-verbal signals from a teacher to write something down?

4. _____

5. _____

Mini Lesson 3: Textbooks and Other Study Material

How can learning this help you? Find the most important information and how to connect it to your life and learning.

CONNECT WHAT YOU LEARN IN YOUR LIFE TO WHAT YOU ALREADY KNOW

Reading notes are invaluable. If allowed, mark up what you're studying. Underline and make notes in the margins or take reading notes.

PAIR Reading Comprehension Process (Prior Understanding, Anticipating, Inputting, Relating): The PAIR Reading Comprehension chapter provides forms (also in the Appendix) and is similar to KWL (what do you know, what do you want to know, what did you learn).

ML 3 Check Understanding: Textbooks and Other Study Material

Take reading notes of a chapter in a textbook from another class.

1. _____

2. _____

3. _____

4. _____

5. Compare your notes with those of a partner.

Mini Lesson 4: Test-Taking

How can learning this help you? Begin these methods now, and improve test scores by 10 to 20 percent.

TEST-TAKING SKILLS ARE CRITICAL

Study the material alone and/or with others.

Relax.

Breathe deeply a few times.

Write your first and last name on the test at the very beginning.

Don't spend too much time on any single question.

Don't rush through the test without reading each question completely.

Be aware of the time you have left for the test.

Guess if you don't know the answer; then move on to the next question.

Statistically, the letters B and C are more frequently the answer than A or D. If you are unsure of the answer, you have a better chance of getting the correct answer by guessing B or C.

Check your answers at the end.

ML 4 Check Understanding: Test-Taking

1. What should you do either alone or with others *before* the test?_____

2. What should you remind yourself to do, especially if you get nervous in a test?_____

3. What should you do at the very beginning of the test?_____

4. If you don't know the answer, should you guess?_____

5. In multiple choice questions, which two answer letters are used the most? A and D or B and C?
_____

Mini Lesson 5: Lowering Test Anxiety

How can learning this help you? Anxiety is one of the biggest problems in test-taking. Studying is the key to being prepared and lowering anxiety. Identify what you know and what you don't know. This kind of knowledge helps you focus your energy on the questions. There are a few other small tips to can follow that may lower any test anxiety before an exam.

BE EARLY, CHECK AND RE-CHECK YOUR ANSWERS, AND USE ALL OF YOUR ALLOTTED TIME

Come early to class on a test day.

Read the instructions carefully, and ask questions if anything is unclear.

When reviewing instructions, note if the exam is timed and how much time you are allotted.

Take a breath, and do not rush—use all of the time you are allotted.

Chewing gum helps some people relieve anxiety when testing.

Use scratch paper to note the questions you want to go back and check if you have time.

Answer all of the questions, even if you have to guess. Research has shown that if you have to guess, B and C are more often the correct answer than A and D.

If you finish early, go back and check your work.

ML 5 Check Understanding: Lowering Text Anxiety

Make a list of which of the test-taking principles you already do well.

1. _____
2. _____
3. _____
4. _____
5. _____

Make a list of which of the test-taking principles you need to improve.

6. _____
7. _____
8. _____
9. _____
10. _____

Mini Lesson 6: Library Reference Skills

How can learning this help you? Library reference skills help increase comprehension and in finding information and improving research; even something as simple as spelling a word correctly, or something more complex, such as finding a source for support.

LIBRARY SKILLS

Libraries include fiction, nonfiction, reference books, magazines, maps, and computers.

Fiction call numbers go by the first three letters of the author's last name.

Information call numbers are arranged with the Dewey Decimal System.

Call Numbers	Subjects	Focus
001-099	Generalities	Prequel to the Dewey Decimal System
100-199	Philosophy	Who am I?
200-299	Religion	Who made me?
300-399	Social Science	Who's the guy in the next cave?
400-499	Languages	How do I talk to that guy?
500-599	Natural Science	Let's talk about the world we see.
600-699	Applied Science	Now, let's make stuff out of what we see.
700-799	Arts and Recreation	Now, let's have some fun.
800-899	Literature	Let's tell our children how wonderful we are.
900-999	Geography and History	Let's tell our future children how wonderful we were.
92 and 920	Biography and Collective Biography	Let's find out about famous people.

LIBRARY DATABASE

Find the topic by looking up the subject, title, or author's last name.

In the reference lesson, the book number is preceded by REF.

ML 6 Check Understanding: Library Reference Skills

1. The name of the library sorting system is the _____ Decimal System.

2. Fiction call numbers are arranged according to the author's last _____.

3. In which group would you find Literature books? (circle) 200-99, 500-599, or 800-899?

4. In which group would you find reference books? (circle) 00-99, 300-399, or 400-499?

5. What three letters precede the reference book numbers? _____

Mini Lesson 7: Reference Materials

How can learning this help you? Reference materials provide a myriad of resources.

A PLETHORA OF REFERENCE MATERIALS IS AVAILABLE!

Encyclopedias: general information on a wide variety of subjects

Specialized encyclopedias: specific information about specific subjects

Atlases: book of maps

Almanacs and yearbooks: yearly, up-to-date information

Dictionaries: important information about individual words

> Each entry contains:
> Entry word and spelling
> Pronunciation
>
> Accent mark follows the emphasized syllable like *Kap'tan*
>
> Schwa sound: every vowel can easily make the schwa sound.
>
> Schwa sounds: *a* is awkwərd, *e* is helmət, *i* is edəble, *o* is lək, and *u* is pət
>
> A long vowel is pronounced as it is said in the alphabet: *tāpe, ēqual, rīce, rōse, Ūtah*

Part of Speech

Word origin or where the word comes from

Definition

ML 7 Check Understanding: Reference Materials

What are two things to learn about each word in a dictionary?

1. _____

2. _____

Write down which type of books the following definition describes:

3. Important information about individual words is called _____

4. General information on a wide variety of subjects is called _____

5. Books of maps are called _____

Mini Lesson 8: Media

How can learning this help you? Media provides many types of resources which may be informative, entertaining, and never-ending! Don't forget to Check content such as books, DVDs, and audiobooks. There are many digital materials, such as archived video footage on streaming sites such as YouTube, digital journal archives, blogs, live events by specialists, podcasts, and many other digital opportunities for your research.

THERE ARE TWO MAIN KINDS OF MEDIA: PRINTED AND ELECTRONIC

Printed sources are newspapers, magazines, and books.

Electronic sources are computers, TV, movies, radio, and today you can include hundreds of thousands of podcasts or other digital media via the Internet. With the explosion of electronic media, we have become a viewing/listening society more than a reading one. We must become critics of what we see and hear, as well as what we read. (Note the chart at the bottom of this page for some interesting sources online.)

EVALUATION OF MEDIA OR LITERATURE THAT WE READ OR VIEW

When evaluating information, the famous German writer and philosopher Goethe suggested we ask three questions:

What is the artist (writer) trying to do?

How well are they doing it?

Is it worth doing?

ML 8 Check Understanding: Media

What are the two main kinds of media?

1. _____

2. _____

What are the three questions Goethe suggests we ask about writers' works?

3. _____

4. _____

5. _____

Mini Lesson 9: Media Reference Skills

How can learning this help you? This is where you put new skills to work. One of the most wonderful experiences one can have is wandering through the "stacks" in the library, scanning the shelves for interesting titles, and finding books that are unexpected treasures. The library can be one of your greatest adventures.

WANDER THROUGH THE LIBRARY AND YOU WILL FIND "WONDERS"

ML 9 Check Understanding: Media Reference Skills

Write down your own personal needs to these questions.

1. What do you need to learn more about in dictionaries? _____

2. What do you need to learn more about in library skills? _____

3. What do you need to learn more about in reference materials? _____

4. Which of the media forms do you need to learn how to use better? _____

5. Use Goethe's evaluation method to evaluate a book or movie. Make your evaluation at least 50 words long.

_____

_____

_____

_____

_____

_____

NAME _____   Language Arts Mini Lessons

Mini Lesson 10: Summary of Reference Skills

How can learning this help you? Practice using all of the resources available to you. Some libraries have special sections that are "reserved" for unique/rare books, documents, etc. These are on reserve for special studies or may be very valuable and require supervision. This is an area you will want to know about and explore someday.

SPECIAL "RESERVED" SECTIONS OF THE LIBRARY

NAME	URL
All Sides/Wikipedia	allsides.com
Google Scholar	scholar.google.com
History	history.com
Internet Archive	archive.org
Internet Public Library	pl.org

ML 10 Check Understanding: Summary of Reference Skills

Work on this exercise with a partner.

1. Open a dictionary to a word. Write down its correct spelling, pronunciation, part of speech, origin, and definition.

_____

_____

2. Find and write down the call number of three fiction books by different authors.

_____

_____

3. Two fiction books

_____

_____

4-5. Find the same information about an example from each of the types of reference books listed in Mini Lesson 7. Use the table below.

Reference Book	Call Number	Title	Topic	Page
Encyclopedia				
Specialized Encyclopedia				
Atlas				
Almanac/Yearbook				
Dictionary				

Get into small groups and compare what you wrote.

Chapter Two: Speed Reading

Why is this chapter important for you? If you can master speed reading, you have the ability to input content in such a way that it is faster to read. *And* your comprehension will increase, and you will be able to accomplish much more. But practice is imperative for improvement.

The Lessons

Chapter Two: Speed Reading 12
    Mini Lesson 11: Speed Reading 13
    Mini Lesson 12: Speed Reading Skills 14
    Mini Lesson 13: Practice Speed Reading 15
    Mini Lesson 14: Speed Reading Drills Part 1 16
    Mini Lesson 15: Speed Reading Drills Part 2 17
    Mini Lesson 16: Speed Read an Entire Passage 18
    Mini Lesson 17: Pushing the Limits Speed Reading 20
    Mini Lesson 18: Pacing 21
    Mini Lesson 19: Chunking 22
    Mini Lesson 20: Conquering Sub-Vocalization 23

Mini Lesson 11: Speed Reading

How can learning this help you? What are some general suggestions for speed-reading? Imagine how wonderful it would be to read your assignments two, three, or sometimes even ten times faster than you do now and still comprehend what you're reading.

HAVE YOU EVER WANTED TO READ MORE? THEN READ FASTER!

Most people read about 300 words per minute. Fast readers typically read around 600 to 800 words per minute. Experienced speed-readers commonly read between 1,000 and 5,000 words per minute! Not only do they finish their reading much more quickly, but they also get more involved in their reading, so they comprehend and enjoy it more.

(For more information on speed reading, see Evelyn Wood's Reading Dynamics Workshop. Pryor Learning, 1972.)

How would you like to read that fast and comprehend as well as enjoy it?

Note from the author: Like most people, I commonly "sub-vocalize" when I read. Also known as "auditory reassurance", it means saying the word you are reading in your head—and it really slows down your ability to read quickly. However, when I took a speed reading class and practiced about an hour a night, I overcame that problem and was regularly reading 4,000 to 5,000 words a minute. When I read that fast, it was almost like having a motion picture flash before my eyes. One night in class, I read a 140-page novel in 45 minutes, averaging 8,600 words a minute! I took a quiz afterward and scored 85% comprehension. Like any skill, it requires regular practice to maintain.

ML 11 Check Understanding: Speed Reading

While the main purpose for speed reading is to read more quickly, what are the two side benefits that many people find, according to the first part of this section?

1. _____

2. _____

3. For most of us, our eyes and minds can read and comprehend much _____ than we think.

4. Most people read about 300 words per minute. Experienced speed-readers read between _____ and _____ per minute.

5. What is an unexpected benefit of speed reading? _____

Mini Lesson 12: Speed Reading Skills

How can learning this help you? Increasing your ability to read and understand quickly will increase your ability to acquire more background knowledge that is required for learning! The following principles briefly tell you what to do, but the key to your improvement is practice. Focusing on the following three skills will increase your reading speed.

THREE EXCELLENT METHODS TO SPEED-READ

Pace yourself by moving a pen, index card, or finger over each line after you read it. We call these *pacers*.

See groups of words at a time, not just one word. This is called *chunking*.

Don't *sub-vocalize*, or move your tongue or lips, silently sounding out the words as you read.

ML 12 Check Understanding: Speed Reading Skills

What are the three main speed reading skills that people can master through practice?

1. _____

2. _____

3. _____

What two parts of your face move when you sub-vocalize?

4. _____

5. _____

Mini Lesson 13: Practice Speed Reading

How can learning this help you? Practice speed reading by diligently using the exercises described in Mini Lesson 14. For more detailed steps, see the speed reading drills in the following lessons and in the Appendix.

USE DRILL CHARTS TO TRACK YOUR IMPROVEMENT

For many people, speed reading may be frustrating at first, but each one of these principles is worth practicing several times.

ML 13 Check Understanding: Practice Speed Reading

Discuss your speed reading experience in a small group or with the whole class.

1. How well did you pace your reading?

2. How well were you able to "chunk," or see groups of words instead of single words?

3. Did you find that you sub-vocalized, or moved your tongue or lips, while you read?

4. How much faster were you able to go?

5. How was your comprehension?

Mini Lesson 14: Speed Reading Drills Part 1

How can learning this help you? Reading drills are critical practice for expertise in speed reading. Like practicing scales in music, they may be tedious, but they can dramatically increase your ability to absorb material more quickly when you are reading, saving you time and effort later.

FOCUS ON ONE OF THESE THREE PRINCIPLES EACH TIME YOU DO A SPEED READING DRILL

Pace. Use a pacer to force yourself to read quickly.

Chunk. See groups of words, not just single words.

Don't sub-vocalize. This is moving your tongue and/or lips as you read.

ONE-MINUTE DRILL

This drill is meant to show you how fast you read for a short amount of time.

1. Set a timer and read for one minute.
2. Start at the top of a page.
3. Read as quickly as you can until the timer goes off.

READING RATE

Calculate your reading rate.

1. Count the number of words in three normal lines. Example: 34 words.
2. Divide those by three to get the average words per line (WPL). Example: 34 words divided by 3 lines equals 11 rounded.
3. Count the number of lines you read. Example: 36 lines. Remember the number of lines in a complete page or column, then if you read more than that the next time, you don't have to count the lines in that page or column again.
4. Multiply the WPL by the number of lines: 11 times 34 equals 374 words.
5. Your reading rate is 374 words per minute (WPM).

ML 14 Check Understanding: Speed Reading Drills Part 1

1-4. What is your WPM?

_____

5. Which element of speed reading—pacing, chunking, or not sub-vocalizing—do you need to work on the most?

_____

NAME _____ Language Arts Mini Lessons

Mini Lesson 15: Speed Reading Drills Part 2

How can learning this help you? Reading drills are critical practice for expertise in speed reading. As has already been said, they may be tedious, but they can dramatically increase your ability to absorb more material when you are reading, saving you time and effort later.

YOU'VE HEARD PRACTICE MAKES PERFECT? IT'S TRUE!

THREE-MINUTE DRILL

1. Set a timer and read for three minutes.
2. Start at the top of a page.
3. Read as quickly as you can until the timer goes off.
4. Calculate your reading rate.
5. Do this the same way as the One-Minute Drill.
6. Count the number of words in 3 normal lines. Example: 32 words divided by 3 minutes equals 11 rounded.
7. Count the number of lines you read: Example: 82 lines. If you read over one page or column, remember the number of lines on that complete page or column, then you won't have to re-count any complete pages.
8. Multiply the WPL by the number of lines, or 11 times 82 equals 962 words.
9. Divide by 3 to get your WPM, or 962 divided by 3 equals 321 WPM.
10. Discuss your experience doing the Three-Minute Drill with your partner.

ML 15 Check Understanding: Speed Reading Drills Part 2

1-4. What is your WPM? _____

5. Discuss your experience doing the Three-Minute Drill with a partner. _____

Mini Lesson 16: Speed Read an Entire Passage

How can learning this help you? This is a drill meant to help you increase your skimming ability. Because you'll read some of the same material three times, you should read much faster than you normally do.

SKIMMING CAN BE VERY USEFUL WHEN SPEED READING

Particularly during research or other reading activities, skimming can help you find the most important information in a passage quickly. Once you have found the information you are looking for, you can slow down your reading and focus more on that area to deepen your comprehension.

THREE-TIMES ONE-MINUTE DRILL: FIRST READING RATE

1. Set the timer for one minute.
2. Start at the top of a page.
3. Read as fast as you can until the timer goes off after one minute.
4. Calculate your reading rate.
5. Count the number of words in three typical lines: Example: 29 words.
6. Divide 29 by 3 to get the average WPL. Example: 29 words divided by 3 equals 10 rounded.
7. Count the number of lines you read. Example: 34 lines. If you read over one page or column, remember the number of lines on that complete page or column, then you won't have to re-count any complete pages.
8. Multiply the number of WPL by the number of lines to get your WPM. Example: 10 times 34 equals 340 WPM.

SECOND READING RATE

For the second timing, start at the same place you did the first time. See if you can read at least 50 percent farther than you did the first time.

1. Set the timer for one minute.
2. Read as fast as you can until the timer goes off.
3. Calculate your WPM again.

THIRD READING RATE

For the third and last time, start at the same place you did the first time. See if you can read at least 100 percent farther than you did the first time.

1. Set the timer for one minute.
2. Read as fast as you can until the timer goes off.
3. Calculate your WPM.
4. Discuss your speed reading experience in groups of 3 to 5 or else with the whole class.

(CONTINUED NEXT PAGE)

ML 16 Check Understanding: Speed Read an Entire Passage

1. What is your WPM? How could skimming be a useful tool for you in an academic setting? Where else could you use this skill outside of your Language Arts Class?

_____

2. Discuss your experience doing the Three-Minute Drill with a partner. _____

_____

Mini Lesson 17: Pushing the Limits Speed Reading

How can learning this help you? This final reading drill is designed to help you finish the entire passage in record time. Attempt to set a new record for yourself.

ONE LAST DRILL: SEE JUST HOW FAST YOU CAN READ

1. Set the timer so you can see how long it takes you to read the entire passage.

2. Read the passage.

3. When you finish the passage, write down the number of seconds, or minutes and seconds, it took you to read.

4. Calculate your WPM by taking the total number of words in the passage by figuring the WPL, then words per page (WPP), then pages per passage (PPP).

5. Suppose the passage you read is 2780 words long.

6. Divide the total seconds into the total words you read in the passage. Carry the divider to the nearest hundredth.

7. Suppose it took you 7 minutes and 40 seconds—or 60 seconds times 7 minutes equals 420 seconds. Add the 40 additional seconds to the 420 seconds, and it took you 460 total seconds.

8. Divide 2780 words by those 460 seconds which equals 6.04.

9. Multiply your answer by 60 (for 60 seconds) or 6.04 times 60 equals 363 WPM. You would have averaged 363 WPM while reading the whole passage.

10. Get into a small group and discuss it.

ML 17 Check Understanding: Pushing the Limits Speed Reading

1-4. What is your WPM?

___

5. Set a few goals on your reading speed by the end of the year.

___

___

Mini Lesson 18: Pacing

How can learning this help you? Your ability to speed-read is enhanced when you learn to pace yourself by using a pacer, such as a pen, index card, or finger. It keeps your eye moving and your mind focused on receiving information.

HOW TO PACE WHEN READING

Pacing involves using an instrument to direct your focus. A pointer such as a pen or a pencil can serve this purpose, or an index card can be used to cover the lines of words you just read. This forces you to go faster.

PACING ACTIVITY

During this speed reading exercise, pay attention to your reading habits. Are you sub-vocalizing? Are you tempted to go back and reread past sections of text? How quickly can you move forward? Are you noticing how these techniques helped speed up your reading?

PART 1

Your teacher will give you a short passage of text and set a timer. When the teacher tells you, read the text normally and see how far you get before the timer goes off.

PART 2

Your teacher will give you a new passage. This time you will read the passage with a pacer—this can be a pen, an index card, a finger, or other items. Hold it above the line you are reading so your hand or the item covers the text as you read.

Start reading when your teacher tells you.

Move your pacer down the first page to force yourself to read faster.

Move the pacer down fast enough so you need to hurry your reading, but slowly enough so you can still comprehend what you are reading.

Your pacer should be covering what you just read. Don't allow yourself to go back and re-read anything. This will help you to focus on what you're reading.

If your teacher is having you calculate your reading speed, do so and record it on your reading speed progress chart (see the Appendix for a sample).

Keep using a pacer when you read. Like learning most skills, it may seem awkward at first and even slow you down, but it will help you increase your reading speed in the long run.

ML 18 Check Understanding: Pacing

1-5. What was your experience during the activity?

Mini Lesson 19: Chunking

How can learning this help you? Chunking helps you see groups of words at a time, not just one word. Most people stop their eyes on almost every word, or even every syllable, as they read. Learn to stop your eyes only once or twice per line and see several words on each stop.

CHUNKING ACTIVITY

Most people stop their eyes on almost every word as they read. Learn to stop and read a few words at a time. It's frustrating at first, but this activity will greatly help you to increase your speed as you practice it.

Read for one minute while you purposely try to read about three words at once; then go on to the next three words.

Read for one minute while you purposely try to read about three words at once; then go on to the next three words.

1. Calculate how many words you read in that minute.
2. Begin at the same starting place and read for one minute again, still trying to read three words at once. Obviously, you will be able to go faster because you're reading much of the same material a second time.
3. Calculate how many words you read in that minute.
4. Begin at the same starting place and repeat this a third time.
5. Calculate how many words you read and see if you're beginning to read a little faster. See if you can get to the place you ended at the first time by the time you get to 30 seconds this third time.

ML 19 Check Understanding: Chunking

1-5. What was your experience during the activity?

_____

_____

Mini Lesson 20: Conquering Sub-Vocalization

How can learning this help you? Sub-vocalizing is when you are either moving your tongue and/or lips to silently "sound out" the words as you read, or doing so in your head. Conquering the habit of sub-vocalization will increase your reading speed.

ARE YOU SUB-VOCALIZING?

Check to see if you are doing this by holding your fingers over your lips and feeling if your lips move. Now, put your fingers at the top of your throat, under your chin, and push up to see if your tongue moves while you read. If your lips and/or tongue move, practice stopping that by checking their movement with your fingers. This will speed up your reading considerably.

ML 20 Check Understanding: Conquering Sub-Vocalization

With a partner, watch each other do the following exercises. For more detailed steps, see the speed reading drills in the Appendix. Try to eventually use all three speed reading skills together.

1. Read a passage your teacher assigns.

2. Have your fingers on your lips or throat.

3. Use a pacer.

4. Try to read three words at once, not one.

5. Discuss your speed reading experience with your partner.

Chapter Three: Writing Process / Pre-Writing

Why is this chapter important for you? Inputting means taking information into your brain—what you read, hear, or view.

The Lessons

Chapter Three: Writing Process / Pre-Writing 24
    Mini Lesson 21: Writing Process / Pre-Writing 25
    Mini Lesson 22: Interesting Your Readers 26
    Mini Lesson 23: Brainstorming for Nonfiction Sources 27
    Mini Lesson 24: Brainstorming for Narrative Sources 28
    Mini Lesson 25: Nonfiction or Expository Outline 29
    Mini Lesson 26: Narrative Outline 30
    Mini Lesson 27: Narrative Outline / Characters and Setting 32
    Mini Lesson 28: Narrative Outline / Plot 33
    Mini Lesson 29: Creating a Web 34
    Mini Lesson 30: Drafting / Stream-of-Consciousness 35
    Mini Lesson 31: Point of View / Person 36
    Mini Lesson 32: Preparing to Draft Your Narrative 37
    Mini Lesson 33: Draft Your Narrative 38
    Mini Lesson 34: Revise a Draft 39
    Mini Lesson 35: Revise Your Own Writing 41
    Mini Lesson 36: Do Not Edit Yet 42
    Mini Lesson 37: Revise, But Don't Edit 43
    Mini Lesson 38: Prepare to Edit 45
    Mini Lesson 39: Edit 46
    Mini Lesson 40: Proofreading 47
    Mini Lesson 41: What Proofreaders Do 48
    Mini Lesson 42: Proofreading Symbols 50
    Mini Lesson 43: Analyzing Your Proofreading 51
    Mini Lesson 44: Practice! 52

NAME _____   Language Arts Mini Lessons

Mini Lesson 21: Writing Process / Pre-Writing

How can learning this help you? Pre-Writing is the best thing you can do before writing an essay, story, poem, etc. Why? It helps you do most of your thinking and organizing before you write many words. It may well be the most important step in the whole writing process, just as the most important part of a building is its foundation.

PRE-WRITING

Choose your topic according to the following criteria: What interests you?

What do you know about, or what do you want to learn about?

Remember that the most powerful and complete sources often come from our own lives. We know more and care more and are generally more concerned about ourselves than we are about anyone or anything else on earth. Even when we are given a topic about which to write, we can still often bring things in from what we have experienced or observed.

ML 21 Student Activity: Writing Process / Pre-Writing

What are two things about your own life that you know a lot about?

1. _____

2. _____

What are three things about your own life that you care a lot about?

3. _____

4. _____

5. _____

Mini Lesson 22: Interesting Your Readers

How can learning this help you? Engage your readers. The way you do that is by finding ways to interest them, giving them a purpose to read your work, and keeping them interested through the end.

GAINING READERS' INTEREST—CONSIDER THE AUDIENCE

We talk to people in different ways—you most certainly do not talk to a six year old the same way that you talk to your parent, a policeman, the teller at the bank, or your teacher . . . and if you do, your teacher probably looks at you a little funny. Aristotle, an ancient Greek philosopher, always admonished his students to pay attention to their language and adapt what they had to say to the specific audience to whom they were speaking. Students should do the same thing. Consider the following questions:

- Are there other people who care about the same thing you want to write about? How would you talk to them about it?
- Are there other people who generally do not care about what you want to write about?
- How would you talk to these people about it?

ML 22 Student Activity: Interesting Your Readers

Write two emails to your principal about something you want to change at school. Write the first email as though it is to a peer, someone your age. Write the second as if it were to your principal. How does your writing change? Which one do you think would be more effective to achieve the change at school for which you are looking? Why?

_____

_____

_____

_____

_____

_____

_____

Mini Lesson 23: Brainstorming for Nonfiction Sources

How can learning this help you? Brainstorming is an activity you can do by yourself or with other people. When you brainstorm, your goal is to bring as many thoughts and ideas together as possible so you can sift through them to find what the most valuable ones are. When you brainstorm with other people, expand your knowledge base by asking them questions about things you do not know, or for their perspective on the ideas you have. Understanding other perspectives will enrich your writing and sharpen your thinking.

THREE SOURCES FROM WHICH PEOPLE DRAW THEIR IDEAS IN NONFICTION

Topic: topics are broad and typically expressed in just a few words. They can be concrete, such as "Eagles", "Baseball", or "Woodworking"; they can also be abstract, such as "Patriotism", "Love", or "Friendship". Many people draw inspiration by making lists of topics, and choosing something from the list, and brainstorming about that chosen topic to narrow their focus.

Theme: a theme is different from a topic. A theme is a statement about a given topic. A theme is expressed as a complete idea or sentence. For example, you might choose the topic 'dogs', and then derive a theme about that topic, such as, "Dogs are the best pets a person can have." Writing about a theme helps make an assertion that you can direct your writing.

Issue: writing about an issue with which you are concerned adds an emotional element to your writing—when you brainstorm about issues, you often identify current situations that you care about one way or another. As you brainstorm about your issue, choose a side to assert or defend. Then ask other people what they think about the issue to learn more about why it is so controversial. Use their point of view to inform your writing.

ML 23 Student Activity: Brainstorming for Nonfiction Sources

Pick one of the three areas and brainstorm a list of five items in that category. Then refine the list and choose one. Ask someone else what they know about it. Open up a discussion.

1. _____
2. _____
3. _____
4. _____
5. _____

Mini Lesson 24: Brainstorming for Narrative Sources

How can learning this help you? Brainstorming is an activity you can do by yourself or with other people. When you brainstorm, your goal is to bring as many thoughts and ideas together as possible, so you can sift through them to find what the most valuable ones are. When you brainstorm with other people, expand your knowledge base by asking them questions about things you do not know, or for their perspective on the ideas you have. Understanding other perspectives will enrich your writing and sharpen your thinking.

FOUR MAIN TYPES OF SOURCES FROM WHICH PEOPLE DRAW THEIR IDEAS

1. Story. Stanley Kubrick, the American filmmaker, was fond of saying, "Everything has already been done. Every story has been told... It's our job to do it one better." Look at your favorite books, and you can usually lump them into one of a few categories by looking at their general arc. Is your story an adventure? A romance? A political thriller? It is okay to use nonfiction or fiction stories you have experienced, heard, seen, or read as a starting point. Use the general idea from those and add your ideas to "do it one better," as Kubrick would say. Make it your story. Often, the best place from which to draw these sources is what you have personally experienced or observed.

2. Person/Character. Use a true person like Dr. Martin Luther King Jr., or your weird aunt, or a fictitious character you've seen in a movie or read about in a book. It may also be someone you've created from your imagination. The most common characters are usually a blend of several sources.

3. Theme. Ray Bradbury was fond of making lists of nouns, and then picking one to inspire his story. *The Veldt, The Wind, The Coffin, The Visitor.* You can also do this with abstract ideas, like patriotism, honesty, or love. The playwright Tennessee Williams said he wrote about what "bugged" him. Charles Dickens wrote *Oliver Twist* (about orphans) and *A Christmas Carol* (about charity). He thought about major problems in his native London, England, and he then wrote novels to try and resolve those problems and feelings. S. E. Hinton wrote about teen violence in her native Tulsa, Oklahoma in her hit book *The Outsiders*.

4. Imagery and Feelings. Starting your story off by describing the setting, or a feeling is a great way to get started. It is an age-old method of setting the stage and is an especially effective source for poetry.

    Examples:
    The Highwayman: "The wind was a torrent of darkness among the gusty trees; . . ."
    The Raven: "Once upon a midnight dreary . . ."

(Get more help on creating and developing your ideas in Chapter 3 Trait I: Idea Development.)

ML 24 Student Activity: Brainstorming for Narrative Sources

What are two (nonfiction or fiction) stories you would like to develop?

1. _____ 2. _____

Who are two (nonfiction or fiction) characters about whom you would like to write?

3. _____ 4. _____

5. What is one image or feeling(s) about which you would like to write? _____

NAME _____   Language Arts Mini Lessons

Mini Lesson 25: Nonfiction or Expository Outline

How can learning this help you? The most common types of expository writing are essays: descriptive, process, comparison, cause/effect, and problem/solution. To keep the reader involved, there must be a beginning, a middle, and a conclusion, and the only way to achieve that is to *outline*.

EXPOSITORY OR ARGUMENTATIVE WRITING OUTLINE

Have a strong introduction.

Catch the reader's interest.

Write a thesis statement. This tells us your stand on the issue.

Explain your points in the body of your essay. Give at least three points. Support each point with logic (reasoning, fact, or statistic) and/or emotion (story).

Make a convincing conclusion.

Restate your points.

Give a final convincing fact or story.

In an argumentative essay, request your readers to help make your plan work. Call them to action.

Follow either the Expository or Argumentative Outline form in the Appendix.

ML 25 Student Activity: Nonfiction / Expository Outline

Fill in the blanks below for an outline of one of your expository or argumentative topics. Use 20 words or less, and purposely use incomplete sentences.

Introduction. Choose an entertainer or athlete and tell us why they are so great.

1. Catch our interest: _____

2. Thesis statement: _____

Body. Explain your points.

3. First point: _____

4. Second point: _____

5. Third point: _____

Conclusion. Convince us.

6. Summarize: _____

7. Final point: _____

8. Call to action for argumentative: _____

9. What is the purpose of the introduction? _____

10. What is the purpose of the conclusion? _____

Mini Lesson 26: Narrative Outline

How can learning this help you? The best way to illustrate something is to tell a story. Narrative stories can be serious, funny, sad, whatever you want them to be. They always have a beginning, a middle, and an end. The narrative outline is no different from any other kind of outline, but it is vitally important, even if you think you know the whole story in advance. Be sure to outline. In a narrative (story) outline, there must be a protagonist and an antagonist. As you develop the qualities and attributes of these characters, you create interest for the reader.

A NARRATIVE OR STORY WRITING OUTLINE

Remember there must be two parties trying to beat each other in the story.

Choose your protagonist (hero) and antagonist (villain).

Give the protagonist at least one admirable quality (courage, honesty, strength, wisdom, loyalty, beauty, etc.) that the reader can respect about them.

Show the quality through descriptive language; don't just "tell" about it.

Remember, the more the reader admires the protagonist, the more they care *about* them. The more they care about the protagonist, the more they care *what happens* to them. The more they care about what happens to the protagonist, the more they care *about the story*.

NARRATIVE PLOT

Exposition: the beginning balance where life is bearable, perhaps even good, but there are hints of future trouble. This also tells us who the characters are at the beginning of the story and how they became that way.

Upsetting Incident: something occurs that upsets the beginning balance and prods your characters into conflict

Rising Action: as the protagonist tries to restore the beginning balance, they encounter a series of crises that get progressively harder to overcome..

Climax: usually the protagonist wins and restores the beginning balance, so life, though now damaged, is bearable again. The climax is really important for both the protagonist and antagonist to "win." Sometimes the protagonist loses and fails to restore the beginning damage. Sometimes he /she even loses their life while trying. That is known as a tragedy.

Resolution: resolving things and tying up any loose ends. Some stories end with the climax and have no resolution. If you have a resolution it is good to have it as short as possible. Once the climax has been reached, it is hard to retain the reader's interest much longer.

FOLLOW THE NARRATIVE OUTLINE FORM IN THE APPENDIX

When creating your outline, you may prefer a formal outline that is in linear (top-to-bottom) form, or you may work better with an informal outline like a web (cluster and spidergram are two other synonyms for the web). Either way, write down your ideas.

(CONTINUED NEXT PAGE)

CHARACTERS AND SETTING

Fill in the blanks below for an outline of one of your narrative topics. Write 20 words or less, and use incomplete sentences.

CHARACTERS

1. Protagonist (hero): _____

2. Antagonist (villain): _____

3. Protagonist's most admirable trait: _____

SETTING

4. Where it happens: _____

5. When it happens: _____

PLOT

6. Beginning balance: _____

7. Upsetting incident: _____

8. Rising action: _____

9. Climax: _____

10. Resolution (optional): _____

ML 26 Student Activity: Narrative Outline

1. Pre-Writing helps you do most of your planning before you have _____ many words.

2. We know more and care more about _____ than we do about anyone or anything else.

What are the four sources people find their ideas from in narrative writing?

3. _____

4. _____

5. _____

6. _____

What are three of the four main parts of a narrative plot?

7. _____ 8. _____ 9. _____

10. In narrative writing, make the climax really important for both the _____ and protagonist to "win."

NAME _____

Mini Lesson 27: Narrative Outline / Characters and Setting

How can learning this help you? When developing an outline, tell who the characters are at the beginning of the story and how they got to be that way; create the setting; inform us about the fragile beginning balance; and begin the action with the upsetting incident.

EXPLORE CHARACTERS AND SETTINGS

ML 27 Student Activity: Narrative Outline / Characters and Setting

Fill in the blanks below for an outline of one of your narrative topics. Write 20 words or less, and purposely use incomplete sentences.

1. Beginning balance: _____

2. Upsetting incident: _____

3. Rising action: _____

4. Climax: _____

5. Resolution (optional): _____

Mini Lesson 28: Narrative Outline / Plot

How can learning this help you? Exposition does three things: it tells us who the characters are at the start of the story and how they got to be that way, it informs us about the fragile beginning balance, and it begins the action of the plot moving with the upsetting incident.

THE PLOT IS WHAT THE BOOK IS ALL ABOUT

ML 28 Student Activity: Narrative Outline / Plot

Write an outline for a poem or short story.

1. Beginning balance: _____

2. Upsetting incident: _____

3 Rising action: _____

4 Climax: _____

5. Protagonist's change and story's resolution (optional): _____

_____

_____

Mini Lesson 29: Creating a Web

How can learning this help you? Brainstorming helps you identify big ideas. Creating a web helps you drill down into a single idea and identify all of its related sub-topics. They can be as broad or as narrow as you wish. The best part of a web is that it is so flexible. You will learn how to make a customized web just for what you want.

WHAT IN THE WORLD IS A WEB?

You can make a web or a cluster any way you want. Start with a single idea in the center, and then draw a line to each new idea that relates to the one in the center. For example, if your center word is "Potato" you could draw a spoke out to the word "French Fry," another spoke to "Tater Tot," and another to "Potato Head." (In February 2021, Hasbro dropped "Mr." from the name of the toy.)

From each of those words, you can make another connection. For example, you might draw a spoke from "French Fry" to "Lunch Food" . . . but wait! Tater Tots are also lunch foods! Draw a spoke from there as well. Then, from Potato Head, you might draw a spoke out to "Iconic Toys," and another to "Movies." Each new spoke represents a sub-point from the main point or topic. The goal is to see how all of these words relate and get your mind moving through as many ideas as possible to inspire your writing. You may not use every idea in your web, but then again, you might come up with a new idea for a story about Potato Head to his Tater Tot children . . . .

ML 29 Student Activity: Creating a Web

Create a web using the same information you used in your formal expository, argumentative, or narrative outline you just made. Use 20 words or less and purposely use incomplete sentences.

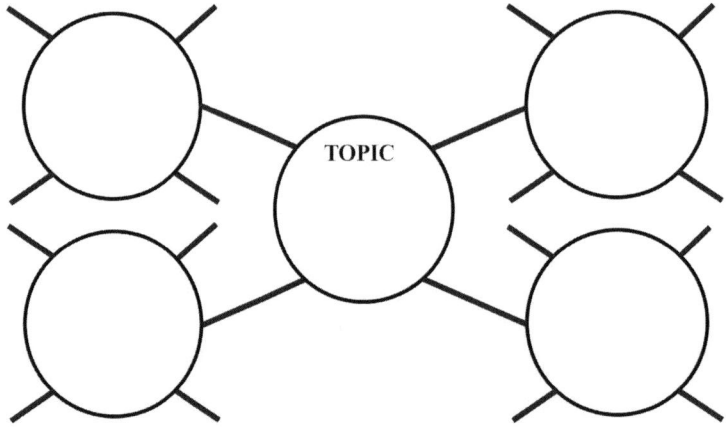

_____
_____
_____
_____

Mini Lesson 30: Drafting / Stream-of-Consciousness

How can learning this help you? Rough drafting is the natural follow-up to outlining. "Roughing in" the content helps you to organize your thoughts in another major step on your way to a final draft. Plus, you will be able to use your creativity to transform your outline into meaningful text.

ROUGH DRAFTING

Many students skip the rough draft and move from their outline to their final copy. *Don't skip the rough draft.* No matter how experienced we are, we can always improve what we have written.

Leave every third line blank for notes.

Use the outline you just made as your "road map."

Follow your outline when it works; depart from it when you have better ideas.

Write your overall thoughts down.

Do you get stressed out when you have to write something? Do you find that it's hard to remember all of the things you are supposed to include? When you're writing, do you get so worried about everything that you forget what you are trying to say? If you follow your outline and focus on your overall ideas and content, you may find that writing will become much easier.

"Don't sweat the small stuff yet." Use your creativity to develop your ideas. Remember, drafting is a right-brained activity. Use the stream-of-consciousness method to draft. Let your overall ideas flow through your mind and onto the paper. Don't worry about conventions like grammar, spelling, and punctuation yet.

Every time you're tempted to stop and check your draft for conventions, imagine you're driving down the highway in a large semi-truck, and suddenly you have to stop. Think of all the work it takes to do that, shifting gears down lower and lower until you stop. Then you slowly shift the gears higher and higher until you're cruising again. That's what happens to your right-brained, creative thoughts and overall ideas when you stop to see if you inserted a comma or spelled a word correctly. It forces your large, flowing ideas to grind to a halt. Then you have to somehow start them up again.

ML 30 Student Activity: Drafting / Stream-of-Consciousness

1. The rough draft is used to transform your _____ into _____ text.

2. What are two of the ways to keep from getting stressed, worried, or anxious when you are writing?
   1. _____ 2. _____

3. Follow your _____ when it works; depart from it when it doesn't work or when you have better ideas.

4. When drafting, is it more important to focus on your overall ideas or on writing conventions? _____
   _____

5. Regarding driving, to what type of vehicle does the book compare drafting? _____

Mini Lesson 31: Point of View / Person

How can learning this help you? Every piece of literature has a point of view. When writing, you must decide which you will employ: first-person, third-person limited, or third-person omniscient.

THERE ARE THREE DIFFERENT POINTS OF VIEW YOU MAY USE WHEN WRITING

First-Person uses the pronouns such as "I," "me," "we," and "us" in order to tell a story from the narrator's perspective. In a first-person narrative, the protagonist may tell of their experiences or another character may do so.

Third-Person Limited reveals the story through the narrator, who knows only the thoughts and feelings of a single character.

Third-Person Omniscient uses mainly one character to tell the story but keeps it in third-person. Writers may maintain this style for the entire narrative or switch between different characters for different sections or when there are scene breaks.

ML 31 Student Activity: Point of View / Person

Work together in a small group and try to find these various points of view.

1-2. Try to find two examples of stories that are written in first-person.

_____

_____

3. Try to find one example of a story that is written in third-person limited.

_____

4-5. Try to find two examples of stories that are written in third-person omniscient.

_____

_____

Mini Lesson 32: Preparing to Draft Your Narrative

How can learning this help you? If the "proof is in the pudding," then the proof of your preparation is in your first draft. Remember that this is your *rough* draft. It's not meant to be polished.

WHEN YOU PREPARE TO DRAFT, LEAVE EVERY THIRD LINE BLANK

When you leave every third line blank, you have that blank line to write on when you revise. If you are typing, double-space your rough draft so you have room to revise.

ML 32 Student Activity: Preparing to Draft Your Narrative

1. Put an _____ at the beginning of every third line and leave it blank for revision space.

2. Use the _____ you created in the Pre-Writing portion of The Writing Process to compose your rough draft.

3. Decide on your story's point of _____: first-person, third-person limited, or third-person omniscient.

4. Stick with your _____ unless you think of something better.

5. Use the _____ method: get the ideas down and worry about the small things like spelling and punctuation later.

6. Reveal the characters of your protagonist and antagonist by _____ what they say and do.

7. Don't just _____ the reader, "She was strong and smart." Say, "Laura kicked in the old door and found the treasure chest that no one else could find."

8. Concentrate on writing down the overall ideas and content.

9. Share your work with a partner and critique each other.

10. Share your work with 3 to 5 other students for comments and suggestions.

Mini Lesson 33: Draft Your Narrative

How can learning this help you? If the "proof is in the pudding," then the proof of your preparation is in your first draft. Remember that this is your rough draft. It's not meant to be polished.

BEGIN TO WRITE YOUR NARRATIVE

Begin with your outline and the web you created and start developing your narrative—your story. This is where the rough draft, the writing, begins.

ML 33 Student Activity: Draft Your Narrative

As you write, you will probably decide to change some things, such as point of view or characters. That's fine. You will be determining your settings/locations as well.

1. Leave every _____ so you have room for revisions.

2. Write a rough draft of your outlined passage.

_____

_____

_____

_____

_____

_____

_____

_____

Mini Lesson 34: Revise a Draft

How can learning this help you? Revising helps you improve the quality and clarity of the thoughts that you have written in your rough draft.

REVISING OVERALL CONTENT

When revising your overall content, read your work from the first four traits: Idea Development, Organization, Voice, and Word Choice. (See the Chapter on The Six Traits.)

Check your overall idea and content as well as its development.

Make sure your organization is clearly showcasing your ideas and content.

Evaluate your piece for how strong your voice is: your opinions, thoughts, and feelings.

Fill in your blank lines, margins, and spaces with revisions and improvements.

Re-read your piece, concentrating on strong, specific words and imagery. Especially evaluate your verbs—use active, specific ones.

Remember, you're trying to improve the big things in your rough draft such as clearer thoughts, better persuasion, stronger characters, and more intense conflicts.

ML 34 Student Activity: Revise a Draft

Write your revisions on the following mediocre piece called "A Minor Football Victory." There are many things you can improve on this. Revise by working on it in the following order:

1. Is there a piece of information that is left out or unclear in the overall idea and content? _____
   _____

2.. What is one way to improve the organization from the beginning, to the middle, and to the end? _____
   _____

3. What is one thing you would change to show the players' bad relationship. _____
   _____

4. What is one image in it that you would improve? _____

5. What is one verb it that you would make more specific? _____

(CONTINUED NEXT PAGE)

A Minor Football Victory

I wasn't very good at football, but in the band I was good. There was this kid who wasn't quite as good as me in the band, but he was good at football. And mean. He would take it out on me at football practice. Once the coach (the coach was mean, too) asked me if I could push the mean kid out of the way if they ran the play through me. It was in practice. I said yes, so they ran the play behind me. I pushed that kid out of the way, so he slugged me hard in the stomach. But it felt good to push that kid out of the way, even if my stomach hurt on account of him hitting me in the stomach. He hit me hard. The coach asked if I could push him out again, and I said yes. I pushed as hard as I could, but I ended up on the bottom of the pile.

Mini Lesson 35: Revise Your Own Writing

How can learning this help you? Revising helps you improve the quality and clarity of the thoughts that you have written in your rough draft.

REVISING OVERALL CONTENT

When revising your overall content, read your work from the first four traits: Ideas, Organization, Voice, and Word Choice. (See the Chapter on the Six Traits.)

Check your overall idea and content as well as its development.

Make sure your organization is clearly showcasing your ideas and content.

Evaluate your piece for how strong your voice is: your opinions, thoughts, and feelings.

Fill in your blank lines, margins, and spaces with revisions and improvements.

Re-read your piece, concentrating on strong, specific words and imagery. Especially evaluate your verbs—use active specific ones.

Remember you're trying to improve the big things in your rough draft such as clearer thoughts, better persuasion, stronger characters, and more intense conflicts.

ML 35 Student Activity: Revise Your Own Writing

Now look at your own rough draft and see how you can revise it. Improve it as you read it, plus revise it according to the following points.

1. How are your ideas and content and their _____?

2. Is your _____ good from the beginning, to the middle, and the end?

3. What is one feeling or thought of the protagonist that you have shared with us? _____

_____

4. What is one of your examples of a good image from this writing? _____

_____

5. What is one of your examples of a good, specific verb from this writing? _____

_____

Mini Lesson 36: Do Not Edit Yet

How can learning this help you? Resist the temptation to edit until you are finished revising. Editing grammar at this point is often counter-productive. If you really revise your piece thoroughly, you'll probably fix little spelling and punctuation mistakes in parts that won't even be used in your final draft. While you're worrying about minor grammar mistakes, you can lose your focus on the more important job of revising the first four traits: ideas, organization, voice, and word choice.

CONCENTRATE ON WRITING WITH YOUR OUTLINE AND WORRY ABOUT EDITING LATER

ML 36 Student Activity: Do Not Edit Yet

What are two of the first four traits the book gives of what to revise?

1. _____

2. _____

3. In addition to the margins, where should you write your revisions? _____

What are the two main reasons to resist the temptation to edit yet.

4. _____

5. _____

Mini Lesson 37: Revise, But Don't Edit

How can learning this help you? You know why you shouldn't edit yet, but see if you can resist the temptation and focus on all of the things to revise.

REVISION IS NOT EDITING

Develop the ideas with originality and clarity.

Organize the thoughts and topics so that each paragraph discusses one topic.

Share your voice. What did the narrator like and dislike? Why?

Check your sentence fluency; also break the article into smaller paragraphs.

There are several ways to revise:

- Improve an idea or idea development.
- Improve the organization.
- Improve the protagonist's voice—sharing their feelings or thoughts.
- Improve the word choice of the imagery.
- Make one of the verbs more specific.

ML 37 Student Activity: Revise, But Don't Edit

1-5. Try to improve the following short piece using the first four of the Six Traits—Idea Development, Organization, Voice, and Word Choice. Break it into into multiple paragraphs according to the topics. Move sentences that are in the wrong place to where they belong. Fix fragments, spelling, grammar, errors, etc. Use the Proofreader Marks when needed.

Yellowsstone

Yellowston National park is neat. It's in Northwest Wyoming. It's pretty I like it. It's also close to The Grand Tetons National Park in Wyoming. They're nice. There's lots of wildlife there. In Yellowstone. Things like buffaloes and bears. When we saw them, I was scarred. It's pretty, too. It has large mountains. The grand Tetons National Park pretty jagged. It also has nice lakes. Yellowstone has lots of famous landmarks. They

(CONTINUED NEXT PAGE)

have geysers, which is where boiling water suddenly shoots up out of the earth in a hole. It shoots up high into the sky. Most of the geysers go off any time. You don't know when it will shoot off. Old Faithful geyser is the most famous geyser, that's because it goes off about every hour. That's why it's called Old Faithful is because it goes off every hour. Almost. There are also wolves, but they mostly come out at night, and people don't see them as much. They also have other famous things like hot pots, which is where little bowls in the ground have boiling water in them that let off a lot of steam. They also have the Grand Canyon of the Yellowstone, which isn't nearly as big as the real Grand Canyon, but it's still pretty Grand. I liked it lots. It also has a gigantic water fall. Wolfs like to hunt in packs, so they can work together. Why is it called Yellowston? Because a lot of the stone and dirt isyellow. Now you know about Yellowstone National Park.

Mini Lesson 38: Prepare to Edit

How can learning this help you? Since the purpose of word choice (strong, specific words that create imagery), involves sentence fluency (well-developed paragraphs and complete sentences) and writing conventions (grammar usage, punctuation, spelling, and capitalization), they help writers clarify their meaning. The more correctly you edit the sentences and conventions in your writing, the clearer and simpler your writing will be.

EDITING PREPARATION

Editing is done after you have revised your paper. All of the large, flowing revisions of the first four traits of writing are complete, and you are now finally ready to "sweat the small stuff" that was discussed in the Rough Draft lesson. Editing is definitely a left-brained activity.

To revert back to the analogy on driving that was given in the Rough Draft lessons, you should now get off the freeway and out of your semi, climb onto a tractor, and slowly "drive" through your writing, carefully sifting through each word to look for every possible mistake in the last three writing traits: Word Choice, Sentence Fluency, and Writing Conventions (see Trait 4 Word Choice, Trait 5 Sentence Fluency, and Trait 6 Writing Conventions), including grammar, punctuation, spelling, and capitalization for more help on editing. Use the proofreading symbols in the Appendix.

These are a few examples of what to edit according to the last two traits.

Read what you have written concentrating on how well your paragraphs are developed. Remember to develop the topic, the whole topic, and nothing but the topic for each paragraph.

Re-read it concentrating on strong, specific words and imagery. Especially evaluate your verbs—use active, specific ones.

Check your writing for incomplete sentences. Find and fix any fragments or run-ons.

Study your writing, focusing on how much variety you have in your sentence beginnings and lengths.

Read your writing again, concentrating on grammar conventions: your errors in grammar usage, punctuation, spelling, and capitalization.

ML 38 Student Activity: Prepare to Edit

1. Should editing be done before or after revising? _____

2. To show how carefully editing should now be done, you were told to get out of the semi-truck used for rough drafting. What vehicle does it say to now "drive?" _____

3-5. What are three of the five examples given of what to edit?

_____

_____

_____

Mini Lesson 39: Edit

How can learning this help you? Editing is the process of refining your writing to eliminate problems with fluency, character development, grammar issues, incorrect spelling and punctuation, and many other problems that seem to crop up when trying to compose a completed, easily read, and understood composition.

NOW EDIT!

ML 39 Student Activity: Edit

1. What is an especially obvious editing mistake you made?

2. In what areas did you find you made the most mistakes according to your editing?

3. In what areas did you find you were the strongest according to what you edited?

What were two sentence or paragraph mistakes you found?

4. _____

5. _____

What were two usage or punctuation mistakes you found?

6. _____

7. _____

What were three spelling or capitalization mistakes you found?

8. _____

9. _____

10. _____

Mini Lesson 40: Proofreading

How can learning this help you? How many times have you searched in vain to find something, only to have someone else see it right before your eyes? Proofreading is like that. After you have done as much as possible to improve your own paper, it's time to let others do what *they* can to help *you*.

PROOFREADING

Look at each other's papers and try to help each other. You will learn from what they tell you about your writing, plus you will learn from proofreading their papers. The key in this is to follow the Golden Rule. Proofread other's papers the way you would want your paper to be proofread.

If possible, have two or more people proofread your paper. Have the first one focus on the principles of revision and the second one focus on suggestions for editing. If there is only time or availability for one person to proofread your paper, then that person should study it according to both the revision and editing principles.

WHEN PROOFREADING SOMEONE ELSE'S WORK

Remember you are simply trying to help the author improve their paper. Be sure to write positive comments as well as negative ones.

Write specific suggestions on ways to improve the writing, especially according to The Six Traits. Don't write what you think they want to hear. Tell them exactly what you feel needs to be improved.

Remember that the author will probably agree with some of your suggestions and disagree with others. It's their paper, and they have the right to have the final say.

If someone is kind enough to give a suggestion, the least you can do is consider it. Don't think you're always right. Appreciate the effort the person made to help you improve your paper.

Remember that it is *your* paper. Use the suggestions you agree with, but don't feel obligated to use the ones with which you disagree. If you're unclear about some of the suggestions, ask the proofreader about them in a friendly, inoffensive manner. Don't be afraid to ask.

ML 40 Student Activity: Proofreading

1. What should the first proofreader focus on? _____

2. What should the second proofreader focus on? _____

3. Remember that you are proofreading to help _____ the author's paper.

4. As an author, you should _____ the proofreaders' efforts, even though you probably won't agree with all of their suggestions.

5. If you're unclear about a suggestion, is it okay to politely ask the proofreader about it? _____

_____

Mini Lesson 41: What Proofreaders Do

How can learning this help you? During the proofreading process, you will need to use the proofreading symbols on page 48 or in the Appendix.

PROOFREADERS USE SPECIFIC MARKS WHEN PROOFING

Get into groups of 3 or 4 and pass your paper to your left.

Proofread the paper given to you according to the principles of revision. Purposely skip any editing problems you see. Pass the paper you just proofread for revision left again. Take the paper from the student on your right and proofread it according to the principles of editing.

After each paper has been proofread for both revision and editing, take your own paper back and study the comments made. See which ones you agree with and which ones you don't.

Thank the students who proofread your paper. Ask them any questions you have. Even though you will undoubtedly disagree with some of their comments, don't discuss those with them unless you need clarification.

See the REP (Revising, Editing, Proofreading) Process Form in the Appendix.

ML 41 Student Activity: What Proofreaders Do

1. What is the sheet of proofreading aids found in the Appendix called? _____
2. How many students should be in a proofreading group? _____ or _____
3. If you have two or more proofreaders, what principles should the first one focus on? _____
4. If you have two or more proofreaders, what principles should the second one focus on? _____
5. What does the initial R stand for in the REP Process Form? _____

PROOFREADER MARKS CHART

Purpose	Symbol	Example
Insert a comma, semi-colon, or colon	/ ,\: / ;\: / :\	Orlando Florida
Insert a hyphen or a dash	/ - \: / — \	one half
Insert parenthesis	( )	prior experience if any
Insert a period	/ . \	Dr
Insert a question mark or exclamation point	/ ? \: / ! \	Did you win
Insert a word	That a book.	That is a book.
Insert an apostrophe or quotation marks	/ ' \: / " \	Jills
Delete	noisy noisy	noisy
Replace	It's loud.	It is loud.
Transpose letters, words, and groups of words	Build the tall shed.	Build the shed tall.
Capitalize a letter	yellowstone	Yellowstone
Make a capital letter lowercase	Yellow bird	yellow bird
Close up space	horse shoe	horseshoe
Use italics	bumblebee	bumblebee

Operational Signs Symbol	Usage	Typographical Signs Symbol	Usage
✎	Delete	ital	Set in italic type
⌒	Close up; delete space	rom	Set in Roman type
⌾	Delete and close up (use only when deleting a word)	bf	Set in boldface type
stet	Let it stand	lc	Set in lowercase
eq #	Make space between words equal; make lines between	caps	Set in capital letters
∽	Trade consecutive words	sc	Set in small caps
ls	Letterspace	wf	Wrong font; change to correct font
¶	Begin new paragraph	X	Check type image; remove blemish
□	Indent type one em from left or right	∨	Insert here or make superscript
⌐	Move right	∧	Insert here or make subscript
			Punctuation Marks
[	Move left	⌄	Insert comma
][	Move center	⌄' ⌄'	Insert apostrophe or single quotation mark
⌐⌐	Move up	⌄'' ⌄''	Insert quotation marks
⌐⌐	Move down	⊙	Insert period
fl	Flush left	Set ?	Insert question mark
fr	Flush right	|;	Insert semicolon
=	Straighten type; align horizontally	|:	Insert colon
||	Align vertically	=	Insert hyphen
tr	Transpose	M	Insert em dash
sp	Spell out	N	Insert en dash
#	Insert space	(|)	Insert parentheses

Mini Lesson 42: Proofreading Symbols

How can learning this help you? Proofreading symbols can save you a great deal of time when marking papers. Writing one symbol may save you from writing a whole sentence. These are definitely worth studying and memorizing.

ML 42 Student Activity: Proofreading Symbols

Write the correct symbol from the Proofreading Symbols in Mini Lesson 41 or in the Appendix.

Put the symbol after the appropriate word.

1. Insert a comma, semicolon, or colon.

    I went to the store and I did my shopping.

2. Insert a period.

    My hair is a mess

3. Insert a word.

    I love to eat my ice cream _____ a cone.

4. Insert an apostrophe or quotation marks.

    Mother said, I am not getting you those shoes!

5. Delete.

    It was a very hot hot day.

6. Replace.

    There's not a place I would rather be.

7. Transpose letters, words, groups of words.

    I liked the building tour for it's unique history.

8. Make a capital letter lowercase.

    My Mother was my favorite person.

9. Close up space.

    When we moved   or had a get together, it was always fun.

10. Use the italics symbol on the following word.

    bumblebee

Mini Lesson 43: Analyzing Your Proofreading

How can learning this help you? The more time you take reading and re-reading your writing, the more mistakes you will find. Even professional proofreaders find errors on their *final* read-through!

THERE IS ALWAYS ANOTHER MISTAKE TO CATCH!

ML 43 Student Activity: Analyzing Your Proofreading

Complete the work on the piece below.

1-9. Mark the story with at least nine appropriate symbols from the Proofreading Chart. You may make other marks in addition to the proofreading symbols,.

10. Get into groups of 3 to 4 students and compare your proofreading revisions. Notice how the space between the lines gives you the room to revise.

This Friendly Girl

There was this here girl she was in are class, she was really Friendly so Friendly she maid other people fill better in the the class, and around her. once a new kid come into our class, he seemed like a kid who has been in alot of trouble. And he din't wanna talk to Nobody. Anyways she up an mov ed over and started talkin to him real friendly like ya know? She says how ya doin and where ya from, all of the time she has this big friendly smile, and she really Listened to his answ ers and cared about him him. well this here kid opened up. He's written alot of poetry an other stuff, he showed other kids in the class and he started to participate. And was all because of this friendly girl.

Mini Lesson 44: Practice!

How can learning this help you? When you work together to improve each other's writing, you all succeed! Get together in groups and proofread each other's work.

PRACTICE, PRACTICE, *PRACTICE*

ML 44 Student Activity: Practice!

1. Get into a group of 3 or 4 students.

2. Finish this word. It's the key to improvement in writing, proofreading, and almost anything.

    P __ a __ t __ c __

3. Write a sentence or two about how you think you did in proofreading for revision principles.

    _____
    _____
    _____
    _____

4. Write a sentence or two about how you think you did in proofreading for editing principles.

    _____
    _____
    _____
    _____

5. Write a sentence or two about how helpful the proofreading changes and suggestions on your paper were.

    _____
    _____
    _____
    _____

Chapter Four: Six Traits of Writing

How can this chapter help you? Next to the Writing Process, the Six Traits of Writing is one of the most revolutionary, helpful programs to ever hit writing. It breaks down your writing abilities into six categories.

The Lessons

Chapter Four: Six Traits of Writing 53
    Mini Lesson 45: Six Traits of Writing 54
    Mini Lesson 46: Trait 1 Idea Development 55
    Mini Lesson 47: Choose an Idea to Develop 56
    Mini Lesson 48: Creating Ideas for Narrative Writing 57
    Mini Lesson 49: Improving Idea Development 58
    Mini Lesson 50: Trait 2 Organization / Expository Writing 59
    Mini Lesson 51: Trait 2 Organization / Narrative Writing 60
    Mini Lesson 52: Improve Organization 61
    Mini Lesson 53: Write and Compare 62
    Mini Lesson 54: Rough Outline 63
    Mini Lesson 55: Trait 3 Voice and Enthusiasm 64
    Mini Lesson 56: Trait 3 Voice / Improvement Suggestions 65
    Mini Lesson 57: Voice in Expository Writing 66
    Mini Lesson 58: Voice in Argumentative Writing 67
    Mini Lesson 59: Voice in Narrative Writing 68
    Mini Lesson 60: Voice in a Story 69
    Mini Lesson 61: Write a Description 72
    Mini Lesson 62: Write a Short Fairy Tale 73
    Mini Lesson 63: Word Choice Using Accurate and Vivid Words 74
    Mini Lesson 64: Show, Don't Tell 76
    Mini Lesson 65: Improve Voice and Imagery 77
    Mini Lesson 66: Expository and Argumentative Word Choice 78
    Mini Lesson 67: Narrative Word Choice 79
    Mini Lesson 68: Trait 5 Sentence Fluency 80
    Mini Lesson 69: Improve Sentence Fluency 81
    Mini Lesson 70: Sentence Length 82
    Mini Lesson 71: Trait 6 Writing Conventions 83

Mini Lesson 45: Six Traits of Writing

How can learning this help you? By learning and incorporating these Six Traits, you will be prepared to use them when writing your piece and be able to create a clear, understandable, informative, interesting, and, hopefully, entertaining result.

TRAIT 1: IDEA DEVELOPMENT

TRAIT 2: ORGANIZATION

TRAIT 3: VOICE

TRAIT 4: WORD CHOICE

TRAIT 5: SENTENCE FLUENCY

TRAIT 6: WRITING CONVENTIONS AND LAYOUT

ML 45 Student Activity: Six Traits of Writing

What do you already know about the Six Traits of Writing?

How many of the Six Traits of Writing can you write down right now?

1. _____
2. _____
3. _____
4. _____
5. _____
6. _____

Try to write down three points about any of the Six Traits you can explain right now.

7. _____
8. _____
9. _____

10. Get with a group of 3 to 5 students and share your answers.

Mini Lesson 46: Trait 1 Idea Development

How can learning this help you? Where can you find interesting, original ideas that you would like to write about? This lesson can help with that. Make sure that whenever possible you choose your ideas from something in which you are interested. Learn to create and develop your writing ideas better.

A THEME IS BEHIND THE MEANING OF YOUR WRITING

Idea development is really about two things: creating a bright, original idea, then going through the real work of developing it. It must have meaning with a theme or an issue to develop it.

ML 46 Student Activity: Trait 1 Idea Development

What is one thing you know a lot about? Perhaps it's a famous patriot, entertainer, or athlete. Maybe a skill like repairing a bike tire or baking a special cake, etc.

1. What is something you are interested in, but need to learn more about? _____

2. Who is someone you are interested in, but want to learn more about? _____

3. What is some information you would like or need to get? _____

4. What is a theme, such as honesty or patriotism, you would like to build a writing assignment around?
   _____

5. What is a "stand" on a controversial issue where you would like to try to persuade your readers that your stand is the best? _____
   _____

NAME _____

Mini Lesson 47: Choose an Idea to Develop

How can learning this help you? Since the idea behind your writing is really your starting point, choose an original idea, do your research, really think about what you want to say, and start writing! This type of writing is called expository, and it explains your idea. So, your job is to investigate or research the idea, evaluate the evidence you discover, present your position on it, and develop an argument concerning it.

CREATING IDEAS FOR EXPOSITORY WRITING

Make sure whenever possible you choose your ideas from something you're interested in. Here are some possible sources.

Information: Get your ideas from ideas you like or things you want to learn.

Theme: Build your writing around a specific person or a certain theme such as honesty or patriotism.

Issue: Take a stand on a controversial issue and try to persuade your readers that your stand is the best.

ML 47 Student Activity: Choose an Idea to Develop

1. Choose one informative topic and tell your readers.

   _____

2. Choose one skill or task you understand.

   _____

3-4. Choose two argumentative topics and take a stand.

   _____

   _____

5. Choose one topic from your list and develop a rough outline.

   _____

Mini Lesson 48: Creating Ideas for Narrative Writing

How can learning this help you? Our best narrative writing often comes from what we've personally experienced or observed. That's because *we know more about ourselves and care more about ourselves than about anyone or anything else.*

NARRATIVE WRITING IS USUALLY DEVELOPED THROUGH ONE OF FOUR METHODS

Other stories. It has been said that Shakespeare never created an original story, but rather, he borrowed stories from other writers and improved upon them. An example of this is what he did with the plots from the great Roman playwright Plautus. Shakespeare took some ideas from Plautus's fine comedies and revised them to make them even better.

Themes. Charles Dickens would look at a social problem such as being kind to others or improving conditions in orphanages and write a story (*A Christmas Carol* or *Oliver Twist*) to encourage people to solve the problem.

Characters. A narrative can be based around a character you know or have read about. It can even be a composite of several people or characters. The great Russian playwright Anton Chekhov usually used this method.

Sensory and emotional imagery. Some writers, especially poets, get their ideas from senses and feelings. Veteran educator Suzan Lake said, "The process of gathering meaning from life always begins with the senses and then passes on to feelings, ideas, thoughts, and judgments."

DEVELOPING YOUR IDEAS

As important as it is to create bright, original ideas, it is even more important to develop them. Here are some ways to do this. Much of this will be covered under Trait 2, Organization. However, here are some basic principles.

Tell your readers something they don't know.

Make your passage focused and specific.

Make sure your writing makes sense to others.

Pick a fairly strong subject to refute.

ML 48 Student Activity: Creating Ideas for Narrative Writing

What are the two parts of Idea Development? 1. _____ 2. _____

3. Our best narrative writing often comes from what we've _____ or observed.

What are two of the four sources from which our narrative writing comes?

4. _____

5. _____

NAME _____   Language Arts Mini Lessons

Mini Lesson 49: Improving Idea Development

How can learning this help you? Idea development is really about two things: create a bright, original idea, then do the real work of developing it. As important as it is to *create* bright, original ideas, it is even more important to *develop* them. There are many ways to do this.

BASIC PRINCIPLES TO DEVELOP YOUR IDEA

Tell your readers something they don't know.

Make sure your writing makes sense to others.

Watch for differences between general and specific details.

Study your topic from several different angles and points of view. That allows you to be knowledgeable (credible) about the topic and also gives you a broad background from which to choose, organize, and draw information.

In an argumentative paper, choose an issue with a fairly strong counterargument that you feel you can refute.

Eliminate redundant (unneeded, overused) information.

Use questions to clarify and expand the main idea.

ML 49 Student Activity: Improving Idea Development

The following possible writing topics may be true, false, or a blend. Choose two and base them on other stories.

1. _____
2. _____

Choose two theme topics. Base them on a theme such as patriotism, courage, or kindness.

3. _____
4. _____

Choose two character topics. Base them on a character or person you know or you create.

5. _____
6. _____

Choose two imagery topics. Base their story on an image such as a certain sight, sound, or touch.

7. _____
8. _____

Choose a narrative idea and another idea from your list of topics and develop a rough outline for each.

9. _____
10. _____

Mini Lesson 50: Trait 2 Organization / Expository Writing

How can learning this help you? Organization is like a skeleton upon which we *flesh out* our ideas. This lesson will help you organize and display your ideas better.

The purpose of organization is to display YOUR ideas clearly and convincingly

Meaning: Organization is the internal structure of your passage. Do this by considering the purpose of writing your passage and the audience for whom you are writing. Then organize the beginning, middle, ending in a way that best holds your readers' attention, displays your ideas, and makes sense. Good organization makes reading your passage as easy to follow as a well-prepared road map.

*Tell us what you're going to tell us about, tell us about it,
then tell us what you've just told us about.*

Expository Writing: This is functional, informative, and argumentative writing. Introduce your topic, develop it (making sure you cover the 5 W's plus H about the topic—who, what, when, where, why, and how), and conclude your paper by briefly restating the different points of it. An argumentative paper is similar, except your purpose is to convince your audience to accept your side of a controversial topic, so write it for that reason. At the end request what you want your reader(s) to do in your call to action.

ML 50 Student Activity: Trait 2 Organization / Expository Writing

1. The purpose of organization is to _____ your ideas.

2. With what part of the body does the text compare organization?

    a. mind   b. heart   c. skeleton   d. bowels

3-5. What are the three types of expository writing?

_____

_____

_____

NAME _____   Language Arts Mini Lessons

Mini Lesson 51: Trait 2 Organization / Narrative Writing

How can learning this help you? Learn how to identify the organizational parts of well-written expository, argumentative, or narrative work.

NARRATIVE WRITING

Follow this plot format.

Exposition: An introduction to the situation, as well as who the main characters are and how they got to be the way they are at the story's start.

Beginning Balance: Life is bearable, but it foreshadows future trouble.

Upsetting incident: Life is no longer bearable. The protagonist (hero) tries to restore the beginning balance. The antagonist tries to permanently destroy it.

Climax: The protagonist wins or loses.

Resolution: Tie up any loose ends. This is optional and only used part of the time.

ML 51 Student Activity: Trait 2 Organization / Narrative Writing

1. The purpose of organization is to _____ your ideas.

What are four of the five parts of a good narrative passage?

2. _____

3. _____

4. _____

5. _____

Mini Lesson 52: Improve Organization

How can learning this help you? Learn how to identify the organizational parts of well-written expository, argumentative, or narrative work.

ORGANIZATIONAL PARTS OF WELL-WRITTEN LITERATURE

Hook your reader with an inviting lead. Make your reader want to finish reading your piece from the first sentence or paragraph to the end.

Cover the Five W's and H (who, what, when, where, why, and how) of journalism. Occasionally one or more is unnecessary, but it's usually essential to cover each one at least briefly.

Practice the art of effective sequencing (putting things in order—first, second, third, etc.).

Use good transition words such as furthermore, next, etc.

Round out your writing with a memorable ending.

If your writing is expository, leave the reader with an *ah-ha!* moment that motivates them to ponder what you've said.

If the writing is narrative, build the conflict so it is really important for the protagonist to win; then have them win or lose.

Student Activity: Improve Organization

Learn the five W's and the H.

ML 52 Student Activity: Improve Organization

What are the five W's and the H?

1. _____
2. _____
3. _____
4. _____
5. _____
6. _____

7. What is the two-word term for putting things in order? _____

8-10. What are three of the ways you can improve your organization?

_____

_____

_____

Mini Lesson 53: Write and Compare

How can learning this help you? When writing a piece, whether expository or argumentative, writers, including you, tend to begin badly, have poor sequencing, unclear development, and an ineffective ending.

HAVE ANOTHER PAIR OF EYES

One of the ways writers improve is by having "another pair of eyes." The job of proofreaders is to "put in their two cents" and help the writer to find a better, clearer way to say the same thing. Comparing your work with other students will give you—and them—a chance to become a better writer.

ML 53 Student Activity: Write and Compare

1. Purposely write something with a poor beginning.

___

2. Write an unclear middle.

___

3. Write an ineffective ending

___

4. Trade papers with someone and improve each other's work.

5. Discuss how and why you made the improvements.

Mini Lesson 54: Rough Outline

How can learning this help you? The entire purpose of an outline is to make writing easier for you. It helps you organize your thoughts and get them on paper eventually. You're creating what some people call a "road map" for your "journey" on paper. The best thing about it is it enables you to return to it and get a new direction when you come to a "roadblock," sometimes called writer's cramp or writer's block. Don't let an outline frighten you. It doesn't have to be overly detailed; the simpler, the better. It is there as a guide to keep your writing on track.

OUTLINING MAKES WRITING EASIER, EVEN THOUGH YOU MAY HATE DOING IT

ML 54 Student Activity: Rough Outline

1. Develop the two rough outlines you made in the Idea Development lesson. To do this, follow the expository and narrative outlines in the Appendix.

2. Develop the rough narrative outline you made in the Idea Development exercise. To do this, follow the narrative outline in the Appendix.

3. Get into a group of 3 to 5 people and explain why you organized your information the way you did. Explain why you chose your introduction and conclusion for the expository paper and why you chose your particular protagonist for your narrative paper.

4. Listen with an open mind to any suggestions your group members offer.

5. Listen to the other group members' papers and respectfully tell them some things you like and dislike about their work.

Mini Lesson 55: Trait 3 Voice and Enthusiasm

How can learning this help you? Professor Donald Graves maintained that voice is the difference between what's read and what's not read. Do you want people to look forward to reading your writing because they find it refreshing? Write with stronger *voice*. Learn to effectively share the opinions and feelings of yours and/or your protagonist's, and *you'll hook your readers.*

Voice [heart] is the difference between what's read and what's not read.

Professor Donald Graves, Writing Education Expert

Voice is a complex combination of your personality and enthusiasm for your topic, your audience, and yourself. Voice is when you (in argumentative or expository writing) or your protagonist (in narrative writing) confidently share your opinions and feelings. The stronger the voice, the more interesting the reading is. Whether people agree with what you write or not, if you write with a strong voice, they will want to read your work.

GENERAL SUGGESTIONS TO IMPROVE VOICE

Study pieces of writing that have strong, but different voices.

Identify, describe, and compare the voices of famous writers.

Practice different voices within the various modes (descriptive, expository, argumentative, narrative, and business) and genres. Learn to match your voice to the mode and genre.

Identify your audience for the piece and write to them.

Purposely write a bland, voiceless piece, then add voice to it. Notice the improvement.

ML 55 Student Activity: Trait 3 Voice and Enthusiasm

1-2. Voice [heart] is the difference between what's _____ and what's not _____.

3-5. Voice is an *enthusiasm* for your _____, your _____, and your _____.

6-7. Strong voice is when you share your _____ and your _____.

8-10. What are three suggestions the book gives to improve your voice?

_____

_____

_____

NAME _____   Language Arts Mini Lessons

Mini Lesson 56: Trait 3 Voice / Improvement Suggestions

How can learning this help you? Study pieces of writing that have strong, but different voices. Identify, describe, and compare the voices of famous writers. Practice different voices within the various modes (descriptive, expository, argumentative, narrative, and business) and genres. Learn to match your voice to the mode and genre. Identify your audience for the piece and write to them. Purposely write a bland, voiceless piece, then add voice to it. Notice the improvement.

GENERAL SUGGESTIONS TO IMPROVE VOICE

Study pieces of writing that have strong, but different voices.

Identify, describe, and compare the voices of famous writers.

Practice different voices within the various modes (descriptive, expository, argumentative, narrative, and business) and genres. Learn to match your voice to the mode and genre.

Identify your audience for the piece and write to them.

Purposely write a bland, voiceless piece, then add voice to it. Notice the improvement.

ML 56 Student Activity: Trait 3 Voice / Improvement Suggestions

1-2. Strong voice is when you share your _____ and your _____.

What are three suggestions the book gives to improve your voice?

3. _____

4. _____

5. _____

Mini Lesson 57: Voice in Expository Writing

How can learning this help you? As the author of your passage, you're supposed to be the expert. Sound like it. First, get your facts straight, dare to take a stand based on your facts, then organize them in the most logical way. Next, plan how to present them in the best, most convincing way. Share your knowledge and opinions about your topic, as well as your desire to communicate these to your readers.

SHARE YOUR OPINIONS AND THOUGHTS BECAUSE *YOU'RE* THE EXPERT

Example: Don't say, "I think school should never start before 9 a.m." If you've written it, we know what you think. Just say, "School should never start before 9 a.m."

ML 57 Student Activity: Voice in Expository Writing

In expository writing what are two things you should share with your readers?

1. _____

2. _____

3. Who is supposed to be the expert of your expository passage? _____

4-5. What are two of the four things you should do with facts in expository writing?

_____

_____

Mini Lesson 58: Voice in Argumentative Writing

How can learning this help you? Argumentative writing is designed to convince or persuade its audience to understand the *other* side of the argument or to support a new belief or idea. Investigate a topic by collecting, generating, and evaluating evidence; then establishing your position on it.

EMOTION

Since argumentative writing usually involves facts, issues, etc., that means there is often emotion associated with it. It may be motivational, scholarly, cynical, and the list goes on. Consider that you are presenting your feelings/opinions/facts as well as acknowledging those of the other side of the issue.

ML 58 Student Activity: Voice in Argumentative Writing

1. Read the following paragraph from an argumentative passage.

Identify and write down two examples of voice in it. If you can't find any, write down two examples of where voice could be used.

2. _____

3. _____

4. Write down one example of weak voice. _____

5. Share with a partner.

United We Stand

In my opinion, the politicians from both the Democrat and Republican parties care much more about building their party than they do about building America. They're all a bunch of selfish jerks. Admittedly, no one is perfect, and each party has flaws. However, the more the two major parties focus on what they agree with each other on, the more they will be able to accomplish for the good of America. If the politicians from each side would look at both the good and the bad on each issue, and then decide for themselves instead of just seeing which way their stupid party wants them to vote, just think how much more needed legislation would be passed and how much more appreciative the citizens would be of their Congress.

Mini Lesson 59: Voice in Narrative Writing

How can learning this help you? The key to making readers care about your narrative writing, or story, is to help them care about the protagonist and their allies.

ONE WAY TO MAKE YOUR READERS CARE ABOUT THE STORY IS TO BUILD UP THE PROTAGONIST

"I look for a story with heart [voice]. It should be a simple story with characters the audience really can care about. They've got to have a rooting interest."

Walt Disney

(Surrell, Jason, Screenplay by Disney. Disney Editions. 2004. P. 12.)

Give the protagonist a major admirable quality. The more the readers care about the protagonist and their friends, the more they care about what happens to them, and therefore the more they will care about what happens in the story. Examples of admirable qualities are the parts of the old Boy Scout Motto—being kind, loyal, trustworthy, brave, etc.

Share the protagonist's or narrator's feelings, opinions, and thoughts.

Show, don't tell. Don't come out and say, "Luke was brave." Show us he was brave by describing something he did or said or what someone else said about his bravery.

Have your protagonist change, usually for the better, during the story.

ML 59 Student Activity: Voice in Narrative Writing

1. What one-word term did Walt Disney say he looked for in a story? _____

2. Give your protagonist an admirable _____ to help us care about them.

3. _____ us, don't just tell us that a character is brave, wise, sly, or scared, etc.

Read a paragraph from a narrative piece (story). Identify and write down two examples of voice in it. If you can't find any, write down examples of where voice could be used.

4. _____

5. _____

NAME _____   Language Arts Mini Lessons

Mini Lesson 60: Voice in a Story

How can learning this help you? How can learning this help you? When deciding how to develop your narrative, your story, one of the first considerations is what "voice" you are going to use to tell it. Most stories have a narrator, and many also use their main character's voice as the narrator. But this is critical: Be sure when you choose what "voice" you are going to write in that you do not deviate from it.

CHOOSE YOUR VOICE CAREFULLY

Beginning writers often fall into the trap of creating the stereotypical protagonist—the high school quarterback or head cheerleader. In reality, a very small percentage of people are the quarterback or head cheerleader. However, everyone has several major qualities. Emphasize one of them. Winnie-the-Pooh, one of the world's most lovable protagonists, isn't strong, handsome, or smart, but he's extremely loyal.

ML 60 Student Activity: Voice in a Story

Answer the questions after reading the following short story, "Another Part of the City" on page 70.

1. Who is the protagonist? _____

2. Who is the antagonist? _____

What are two examples of strong voice?

3. _____

4. _____

5. Share and compare with a partner.

(CONTINUED NEXT PAGE)

Another Part of the City

Seth looked around and quickened his pace. He knew he'd made a mistake. He had thought this route would take him to his home on the other side of the city more quickly, but he now realized he was in a very rough neighborhood, and the sooner he could get out of it, the better. As he turned a corner he heard a car trying to start at the other end of the block. It was soon evident that the car wasn't going to start. A girl got out of the car, grabbed her purse, slammed the door, and started walking.

Just then five boys came around the corner right in front of her. Seth immediately stepped into the shadows. When the boys saw the girl, they started whistling and quickly surrounded her. The boys, like the girl, were all a few years older than Seth and several inches taller.

"Well, looky what we got here," said a boy, and he whistled.

Seth slunk down further into the shadows. He knew he was safe there because they couldn't see him.

The girl tried to walk between them, but another boy stepped in front of her. "Where you goin' in such a hurry, girl?" he asked.

"Please," the girl pleaded. "Please let me go."

Seth felt bad for the poor girl.

"You a pretty girl," said another boy as he sauntered up to her. "You gotta say, "Pretty please." The other boys laughed and smirked.

"Pretty . . . please," said the girl, and she started to whimper.

Seth couldn't stand there any longer. He stormed up to the group, pushed one of the bigger boys out of the way a little, and stepped right up to the girl, looked up at her, and asked, "Sister, where you been? We got a big group o' family out lookin' all over for you. I'm surprised they haven't found you by now."

The boys were visibly disappointed, but the girl quickly caught on and stammered, "Wh-why, I didn't know they was all out lookin' for me."

"Oh, yeah," said Seth. "Even Uncle Charlie an' a half dozen o' his big ol' friends is out lookin.' They likely be along here any minute. He mad 'cuz he had to miss part o' the game on TV to come out lookin' for you. They likely to take out their anger on whomever is around."

"Oh, no," said the girl. "Uncle Charlie, he's mean, an' his friends is even meaner."

(CONTINUED NEXT PAGE)

One of the boys gave a signal, and the group quickly faded away into the darkness leaving Seth and the girl alone. The girl put her head down on Seth's shoulder and sobbed.

After a few moments, Seth said, "We'd better get out o' here. No tellin' when them big guys 'll come back."

The girl hurried after him. "Can I come with you for a while? I don't wanna walk alone."

"Sure. It's a free sidewalk," he answered.

After they had walked a little way, the girl said, "I can't believe you were brave enough to walk into the middle of all those big guys. How did you ever think of that idea?"

"Uncle Charlie. He told me."

"You mean there really is an Uncle Charlie?"

"Yup."

"Is he as big and mean as you said?"

"No. He's a little scrawny dude who uses a walker, but he has good ideas."

The girl laughed. "I'll say he does."

Mini Lesson 61: Write a Description

How can learning this help you? ? Using voice in your descriptions helps your writing be more authentic and emotionally relatable.

DESCRIPTION SETS THE STAGE IN THE READER'S MIND; EVEN TAKES THEM DOWN MEMORY LANE

ML 61 Student Activity: Write a Description

1. Leave every other line blank. Describe a good teacher you once had. Write this in 50 words or less.

_____

_____

_____

_____

2. Revise your piece so that it is weak. Use a hesitant, apologetic manner to describe them. Include terms like "I think . . ." and "I'm not sure, but . . ."

3. Revise your piece about the same former good teacher, but this time use a confident, emotional manner to describe them. Give us your opinions in no uncertain terms.

_____

_____

_____

_____

4. Get into a small group and read the two versions to compare them.

5. Change to a different group and have everyone in that group read their two versions.

NAME _____   Language Arts Mini Lessons

Mini Lesson 62: Write a Short Fairy Tale

How can learning this help you? Write a short fairy tale or some other fantasy story you know, focusing on using voice.

FANTASY, ADVENTURE, AND FAIRY TALES ARE FUN TO WRITE BECAUSE YOU USE IMAGINATION!

ML 62 Student Activity: Write a Short Fairy Tale

Write a short version (50 to 100 words) of a fairy tale such as "Hansel and Gretel," but make the protagonist really bland.

_____

_____

X_____

_____

_____

X_____

2. Mark every third line with an X and leave it blank so you have room to insert revisions.

3. Write the fairy tale with the bland protagonist.

_____

_____

X_____

_____

_____

X_____

_____

_____

X_____

_____

4. Trade papers with another student and improve the voice in each other's narratives by showing an admirable trait the protagonist has, plus by sharing their feelings and thoughts.

5. Discuss the voice improvements with your partner.

Mini Lesson 63: Word Choice Using Accurate and Vivid Words

How can learning this help you? The more accurate and vivid your words are, the more clear and interesting your writing is for your readers. The more vivid the images are, the longer your readers will remember them. Voice and word choice are the two traits that will probably keep readers' interest in your writing the most.

USE ACCURATE AND VIVID WORDS

Your writing should be clear, exact, and interesting. Choose the best, most specific words possible. This is especially important with verbs and nouns. Another point is to make sure your words fit your topic and your audience. Don't use words that are too hard or too simple for your readers

EXPOSITORY WRITING

There is a different purpose for good word choice in expository writing than in narrative writing. In expository writing, the purpose should be to give us clear, specific imagery that helps us understand what you are trying to tell us without a lot of excess words. Try to not use technical jargon (words familiar to only a small part of your readers).

NARRATIVE WRITING

In narrative writing, wonderful imagery is imperative. Make sure it either furthers the plot, develops the characters, describes the setting/time, and/or creates the feelings and responses you desire. Don't use imagery just for the sake of having imagery. That is like driving down a dead-end street.

ML 63 Student Activity: Word Choice Using Accurate and Vivid Words

What are the two traits that will probably keep your readers' interest the most?

1. _____
2. _____

Which two parts of speech especially need strong and specific word choices? (Your choices are adjectives, adverbs, conjunctions, interjections, nouns, prepositions, pronouns, and verbs.)

3. _____
4. _____

5. In both expository and narrative writing, imagery should have _____.

6. In expository writing, imagery should help _____ what you are trying to tell us.

What are three of the four purposes of imagery in narrative writing?

(CONTINUED NEXT PAGE)

NAME _____   Language Arts Mini Lessons

7. _____

8. _____

9. _____

10. Don't use imagery just for the sake of _____.

Mini Lesson 64: Show, Don't Tell

How can learning this help you? The more you show something, the better readers will be able to imagine it, and the more interesting they will find your writing.

GIVE YOUR READERS A CHANCE TO USE THEIR IMAGINATION

Show key parts; don't just tell about them.

Example: Jared took a bite of the juicy peach. (Adequate)
Example: As Jared bit deeply into the ripe peach, he felt its rich juice run down his throat. (Strong)

Create strong images. The more specific your images, the more interesting your readers will find your writing. Strong images generate strong emotions and memories for your readers.

Remember that there are two types of imagery. Create both in your writing.

1. Sense imagery: see, hear, feel, taste, and smell.
2. Emotional imagery: fear, joy, sadness, anger, etc. These trigger memories of emotions we have felt in our lives. Remember, emotional memory is very similar to voice.

Choose strong, specific words, especially with your verbs and nouns.

Make a list of words and phrases you especially like.

Make a list of overused words and phrases that you can quit using

ML 64 Student Activity: Show, Don't Tell

What two parts of speech are especially important with which to use strong and specific word choices? Your choices are adjectives, adverbs, conjunctions, interjections, nouns, prepositions, pronouns, and verbs.

1._____ 2._____

3. The more you show something, the better readers will be able to _____ it.

4. The more specific your images, the more _____ your readers will find your writing.

5. Strong _____ generate strong emotions and memories for your readers.

Mini Lesson 65: Improve Voice and Imagery

How can learning this help you? Learn to read through your writing at least once just to look for stronger word choice, especially with your verbs and nouns. Re-read your writing once to improve the voice and once to improve your imagery, and it will really make your writing stand out more.

MAKE NOUNS AND VERBS REALLY COUNT!

Here are examples of sentences with weak word choice, followed by a revised version.

Example: The highway patrol needs to stop teenage motorists from speeding. (Weak)
Example: Our diligent highway patrol needs to bring speed-crazed teenage drivers to a screeching halt. (This shows us the author's opinion of the highway patrol and teenage drivers.)

Here are examples of sentences using boring word choice in argumentative writing. Revise the words, especially the verbs and nouns, to make them stronger. *Show* us the author's opinions and thoughts.

Example: Maybe the principal could help the struggling students more.
Example: Congress should reduce poverty.

Here are examples of sentences with weak word choice in narrative writing. Revise their words, especially the verbs and nouns, to make them stronger. *Show* us *imagery*, as well as their feelings.

Example: The girls walked down the hall laughing.
Example: The teacher took off his glasses and looked angrily at the boy.

ML 65 Student Activity: Improve Voice and Imagery

Underline each word that shows strong word choice in the two following sentences.

1. Stella slipped on her pink sandals and carefully stepped over the rough coral stones.

2. The bent old man slowly picked up another dying starfish and painfully threw it back into the waiting waves.

3. Write a sentence about the beach. Have at least three underlined examples of strong word choice in it.

_____

4. Write three examples of strong word choice from the following sentence.

Despite the initial cost, a connector road from our town to the freeway will bring in more business and make it more convenient for residents and travelers alike to journey to and from our little corner of the world.

_____

5. Write an expository or argumentative sentence with at least three examples of strong word choice in it.

_____

Mini Lesson 66: Expository and Argumentative Word Choice

How can learning this help you? Expository and argumentative word choice may not seem as important as narrative or descriptive word choice, but it may be even more so. Clarity is extremely critical in expository and argumentative writing, and one of the best ways to get clarity is with specific words.

CLARITY IS IMPERATIVE IN EXPOSITORY AND ARGUMENTATIVE WRITING

Mark Twain said that the difference between the right word and the nearly right word is as different as lightning and a lightning bug.

ML 66 Student Activity: Expository and Argumentative Word Choice

1-3. Write a paragraph of argumentative or expository writing that has strong word choice.

_____

_____

_____

_____

4-5. Change the word choice to be vague and bland.

_____

_____

_____

_____

NAME _____   Language Arts Mini Lessons

Mini Lesson 67: Narrative Word Choice

How can learning this help you? In stories, and even more so in poems, possibly the most important trait to use in improving the writing's quality is word choice. Put your reader *right inside the poem or story*. The best way to do that is through strong imagery and specific, strong words.

EXCELLENT WORD CHOICE CAN PUT THE READER RIGHT INSIDE THE STORY!

ML 67 Student Activity: Narrative Word Choice

1-2. Find a poem that is strong in word choice.

_____

_____

3-4. Change one stanza to unspecific and boring word choice.

_____

_____

5. Exchange your poem with someone else and look at the changes they made.

NAME _____

Mini Lesson 68: Trait 5 Sentence Fluency

How can learning this help you? Just as it is hard to listen to a monotone speaker, sentences that start with the same types of words each time and are each of comparable length bore the reader. This lesson will help you inject variety into your sentence types so they will become more fluent.

MEANING

Weave your sentences with natural fluency and variety. Use crisp, clear sentences that start in different ways and vary in length. To use some musical terms, short, choppy sentences give a crisp, staccato effect. These are especially effective in emotional pieces. Longer, flowing, legato sentences work well in less emotional, more descriptive sentences.

ML 68 Student Activity: Trait 5 Sentence Fluency

Fill in the correct blanks of the following sentence from the text.

1. Sentences that _____ with the same types of words each time become boring.

2. Sentences that are each of comparable _____ become boring.

3-4. Use clear sentences that _____ in different ways and _____ in length.

5. Short, choppy sentences are especially effective in _____ passages.

NAME _____   Language Arts Mini Lessons

Mini Lesson 69: Improve Sentence Fluency

How can learning this help you? Sentence fluency means having a variety of words and sentence lengths in your sentences. Purposely plan to have variety in your sentences.

SENTENCE BEGINNINGS

Make sure you don't start consecutive sentences with the same word.

Don't always start a sentence with the subject. Start in different ways, like the following examples.

Example 1. "He decided the . . ."	(Subject)
Example 2. "The strange kid wanted to . . ."	(Two adjectives, then subject)
Example 3. "After the party ended, John went . . ."	(Dependent clause, then subject)

SENTENCE VARIETY

Purposely vary the sentences in most paragraphs between short, medium, and long..

It's good to combine several short, choppy sentences into one smooth sentence.

Use connecting words and phrases (but also, nevertheless, however, in addition to) to show how ideas relate.

Watch out for sentence fragments (incomplete sentences).

Watch out for run-on sentences (multiple sentences jammed together).

Get rid of deadwood. Be as brief and concise as possible.

ML 69 Student Activity: Improve Sentence Fluency

1. What is one way to improve the fluency of your sentence beginnings? _____

What are two ways to improve your sentence variety?

2. _____

3. _____

4. Create a 5 to 10 sentence paragraph with each sentence starting with the same word.

_____

_____

_____

5. Trade paragraphs with another person or group and revise most of their sentences so they start in different ways.

Mini Lesson 70: Sentence Length

How can learning this help you? Have you ever read a bunch of short sentences? They get really boring, don't they? It is the same thing with long sentences; we sometimes need sentences to stop so we can mentally breathe. We should mix up our sentence lengths between short, medium, and long.

VARY THE LENGTH OF SENTENCES TO ADD INTEREST

ML 70 Student Activity: Sentence Length

1. Read a 5 to 10 sentence paragraph from a professional writer and record the number of words in each sentence. _____

2. Find the average by totaling all of the words in the paragraph and dividing them by the number of sentences. _____

3. Get with a partner who read something by a different writer and compare the two writers' lengths to see how close they are.

Mini Lesson 71: Trait 6 Writing Conventions

How can learning this help you? Writing Conventions will be discussed in detail in later chapters but will be addressed briefly here as we study the basic part of writing: the sentence. Poor writing conventions and sloppy work not only make your writing harder to follow, they are also the first weaknesses most people notice in your writing. This lesson gives an introduction for what to work on. This trait will help make your writing clear.

MAKE YOUR WRITING CLEAR AND APPEALING

The two purposes of writing conventions and good layout are to make your writing clear and appealing. They include capitalization, layout, paragraphing, punctuation, spelling, and word usage. Layout is also essential has as much to do with understandable text as any other convention. Layout includes neatness, illustrations, good font choice, graphic organizers like numbers or bullets, and the general appearance of the page.

Weak	Strong
The girl nelt at the the stream. Suddunly a Bear rose up from behind the bushes, he roared and the girl, she wuz scared, and . . .	The girl knelt at the stream. Suddenly a bear rose up from behind the bushes. It roared, and the girl was scared. She . . .

ML 71 Student Activity: Trait 6 Writing Conventions

Find five mistakes in the weak piece above (left) about a girl at a stream. Compare it to the second strong one about the same topic.

1. _____
2. _____
3. _____
4. _____
5. _____

What are the two purposes of writing conventions and layout?

6. _____
7. _____

What are three of the types of convention weaknesses?

8. _____
9. _____
10. _____

Chapter Five: Modes and Genres

Why is this chapter important for you? Learn to categorize your writing into modes, then sub-categorize each mode into genres, while learning keys to writing these modes and genres successfully.

The Lessons

Chapter Five: Modes and Genres	84
Mini Lesson 72: Modes and Genres	86
Mini Lesson 73: Experience with Modes and Genres	87
Mini Lesson 74: The Descriptive Mode	88
Mini Lesson 75: The Importance of Description	89
Mini Lesson 76: Creating Description	90
Mini Lesson 77: Prose	91
Mini Lesson 78: Imagery in Poetry	92
Mini Lesson 79: Describing / Images	94
Mini Lesson 80: Create a Free Verse Poem	96
Mini Lesson 81: Expository Mode	97
Mini Lesson 82: Expository / Functional Genre	98
Mini Lesson 83: Expository / Informational Genres	100
Mini Lesson 84: Argumentative Mode	101
Mini Lesson 85: Argumentative Mode Genres	102
Mini Lesson 86: Essay Outline	103
Mini Lesson 87: Three Parts of an Essay	104
Mini Lesson 88: Create an Essay Draft	105
Mini Lesson 89: See All Sides of an Issue	106
Mini Lesson 90: Narrative Mode	107
Mini Lesson 91: Genres in the Narrative Mode	108
Mini Lesson 92: Drama	109
Mini Lesson 93: Fantasy	110
Mini Lesson 94: Folklore	111
Mini Lesson 95: Horror	112
Mini Lesson 96: Mystery	113
Mini Lesson 97: Personal Narrative	114
Mini Lesson 98: Poetry	115

Mini Lesson 99: Poetry Terms ... 117
Mini Lesson 100: Science Fiction ... 118
Mini Lesson 101: Young Adult Literature ... 119
Mini Lesson 102: Reviewing Narrative Writing Genres ... 120
Mini Lesson 103: Business Mode ... 121
Mini Lesson 104: Block Business Letter Format ... 122
Mini Lesson 105: Business Email Format ... 124
Mini Lesson 106: Friendly Letter Format ... 125

Mini Lesson 72: Modes and Genres

How can learning this help you? From the beginning of your writing, you must decide on the mode most applicable to your end result. As an example, should you choose narrative as your mode, then you proceed to choose a genre, or type of narrative writing, such as science fiction.

MODES AND GENRES

A mode is a major form of writing under which all other types may be subdivided. There are five modes of writing: descriptive, expository, narrative, argumentative, and business (recently added because of its own uniqueness).

A genre is the category of writing.

Each mode is subdivided into genres. Some genres fit into several modes. Usually, each genre fits into one mode more than it does the others. For instance, five of these genres in the narrative mode (and there are more) are poetry, drama, prose, fantasy, and young adult.

ML 72 Student Activity: Modes and Genres

What are the five modes of writing? Name two genres in each mode.

1. _____ a. genre _____ b. genre _____
2. _____ a. genre _____ b. genre _____
3. _____ a. genre _____ b. genre _____
4. _____ a. genre _____ b. genre _____
5. _____ a. genre _____ b. genre _____

3. Write down at least one example you have read from each genre.

   1. _____ 2. _____ 3. _____ 4. _____ 5. _____

4. Write a description of your kitchen after breakfast this morning.

   _____
   _____
   _____
   _____
   _____
   _____

5. Share your description with a partner.

NAME _____   Language Arts Mini Lessons

Mini Lesson 73: Experience with Modes and Genres

How can learning this help you? John Goodlad, considered the father of American education, said that the way to learn is to combine what we already know about a topic with what we don't know. If you can connect what you are learning now with what you already know, it makes the learning easier and more complete.

COMBINE WHAT YOU KNOW WITH WHAT YOU DON'T KNOW

ML 73 Student Activity: Experience with Modes and Genres

Write down the title or a very brief description of an example you have read from each genre.

1. Descriptive: _____

2. Expository: _____

3. Argumentative: _____

4. Narrative: _____

5. Business: _____

Mini Lesson 74: The Descriptive Mode

How can learning this help you? This short lesson on the Descriptive Mode helps teach you how to describe things more vividly and accurately in your writing. The Word Choice portion of the Six Traits lesson also gives suggestions for the Descriptive Mode.

DESCRIBE THINGS VIVIDLY AND ACCURATELY

The Descriptive Mode is used when describing things with specific words, images, and/or emotions. This is especially important in poetry. Whenever your purpose is to help your readers imagine something, or whenever you want to describe something to your readers, you will be writing descriptively.

Descriptive writing supports all of the other modes. Everything needs to be described to some extent.

Imagery's importance to descriptive writing is in the use of crisp, clear images which help us to see, hear, feel, smell, or taste something (sense imagery). Sharing the joy, sadness, or anger of someone (emotional imagery) also helps describe a situation.

ML 74 Student Activity: The Descriptive Mode

1. Which of the Six Traits fits best with the Descriptive Mode? _____

2. What mode describes things with specific words, images, and/or emotions? _____

3. Through what means does the Descriptive Mode support all of the other modes? _____
   _____

4. The best way to describe something is through crisp, clear _____

5. What is one of the main genres of the Descriptive Mode? _____

Mini Lesson 75: The Importance of Description

How can learning this help you? Have you ever read something that had promise but just wasn't "cutting it?" In your mind you might be thinking, *If I could have written this, I would have said it this way.* How would you do it? Make it more descriptive.

USE DESCRIPTION TO MAKE YOUR WRITING MORE INTERESTING

ML 75 Student Activity: The Importance of Description

The short piece below has enough action that it could really be exciting, but the words in it are dull and boring. Take this bland passage of writing and give it at least three specific uses of sense imagery and at least two of emotional imagery. Add your improved words above the current bland ones.

    The girl left her friends and started walking through the park toward her home. It was a stormy, autumn night. All of a sudden, the lights in the park turned off. Then she heard some footsteps on the leaves behind her. She started walking faster when she heard a voice.

Identify or create at least three specific examples of sense imagery in this piece.

1. _____

2. _____

3. _____

Identify or create at least two specific examples of emotional imagery in this piece.

4. _____

5. _____

Mini Lesson 76: Creating Description

How can learning this help you? Descriptive verbs and nouns allow us to be very specific in our word choices, but you must concentrate on using descriptive verbs and nouns more than you concentrate on descriptive adverbs and adjectives. Why? Because verbs and nouns make your writing more interesting.

USE DESCRIPTIVE VERBS AND NOUNS MORE THAN ADVERBS AND ADJECTIVES

ML 76 Student Activity: Creating Description

Make these five bland sentences into something very descriptive.

1. A girl tried to climb onto a horse from its front.

2. The horse kept its head up high.

3. She then tried to climb on from the back.

4. The horse swatted her with its tail.

5. She tried again, and the horse kicked her.

Mini Lesson 77: Prose

How can learning this help you? A common definition of prose is writing that is not poetry, but it is also simple and natural description based on strong imagery.

PROSE IS DESCRIBING SOMETHING FOR ITS OWN SAKE

Use the following description of an experience at Bryce Canyon to answer the questions.

Bryce Canyon National Park

If you have ever been to Bryce Canyon National Park, Utah, you know that beautiful pine trees take you right up to the edge of the canyon rim where bright orange cliffs suddenly drop 300 feet straight down.

On a glorious dawn one morning, I sauntered out to the canyon rim of Bryce Canyon National Park. It had been rainy and foggy all night, but now it was clear. However, as I approached the rim, I quickly saw that the fog had settled down into the canyon beneath me. It was so thick that it looked like I could wander out onto it without falling three hundred feet to the canyon floor.

Slowly as the sun rose, the fog settled lower. First the tip of one giant, orange spire appeared, then another. Each one now looked like an orange ship sailing across the sea. Gradually the fog descended the spires, and I could see more and more until after an hour of transfixed gazing I could see clear to the canyon's bottom.

ML 77 Student Activity: Prose

Find five descriptive places in this writing and substitute bland, unimaginative words for them. Notice the difference between the descriptive and bland words.

1. _____
2. _____
3. _____
4. _____
5. _____

Mini Lesson 78: Imagery in Poetry

How can learning this help you? Many people often describe something using the poetic form. Since the key to poetry is to show meaning while using as few words as possible, it is usually extremely descriptive. It does *not* have to rhyme.

POETRY DOES *NOT* HAVE TO RHYME

The following is an example of a free verse poem. Notice the imagery in it.

Apricots and Jungle Jim

One summer morning when I was five we were going to a family picnic,
and I put on my brand new Jungle Jim clothes.
They were matching tan shorts and shirt,
and I had two pockets in my pants and two pockets in my shirt.

I was so proud in my new clothes
because I knew I looked like the old movie hero, Jungle Jim,
who fought bad guys and bad animals
over in the African jungles.

We went out to our shop and orchard
to pick up my dad for the picnic.
Well, apricot season was on,
and our trees were full of the luscious fruit.

I went out, devoured many, and was soon full.
I filled one pants pocket and then the other.
I then stuffed apricots into both shirt pockets,
Now my bulging pockets were full of snacks.
Just then my dad called me to go to the picnic.
I turned . . . and ran . . . and TRIPPED!
I fell down onto the ground,
and all of my apricots made a gooshing sound.
When I stood up, all the juice started to drip down my front, all gooey.

I sniffed, and I stomped, and I bawled.
Instead of going to the picnic and showing off my Jungle Jim outfit,
I had to go home, bathe, and change.
Jungle Jim's gooey clothes were left behind.

(CONTINUED NEXT PAGE)

NAME _____ Language Arts Mini Lessons

ML 78 Student Activity: Imagery in Poetry

Find three examples of different kinds of sense imagery in the above example of free verse poetry.

1. _____

2. _____

3. _____

Find two examples of different kinds of emotional imagery in the above poem.

4. _____

5. _____

NAME _____   Language Arts Mini Lessons

Mini Lesson 79: Describing / Images

How can learning this help you? If you specifically try to make a bland piece of writing interesting, it will help you to realize how to write your own in a descriptive manner.

CREATE A BLAND PIECE AND MAKE IT INTERESTING

ML 79 Student Activity #A: Describing / Images

1. Put an X at the start of every third line of your paper, and don't write on it. Then you have room for revision.

_____

_____

X_____

_____

_____

X_____

2. Purposely write a vague, uninteresting, short description of something that is 50 words or less.

_____

_____

X_____

_____

_____

X_____

3. Trade papers with someone and make each other's paper specific and interesting.

4. Compare how you improved each other's paper.

5. With the intent of finding imagery, read the description on the next page and answer the questions.

(CONTINUED NEXT PAGE)

NAME _____   Language Arts Mini Lessons

    Look down on a small valley. See snow at the top, pine trees, rock cliffs, and a stream running through the bottom. Perhaps you see some trout jumping out of the stream to catch flies. By the stream is a log cabin with smoke coming out of the chimney.

ML 79 Student Activity #B: Describing / Images

Try to list examples of three senses that the above description suggests or infers (see, hear, touch, smell, taste).

1. _____

2. _____

3. _____

Try to list specific examples of two kinds of emotional imagery (joy, anger, fear, excitement, etc.) the picture shows or infers.

4. _____

5. _____

Mini Lesson 80: Create a Free Verse Poem

How can learning this help you? Free verse is not prose. As with other types of poetry, it is language writing which irregularly uses rhythm and sound with no fixed pattern. It is a form of poetry that is really devoid of any hard and fast rules.

USE YOUR IMAGINATION

ML 80 Student Activity: Create a Free Verse Poem

Try writing your own free verse poem.

1. Think of a single incident, whether true, fictitious, or a blend of both.

2. Make sure the incident has a lot of possibilities for both sensory and emotional imagery.

3. Leave every third line blank for revising. Write it as a story to get all of the facts down on paper.

4. Revise it for both sensory and emotional imagery.

5. Revise it for strong, specific verbs and other words.

6. Break it into one thought per line.

7. Make your groups of lines consistent (the same number of lines in each stanza).

8. Make sure it is at least eight lines long.

9. Polish it.

10. Share it in groups of 3 to 5 students.

NAME _____   Language Arts Mini Lessons

Mini Lesson 81: Expository Mode

How can learning this help you? Why is the Expository Mode important for you? It will help you to explain things to your readers (audience) more clearly.

EXPOSITORY MODE

The Expository Mode is used when explaining things with facts and examples, as well as giving directions. The vast majority of the writing done in the world is expository writing. Here are some basic suggestions for successful expository writing of any kind.

Be clear to your intended audience.

Be brief.

Be complete. Cover your topic, your whole topic, and nothing but your topic.

Be fair and impartial.

Be credible (trustworthy and deserving of the trust your readers place in you).

ML 81 Student Activity: Expository Mode

Make a list of at least five things you need/want to do today after school is out.

1. _____

2. _____

3. _____

4. _____

5. _____

NAME _____

Mini Lesson 82: Expository / Functional Genre

How can learning this help you? The Functional Genre of the Expository Mode is probably the most used of all genres, yet we almost overlook it as a type of writing because it's so brief and often so informal. The purpose of functional writing is to give directions, often to ourselves. It doesn't always have to be neat or formal, just clear.

THE MAIN TYPES OF FUNCTIONAL WRITING ARE:

Lists: grocery lists, "to-do" lists, etc.

"How-to" instructions

Recipes

Schedules—class, airline, event, etc.

Travel itineraries.

ML 82 Student Activity #A: Expository / Functional Genre

1. What is the most used of all modes? _____

2. Which genre in that mode is the most used genre? _____

What are three examples of functional writing?

3. _____

4. _____

5. _____

ML 82 Student Activity #B: Expository / Functional Genre

Make a list of at least five things you must do, should do, or want to do to clean or organize your bedroom.

1. _____ 2. _____

3. _____ 4. _____

5. _____

(CONTINUED NEXT PAGE)

NAME _____   Language Arts Mini Lessons

ML 82 Student Activity #C: Expository / Functional Genre

What are three of the suggestions the book gives to use in your expository writing?

1. _____

2. _____

3. _____

4. Write instructions on how to prepare a peanut butter and jelly sandwich.

   _____

5. Give directions to get from the principal's office to your language arts classroom. _____

   _____

Mini Lesson 83: Expository / Informational Genres

How can learning this help you? The Informational Genre, except for in functional writing, is what adults do most. It shares knowledge and explanations.

SHARE KNOWLEDGE AND INFORMATION

1. "How-to" Manuals

    These manuals are written to explain how to perform a task, follow some directions, or develop a skill. Examples are manuals for household appliances and automobiles.
    These are books written to explain the various parts of a topic in a clear, concise way. This book is an example of an informational sourcebook.

2. Research papers

    Research papers are based upon formal research with proper credit given for sources.

3. Documentaries

    These are nonfiction works of literature, such as a book, article, motion picture, or television program that show or analyze news events, people's lives, social conditions, scientific information, etc. They have little or no fiction and usually have some type of organization, such as plot, description, chronology, etc.

4. Informational essays

    These essays are like speeches or reports. Their purpose is to share knowledge or understanding. Here is the basic organization of an informational essay.

    Introduction: Catches our attention and informs us about the purpose of the essay through the thesis statement

    Body: Gives 3 to 5 points using logic and/or emotion to convince us of the point. This is usually about 75 percent of the essay

    Conclusion: Sums up the points and leaves us with something important to think about regarding the topic

ML 83 Student Activity: Expository / Informational Genres

1. What is one of the terms for a report written to share knowledge or enlightenment? _____

2. What is the term for a book that explains how to perform a task or develop a skill? _____

3. What is the term for a book that explains the different parts of a major topic? _____

4. Create an outline for a report about a famous person—politician, religious leader, athlete, or entertainer—about whom you already know something.

5. Get into a small group and compare your expository outline.

Mini Lesson 84: Argumentative Mode

How can learning this help you? Argumentative writing is the most important writing any of us will ever do because it's about convincing others. Unfortunately, it's the genre that many of us have done the worst at and where most of us have done the most poorly on our school standardized writing tests.

THE MOST IMPORTANT WRITING YOU WILL EVER DO

Argumentative writing persuades, motivates, and/or convinces people to accept their own opinions or products. The writer must take a stand on a controversial issue and attempt to convince the reader of that stand through logic and emotion. Examples of these argumentative topics could include such things as mandatory schooling through grade 12, school competency attached to driver's licenses, or key national issues about taxes or foreign policy, etc. No matter what the issue is, the better you can show your solution's plan and benefits, the more people you will persuade.

ML 84 Student Activity: Argumentative Mode

Choose one of the school's extracurricular activities, like basketball, choir, drama, etc.

1-4. Write about why it's the most outstanding extracurricular activity in your school. Be as convincing as you can. Try to use both logic and emotion to convince us.

_____
_____
_____
_____
_____
_____
_____
_____
_____
_____

5. Get into groups of 4 to 5 students and share your writing with your group.

Mini Lesson 85: Argumentative Mode Genres

How can learning this help you? The two main genres in the Argumentative Mode are advertisements and argumentative essays.

ADVERTISEMENTS AND ARGUMENTATIVE ESSAYS

Advertisements are usually brief statements created for the purpose of convincing the readers to buy a product or endorse an idea or candidate.

As important as advertisements are, much more of our writing deals with argumentative essays. Argumentative essays are like speeches in writing. The goal is to convince readers of something by using both logic (statistics, facts, etc.) and emotion (stories, etc.).

An argumentative essay is usually written when the view or opinion expressed has the potential for controversy. It addresses a split audience: those who agree with the writer's views, those who oppose the writer's views, and those who are undecided or don't know or care. Don't expect to win everyone over to your side, but hope to at least gain empathy (understanding) from your opposition.

ML 85 Student Activity: Argumentative Mode Genres

1. Write an advertisement about a fictitious candy bar.

   _____
   _____

2. Tell why it's the best candy bar to buy.

   _____
   _____

3. Create your ad to reach one of these age groups: children, teens, mothers, grandparents.

   _____
   _____

4. Now create an ad for the same candy bar, but for a different audience. Be as convincing as you can. Try to use both logic and emotion to convince the reader.

   _____
   _____

5. Get into groups of four to five students and share both of your ads with your group.

NAME _____   Language Arts Mini Lessons

Mini Lesson 86: Essay Outline

How can learning this help you? Here's a good sequence for creating an outline for your essay. Before you write the paper, make an outline (cluster or formal) of the points you want to make. It will make your actual essay much more organized and understandable to the reader.

A GOOD SEQUENCE FOR CREATING YOUR OUTLINE

Decide on your stand.

Analyze your audience. Where do most of them stand on this particular issue?

Write down the essay body's outline of the 3 to 5 points of your plan and its benefits.

Now that you have a rough outline, write down and solidify your thesis statement.

Develop the rest of your introduction's outline.

Develop your conclusion's outline.

ML 86 Student Activity: Essay Outline

1. Which writing mode is usually most poorly done by American writers? _____

2. The argumentative writer attempts to _____ the readers that their thoughts or products are the best.

What are two of the steps recommended in the suggested sequence for writing your essay?

3. _____

4. _____

5. Using the steps above, write a 50-100 word essay convincing us who was one of your best elementary teachers.

_____

_____

_____

_____

_____

_____

Mini Lesson 87: Three Parts of an Essay

How can learning this help you? Tie everything into your thesis statement. That helps both your thesis statement and the rest of your essay.

THREE PARTS OF AN ESSAY

1. Introduction: its purpose is to catch the reader's attention, briefly explain the problem, and state your position in a thesis statement, which is a statement to be proved or maintained against objections.

Catch the readers' attention and connect them to your topic with a story, quote, fact, etc. You can produce a powerful psychological impact with a well-constructed introduction. Most readers come to the written text carrying their own opinions about the subject. You can help them change that.

Briefly acknowledge the opposing viewpoint(s). The reason the topic is controversial is that there are valid and invalid points on each side.

Your thesis statement should make your position clear on the problem you're addressing.

Creating a strong thesis statement is the heart of argumentative writing.

Clearly present the thesis statement in the introduction. It is the touchstone for you, the writer, to keep returning to throughout the essay.

2. Body: this is where the points of your plan and its benefits appear. It is usually about 75 percent of the paper's length.

Acknowledge the opposition, then expand upon your thesis by explaining your plan and its benefits. It is usually composed of 3 to 5 points. Each point is like a mini-paper with a body of its own. Each point should be supported with logic and/or emotion. That will make your essay more convincing.

3. Conclusion: this is where you make your final summation and appeal to your audience.

Restate your thesis and reaffirm why your plan is the most beneficial.

Emphasize your plan by leaving your audience with a key fact or story to convince them to accept your point of view.

Request your audience's help to bring your plan to fruition. That's what is called the "call to action."

ML 87 Student Activity: Three Part of an Essay

1. What is the heart of argumentative writing? _____
2. What is one of the parts of the introduction besides the thesis statement? _____
3. Approximately what percent of an essay's length should the body be? _____
4. How many points or reasons should a good essay typically have? 2-4, 3-5, 4-6, or 5-7? (circle)
5. What is one of the four things the book suggests to include in the conclusion? _____

Mini Lesson 88: Create an Essay Draft

How can learning this help you? What are the main points your opponent will make against your points for his or her side? One of the most important items in any confrontation, whether spoken or written, is that your opponent will have counterarguments to every good point you make. Otherwise, it wouldn't be a controversial issue.

IDEAS FROM TEACHER AND WRITER KELLY GALLAGHER:

Mr. Gallagher gives his students an exercise somewhat like this in his book entitled Write Like This.

What are the main points of your argument?

What are your opponent's counterarguments?"

What are your opponent's main points? (Similar to counterarguments.)

What are your counterarguments? (Similar to your main points.)

ML 88 Student Activity: Create an Essay Draft

Use these statements to create your own essay rough draft. You will find a copy of the Argumentative outline for your essay in the Appendix.

1. Choose a controversial issue, such as an international or national problem, or which entertainer, athlete, or team is best. _____

2. Choose a side to take a stand on. _____

3. Use a copy of the Argumentative outline form to create an outline of how you could best persuade others to agree with you. _____

_____
_____
_____
_____
_____
_____
_____

4. Write a rough draft based on your outline.

5. Get with another student and evaluate each other's outlines according to the principles just presented.

NAME _____

Mini Lesson 89: See All Sides of an Issue

How can learning this help you? One of the most helpful things debate classes do is to help the participants learn to see all sides of an issue.

THERE ARE ALWAYS AT LEAST TWO SIDES TO ANY ARGUMENT

Debate students go into one round of competition and debate for an issue. During this, they give every major fact, statistic, and emotional reason to agree with that side.

In their next round, they may debate against the same issue, and give every major fact, statistic, and emotional reason to fight against that issue. With this practice, they learn that there are usually many valid and invalid points to every controversy.

ML 89 Student Activity: See All Sides of an Issue

Present both sides of the same issue. It is similar to debate except it is written, not spoken.

Choose a controversial issue, such as an international or national problem, school issue, or which entertainer, athlete, or team is best.

1. Choose a side to take a stand on and write an outline of how you could best persuade others to agree with you. Follow the Argumentative outline form in the Appendix.

2. Next, write an outline trying to persuade others that the opposite side of the issue is better. Follow the Argumentative outline in the Appendix.

3. Get with another student and evaluate each other's outlines.

4. Make any final revisions your partner suggested with which you agree.

5. What is one of the four things the book suggests to include in the conclusion? _____

_____
_____
_____
_____
_____
_____
_____

Get with another student and evaluate each other's outlines according to the principles just presented.

Mini Lesson 90: Narrative Mode

How can learning this help you? How many times have you read or written a story that was uninteresting or unclear? This lesson will help you to differentiate between the nine types of narrative genres. It will also teach you to better identify and comprehend narrative writing by others and help you write better narrative passages yourself.

NARRATIVE MODE

A narrative is basically a story. A short narrative usually covers a single incident, while a long one covers a longer period of time. Here are the general elements of their structure.

Characterization: Who is this about?

Protagonist (usually the hero): Give the protagonist at least one admirable quality (wise, brave, strong, etc.). Show us that quality through what the protagonist does and says, and what others say about them. Share some of their feelings and thoughts with the readers. Show how they change during the story.

Antagonist (usually the villain): Give the antagonist strong reasons to overcome the protagonist's desires. Let the antagonist try hard to overcome the protagonist.

Plot: What happens?

Exposition: introduces us to the situation, as well as who the main characters are and how they got to be the way they are at the story's start.

Beginning Balance: Life is bearable, but it foreshadows future trouble.

Upsetting Incident: Life is no longer bearable.

Rising Action: How the protagonist (hero) tries to restore the beginning balance. The antagonist tries to permanently destroy the balance.

Climax: When the protagonist wins or loses.

Resolution: Tie up any loose ends. This is an optional element used part of the time.

ML 90 Student Activity: Narrative Mode

Identify the general plot elements of each of these definitions.

1. Protagonist wins or loses. _____
2. Life is good, or at least bearable, but it has foreshadowing of future trouble. _____
3. Something happens that makes life no longer bearable. _____
4. The protagonist (hero) tries to restore beginning balance. _____
5. What is the situation, who are the characters, and how did they get to be that way at the story's start?
   _____

NAME _____

Mini Lesson 91: Genres in the Narrative Mode

How can learning this help you? While the plot structure of the Narrative Mode is listed in a previous Mini Lesson, there are several different kinds of genres within this mode. They are presented alphabetically.

NINE GENRES OF NARRATIVE WRITING

- Drama
- Fantasy
- Folklore (fables, legends, myths)
- Horror
- Mystery
- Personal narrative
- Poetry
- Science fiction
- Young Adult

ML 91 Student Activity: Genres in the Narrative Mode

Alone or with a partner, remember and write the title of an example of each of the nine types of narrative writing listed. Don't use the sample titles previously mentioned.

Number	Narrative Type	Title
1		
2		
3		
4		
5		
6		
7		
8		
9		

10. Get with a partner and share your sample titles.

Mini Lesson 92: Drama

How can learning this help you? Plays are narratives written for the main purpose of being performed for groups of people. Historically, the most famous writer of all time is the playwright William Shakespeare.

PERFORMANCE ART IS DRAMATIC, POETIC, MUSICAL, COMEDIC, AND MORE.

A few of the most famous American playwrights and some of their works are Arthur Miller (The Crucible and Death of a Salesman), Tennessee Williams (The Glass Menagerie and Streetcar Named Desire), Neil Simon (The Odd Couple and Barefoot in the Park), and the musical tandem of Richard Rodgers and Oscar Hammerstein (Oklahoma!, South Pacific, and The Sound of Music). Although they wrote in the mid-twentieth century, their plays continue to stand as landmarks.

Plays are made up of dialogue and stage directions. Effective dialogue constantly moves the story forward, shows a character's development, or brings forth an emotion from the audience.

Musical plays are generally much more involved than non-musical plays. Here's why: most non-musical plays have one interior set, which makes it easier to produce, and ten or fewer characters, which also makes it easier to produce. Musical plays usually have multiple sets that must be moved on and off the stage quickly. They also usually have 40 to 80 people in the cast.

ML 92 Student Activity: Drama

1. Read the following sample of a part of the fable "The Three Little Pigs" (56 words below). Read it to get a feeling for the drama genre.

   (The first Little Pig is snoring in his chair. The Wolf enters, very businesslike, and knocks on door. Little Pig rises fearfully.)

   Wolf: Little Pig, Little Pig! Let me come in!

   First Little Pig: (hiding behind the chair) No! Not by the hair of my chinny chin chin!

   Wolf: (angry) Then I'll huff, and I'll puff, and I'll blow your house in!

2. Choose another children's story and write your own 50+ word sample in the drama genre.

3. Choose a fairy tale, such as "Jack and the Bean Stalk" or "Little Red Riding Hood." Write down which fairy tale and write it as a play, i.e. dialogue and stage directions.

4. Write stage directions in the present tense and in italics.

5. Share your play in groups of 3 to 5 students.

Mini Lesson 93: Fantasy

How can learning this help you? Fantasy is currently a very popular genre, so if you want to pursue it, you will learn that fantasy's purpose is to depart from reality as we know it. If you can imagine something, fantasy can take you there. Fantasy may take place in ancient times, present time, or future times. It may have mythical characters and places, and the characters may have exaggerated powers. Two of the most successful fantasy writers are J. R. R. Tolkien (*Lord of the Rings* series) and J. K. Rowling (Harry Potter series).

TAKE A BREAK FROM REALITY AND TRY THE FANTASY GENRE

ML 93 Student Activity: Fantasy

Choose another children's story. Write down which story you chose and write your own 50+ word sample in the fantasy genre. Share in groups of 3 to 5 students.

Mini Lesson 94: Folklore

How can learning this help you? These are types of stories usually spoken and/or written by more primitive cultures and are passed on from one generation to another. They include fables, legends, and myths. Along with the fact that folklore was mankind's first fictional literature, there are some nice works in this genre.

MANKIND'S FIRST FICTIONAL LITERATURE

Fables. These are brief folklore stories that teach a moral or practical lesson about how to get along in life. The characters of many fables are animals that speak and behave like people. Examples include Brier Rabbit and Little Red Riding Hood.

Legends. Legends are folklore stories about characters who perform extraordinary deeds. These are often based to some extent on real people and their adventures, but they are usually greatly exaggerated. Examples include Pocahontas, Robin Hood, and Davy Crockett.

Myths. Myths are folklore stories that explain something about a primitive culture's world and beliefs and generally involve their gods or other supernatural beings. The Greeks were especially successful at writing myths. Examples of this include Hercules, Medea, and Jason and the Golden Fleece.

Fairy Tales. Walt Disney made many of these famous with his glorious cartoons like Sleeping Beauty, Cinderella, and Snow White and the Seven Dwarfs.

ML 94 Student Activity: Folklore

1. Think of a fable—perhaps about a family pet or a fascinating aunt or grandparent—you could write a rough outline for, or choose a character and write a legend or a myth about them and briefly write their story in 30 to 50 words.

2. Write in any of these genres: fantasy, fable, legend, myth, horror, mystery, personal narrative, science fiction, or young adult.

3. Use the key points of whatever genre you choose, so others can easily identify in which genre you're writing.

_____

_____

_____

_____

_____

4. Revise your story to improve it.

5. Get into groups again of 3 to 5 students and share your stories. Have everyone guess the genres.

Mini Lesson 95: Horror

How can learning this help you? If you want to write in the horror genre, your goal is to give your readers a desired terrifying experience based on what they read or view without having to experience it. The stories usually have violence and often revolve around the supernatural: ghosts, witches, vampires, etc.

IT'S ALWAYS FUN TO "WRITE A GOOD SCARE!"

Edgar Allen Poe popularized this genre in America. Stephen King is one of the current masters of it. R. L. Stine was the master for younger audiences for many years. Often the protagonist becomes isolated from everyone else and becomes exceedingly vulnerable.

ML 95 Student Activity: Horror

1. Think of a good protagonist for a horror story. _____

2. Think of a good antagonist for a horror story. _____

3. What is a good upsetting incident for a horror story? _____

4. What is a good rising action for a horror story? _____

5. What is a good climax for a horror story? _____

NAME _____ Language Arts Mini Lessons

Mini Lesson 96: Mystery

How can learning this help you? When you choose to write in the mystery genre, one of your challenges will be to keep the plotline clear since there are many parts to building the actual "mystery." Mysteries usually start by telling us of an act of violence, and they foreshadow more violence in the future. The protagonist tries to figure out who the antagonist is and catch them before more victims are attacked. *And Then There Were None* (also called *Ten Little Indians* in the play and movie versions), by Agatha Christie, is one of the most famous mystery novels.

WHO DONE IT?

ML 96 Student Activity: Mystery

1. Think of a good protagonist for a mystery story. _____

2. Think of a good antagonist for a mystery story. _____

3. What is a good upsetting incident for a mystery story? _____

4. What is a good rising action for a mystery story? _____

5. What is a good climax for a mystery story? _____

NAME _____

Mini Lesson 97: Personal Narrative

How can learning this help you? You will not only learn more about writing, but it will help you remember things about yourself. Don't forget, we know more about ourselves, and we care more about ourselves than we do about anyone or anything else in life. That's what helps us to survive, succeed, and serve others.

THREE TYPES OF PERSONAL NARRATIVE

Short personal narrative or writing about a single incident in your life

Autobiography or writing your whole life's story

Memoirs which focus on a key time or series of related times of your life: they are often about famous people, but they can be about ordinary people like us

Whatever type of personal narrative you write, tell it with honesty and emotion. However, write only what you don't mind sharing with others. Don't include anything that's too personal. Tell the truth and nothing but the truth but not necessarily the whole truth.

ML 97 Student Activity: Personal Narrative

Write down three ideas of events from the first half of your life for your autobiography.

1. _____
2. _____
3. _____

Write down three ideas of events from the last half of your life for your autobiography.

4. _____
5. _____
6-10. _____

Choose one of these incidents and make an outline of how you can write this best.

_____
_____
_____
_____

Mini Lesson 98: Poetry

How can learning this help you? Many writers who write other genres *also* write poetry. Since poetry is the most descriptive genre in the Narrative Mode, it is also usually the shortest in length. There are many great poems that are only eight or so lines long. Focus on a short piece of quality writing with a poem.

>Poets must give the same careful attention to words
>
>that composers give to melody,
>
>that painters give to color,
>
>that sculptors give to shape,
>
>and that dancers give to movement.
>
>John Malcolm Brinnin
>
>Holt, Rinehart, Winston, *Elements of Poetry*, Course Two, p. 341

Poetry focuses on giving as much meaning within as short a space as possible. Great attention is paid to word choice. The writing has its own form with each thought usually receiving its own line. Often the writing has rhyme and rhythm, but neither is required for a good poem.

Because of the originality and importance of poetry, some additional principles of poetry are included.

FIVE KEYS TO GOOD POETRY

1. Words in a poem are like the tip of an iceberg; most of the meaning lies beneath the surface.

2. Economy of words means saying a lot with relatively few words.

3. Lines are used to separate each thought.

4. When rhyming, never sacrifice meaning for the rhyme; meaning is more important than rhyming.

Along with all of the great poems that rhyme, there are also many great ones that don't rhyme.

5. Rhythm is critical to poems that rhyme and also need to have rhythm patterns.

(CONTINUED NEXT PAGE)

ML 98 Student Activity: Poetry

Identify the correct poetry term for each of these statements.

1. In poetry each _____ usually receives its own line.

2. Words in a poem are like the tip of an _____.

3. Most of the meaning lies beneath the _____.

4. Meaning is more important than _____.

5. Poems that rhyme also need to have _____ patterns.

6. Are most poems meant to be read aloud or silently? _____

7. When reading a poem aloud, should you pause when the meaning and punctuation call for it? _____

8. Read the first stanza of Alfred Noyes's famous poem, "The Highwayman" aloud in a sing-songy, galloping manner.

The Highwayman

Alfred Noyes

The wind was a torrent of darkness among the gusty trees.

The moon was a ghostly galleon tossed upon cloudy seas.

The road was a ribbon of moonlight over the purple moor,

And the highwayman came riding—

Riding—riding—

The highwayman came riding, up to the old inn-door.

9. Now read the first stanza of *"The Highwayman"* aloud as though it's in prose (paragraph) form.

10. Notice how much more meaning comes by reading the poem as if it's prose.

Mini Lesson 99: Poetry Terms

How can learning this help you? There are quite a few different terms used in poetry. These terms give you an idea of how to compose your poem and the methods that many poets incorporate in their poetry to for interest and variety.

SO MANY TERMS

Alliteration. The repetition of sounds at the beginning of words. ("A big, black, bug bit a big, black bear," "The silken, sad, uncertain rustling . . .")

Assonance. The repetition of sounds within words. ("How now, brown cow?")

Free Verse. A poem that does not have a regular rhythm or rhyme pattern. It tries to use the natural rhythms of ordinary speech and relies heavily on imagery.

Inversion. Change normal word order so the words rhyme or give emphasis.

Metaphor. A comparison of two unalike things by suggesting they are the same thing. ("His hand is a wet fish.")

Onomatopoeia. Words and phrases that make the sounds of their definitions (boom, buzz, sizzle).

Personification. Give non-human things human-like qualities. (The tree rocked itself in the wind.)

Simile. A comparison of two unalike things linked together by like or as. ("His hand is like a dead fish" or "I'm as hungry as a horse.")

Rhythm. The constant repetition of stressed and unstressed syllables.

Rhyme. Words that have similar sounds, especially at their ends.

Rhyme and rhythm are very complicated so our exploration will end here but the main point is that if you choose to rhyme, you also need rhythm, and you need to keep your rhyme and rhythm consistent. Re member, meaning is much more important than rhyming.

ML 99 Student Activity: Poetry Terms

Identify the correct poetry term for each of these statements.

1. Words and phrases that make the sounds of their definitions. _____

2. A comparison of two unlike things, linked together by like or as. _____

3. The repetition of sounds at the beginning of words. _____

4. These poems do not have a regular rhythm or rhyme pattern but rely heavily on imagery. _____

5. Constant repetition of stressed and unstressed syllables. _____

NAME _____

Mini Lesson 100: Science Fiction

How can learning this help you? Writing in the Science Fiction genre is a lot of fun. You can let your imagination run wild. It is usually about the exploration of future life and developments, but can also be about the past when you approach stories that include time travel, also very fascinating.

EXPLORE THE FUTURE WITH THE SCIENCE FICTION GENRE

Science fiction is mainly based on future scientific advancements which both help and hinder the protagonist, but that does not prevent writers from exploring the past, as well.

The plot is usually full of high adventure.

There is often a theme or moral to be learned by the reader.

Mary Shelley's Frankenstein is considered the first great science fiction novel. George Orwell's 1984 and H. G. Wells's War of the Worlds are also famous. George Lucas (Star Wars) is the most successful story/movie creator of science fiction. The Avengers series is also very popular science fiction.

ML 100 Student Activity: Science Fiction

1. Think of a good protagonist for a science fiction story. _____

2. Think of a good antagonist for a science fiction story. _____

3. What is a good upsetting incident for a science fiction story? _____

4. What is a good rising action for a science fiction story? _____

5. What is a good climax for a science fiction story? _____

NAME _____   Language Arts Mini Lessons

Mini Lesson 101: Young Adult Literature

How can learning this help you? This is a relatively new genre about teenagers and teenage problems. It really got started in 1967 with S. E. Hinton's young adult hit *The Outsiders*. Below is an example of young adult literature using a small portion of the fable *"The Three Little Pigs."* Of course, this little piece is meant to be a stereotype of young adult literature.

THE YOUNG ADULT GENRE IS RELATIVELY NEW; SINCE THE MID-1960s

So, my bro and I were chillin' in my new shack made of cool sticks, you know? And all of a sudden, this big, bad (and I mean BA-A-AD) wolf came waltzing up to the door. He said, "Yo, Little Pig, Little Pig. Like, let me come in."

We looked at each other like, "Dude! What is going on here?"

ML 101 Student Activity: Young Adult Literature

1-2. Read the preceding part of an updated version of the fable "The Three Little Pigs." Get a feeling for the young adult literature genre and write 50+ words of your own about a section of some story you have read before.

_____

_____

_____

3-4. Choose another children's story. Write down which story you chose and write a section of your own 50+ word sample in the young adult genre style.

_____

_____

_____

5. Share in groups of 3 to 5 students.

Mini Lesson 102: Reviewing Narrative Writing Genres

How can learning this help you? Reviewing is invaluable. The more you do it, the more it cements the content into your brain. Remember "practice makes perfect?" Well, reviewing makes "perfecter . . .," and, by the way, that is not a word.

REVIEWING GENRES

ML 102 Student Activity: Reviewing Narrative Writing Genres

Write down the correct genre for each of these types of stories.

1. Exploration of the future where scientific developments both help and hinder the protagonist:
   _____

2. Start with an act of violence that will foreshadow more violence in the future: _____

3. A story about you: _____

4. Scare your readers without making them actually experience something: _____

5. Figure out who the antagonist is before they attack someone else: _____

6. A relatively new genre about teenagers and teenage problems: _____

7. Often takes place in ancient times and has mythical characters with exaggerated powers:
   _____

8. Brief folklore stories that teach a moral or practical lesson, where the characters are often animals:
   _____

9. Folklore stories about a primitive culture's world, beliefs, and gods: _____

10. Written for the main purpose of being performed for groups of people:_____

Mini Lesson 103: Business Mode

How can learning this help you? You will learn formatting tips for communicating in the business world.

The Business Mode is literature written for the specific purpose of conducting various forms of commerce. This has only been considered its own mode for a short time, yet it's been used since mankind started doing trade. The writing's purpose is usually functional, informative, and/or argumentative. Clarity and brevity are typically the keys; little time is spent on writing for entertainment, description, or aesthetic value.

GENRES IN BUSINESS MODE

Memos: Brief notes written to convey business points

Emails: Brief notes written over the Internet

Reports: organized papers, usually researched, used to support facts or opinions

Business letters: letters written for the purpose of transacting or improving business

ML 103 Student Activity: Business Mode

What are the two keys to good business writing?

1. _____

2. _____

Match the business writing term with these definitions.

3. Brief notes written to convey business points. _____

4. Letters written for the purpose of transacting or improving business. _____

5. Organized papers, usually researched, used to support facts or opinions. _____

Mini Lesson 104: Block Business Letter Format

How can learning this help you? You will learn important formatting tips for communicating by letter or memos in the business world.

COMMUNICATING IN THE BUSINESS WORLD

Notice how everything starts on the left. It's also fine to have the heading and closing on the right, but everything else should be on the left.

Return Address	Smith Engine Repair
	562 Harper Road
	La Grange, GA 30240
	(1 space)
Date	September 8, 2020
	(2 spaces)
Heading	Juanita M. Lopez
	Administrative Assistant
	Chamber of Commerce
	P.O. Box 465
	Solvang, CA 93463
	(2 spaces)
Greeting:	Dear Ms. Lopez:
	(1 space)
Body.	What you say in your letter. (This is usually 90% of the letter.)
Paragraph 1.	Clear, friendly introduction. Briefly state the letter's point.
Paragraph 2.	Explain the importance of the main point of the letter.
Paragraph 3.	(If needed.) Provide more details and background.
Paragraph 4.	Restate the main points and include a call to action.
	(Double-space for a new paragraph instead of indenting.)
	(1 space)
Closing,	Sincerely,
	(2 spaces)
Signature	*Charles D. Smith*
Printed name	Charles D. Smith
Position	President, Smith Engine Repair

(CONTINUED NEXT PAGE)

NAME _____   Language Arts Mini Lessons

ML 104 Student Activity: Block Business Letter Format

Follow the Block Business Letter Format for the assignments below.

1. Write down the terms of five of the seven parts of a business letter. _____

_____

2. Write down the parts for a fictitious business letter. Use real or made-up names, etc.

_____

_____

3. Just write "Body" where the body of the letter goes.

4. With a partner, evaluate each other's letters.

5. Take the evaluation from your partner and make the changes in your own letter.

NAME _____

Mini Lesson 105: Business Email Format

How can learning this help you? You will learn important formatting tips for communicating with email in the business world.

COMMUNICATING PROFESSIONALLY THROUGH EMAIL

Date:	September 8, 2020
	(2 spaces)
Subject:	Subject of email
	(1 space)
Greeting:	Dear Ms. Lopez:
	(1 space)
Body:	What you say in your email. (This is usually 90% of the email.)
Paragraph 1:	Clear, friendly introduction. Briefly state the email's point.
Paragraph 2:	Explain the importance of the main point of the email.
Paragraph 3:	If needed, provide more details and background.
Paragraph 4:	Restate the main points and include a call to action.
	(Double-space for a new paragraph instead of indenting.)
	(1 space)
Closing:	Sincerely,
	(1 space)
Printed Signature:	Charles D. Smith
Position:	President, Smith Engine Repair

ML 105 Student Activity: Business Email Format

1-5. Using the Business Email letter like the one above, create one using all of the points.

_____

_____

_____

_____

_____

(CONTINUED NEXT PAGE)

NAME _____   Language Arts Mini Lessons

Mini Lesson 106: Friendly Letter Format

How can learning this help you? Learn formatting tips for communicating with family and friends.

HOW TO COMMUNICATE INFORMALLY WITH A LETTER

Including the address is not necessary but is acceptable.

Heading:	110 Willowbrook Road
	Battleground, IN 47920
	(1 space)
Date:	May 5, 2005
	(1 space)
Greeting:	Dear Linda,
	(1 space)
Body:	What you say in your letter. (This is usually 95% of the letter.)
	(Double-space for a new paragraph instead of indenting.)
	(1 space)
Closing:	Yours sincerely,
Signature:	*Ashley*

ML 106 Student Activity: Friendly Letter Format

1-4. Using all of the points of the Friendly Letter Format like the one above, compose a brief friendly letter to a relative thanking them for a present sent to you.

_____
_____
_____
_____

5. Trade letters with another student and evaluate each other's work.

Chapter Six: Contest Writing

What should you learn from this chapter? A letter from the author:

Dear Students,

While literature is usually most kids' favorite part of language arts, many will probably like contest writing as well. Not only do you have the opportunity to learn all the elements necessary to write well (which will be invaluable to you throughout your life), but you will have the added opportunity to read literary masterpieces and learn from many great writers. As a bonus, I found that many students discover that writing, especially for contests, is even more enjoyable and motivating, and they learn a great deal about writing and grammar while working on their contest writing.

I sincerely hope you are learning some helpful language arts concepts from your teacher and this book.

Neil Johnson
Teacher, Author, Mentor

The Lessons

Chapter Six: Contest Writing 126
    Mini Lesson 107: Why Enter a Contest? 128
    Mini Lesson 108: Writing Process for a Contest 129
    Mini Lesson 109: Pre-Writing Introduction 131
    Mini Lesson 110: Three Main Categories of Contests 132
    Mini Lesson 111: Essay Outline 133
    Mini Lesson 112: Trait 1 Ideas 135
    Mini Lesson 113: Trait 2–Organization / Outline 136
    Mini Lesson 114: Trait 2 Organization / Plot 139
    Mini Lesson 115: Poetry Organization 143
    Mini Lesson 116: Rough Draft 145
    Mini Lesson 117: Stream-of-Consciousness Writing 146
    Mini Lesson 118: Rough Draft Review 147
    Mini Lesson 119: Trait 3 Voice 148
    Mini Lesson 120: Revising Overall Content 151
    Mini Lesson 121: Trait 4 Word Choice 153
    Mini Lesson 122: Editing Paragraphs and Sentences 156
    Mini Lesson 123: Editing Usage and Punctuation 158

Mini Lesson 124: Editing Spelling and Capitalization 159
Mini Lesson 125: Editing Rhyme and Rhythm 160
Mini Lesson 126: Proofreading 161
Mini Lesson 127: Proofreading Each Other's Papers 162
Mini Lesson 128: Proofreading Ideas and Organization 163
Mini Lesson 129: Proofreading–Voice and Word Choice 164
Mini Lesson 130: Proofreading Paragraphs and Sentences 166
Mini Lesson 131: Proofreading Usage and Punctuation 167
Mini Lesson 132: Proofreading Spelling and Capitalization 168
Mini Lesson 133: Trait 5 Sentence Fluency 169
Mini Lesson 134: Proofreading Rhyme and Rhythm 171
Mini Lesson 135: Word Choice in Poetry 172
Mini Lesson 136 Some of the Best Writing Contests 173

Mini Lesson 107: Why Enter a Contest?

How can learning this help you? You know the good and bad feelings you get when writing something for your teacher? After hard work and a lot of personal investment of yourself, the teacher makes some comments to help you, then quickly moves on to the next paper in the huge stack that awaits them. You may be happy with your grade and pleased with your work, but the teacher is the only person other than you to *see* it. When you enter a contest, all that changes.

When you submit your writing to a contest, judges reading and evaluating your work whom you will never see, but they will be scrutinizing it and comparing it with work by other students from other schools, and even other states. If (or when) you are a winner, it's very exciting, and you feel your time and effort were worth it.

YOUR AUDIENCE—THE JUDGES

If you're writing for a contest, your audience will be judges who will likely be busy adults who are kind enough to spend several hours reading a stack of contest entries. They are probably good with writing and grammar skills, and they like to read, but it is still a daunting task to read all of those contest papers and choose the best ones. Try to imagine these judges and write considering them. What can you write about that will make your writing piece stand out to your judges from all of the other contest pieces they read?

Good luck! May you write some things you are genuinely proud of and may you learn a lot about writing and grammar from this work.

ML 107 Student Activity: Why Enter a Contest?

1. What is usually the favorite part of language arts for most students? _____

2. What did this book's author find was usually his students' favorite part? _____

3. With whom does a contest judge compare your contest piece? _____

   a. Students in your classroom

   b. Students from your school or even students from other states

   c. They don't compare it; they just read it for its own merits.

4. Are the judges usually skilled with writing and grammar? _____

5. Should you try to write something that will stand out for your judges? _____

Mini Lesson 108: Writing Process for a Contest

How can learning this help you? If you use the Writing Process to create a strong piece of writing, and you then use the principles from the Six Traits of Writing to polish it, you will have an excellent chance of writing an outstanding piece. In this Chapter, there will be sample poems that won contests to show how these writers excelled in one or more of the Six Traits.

WINNING A CONTEST IS SUCH A THRILL!

Student author McCall Bowcut has written a very sophisticated poem. As you read "I Saw a Baby Unicorn," notice the beautiful imagery created by the strong, specific word choices McCall made.

Since this is a rhymed poem, see how she never sacrifices meaning for the sake of a rhyme. She also has fine sentence structure. McCall's poem was chosen as a "Top Ten Poem" from over a thousand entries.

I Saw a Baby Unicorn

McCall Bowcut

I saw a baby unicorn, lying in the shade.
Its coat was sleek and shiny,
and its eyes like bottled jade.

Its hooves were white as icicles, with little flecks of gray.
Its tail shone brighter than the sun
on a summer day.

It smelt of fragrant flowers with the slightest hint of rain
and tiny dots of starlight
danced upon its mane.

It was the most enchanting beast that I had ever seen.
It had a horn upon its nose
and sported tiny wings.

(CONTINUED NEXT PAGE)

I quickly yelled for all my friends. I felt I had to share

this tiny creature I had found

lying sweetly there.

Until one girl said with a sniff, "Unicorns do not exist.

They never have, they never will.

We all know they're just a myth!"

We saw a baby unicorn, but just as I had feared,

the unicorn quaked as it heard her words

and, with a pop, it disappeared.

ML 108 Student Activity: Writing Process for a Contest

List two examples of strong imagery from the poem, "I Saw a Baby Unicorn."

1-2. _____

_____

List two examples of original word choices.

3-4. _____

_____

5. If the baby unicorn is a metaphor, what do you think it represents in today's world?

_____

NAME _____   Language Arts Mini Lessons

Mini Lesson 109: Pre-Writing Introduction

How can learning this help you? Pre-Writing is the best thing you can do before writing an essay, story, poem, etc. Why? It helps you do most of your thinking, creating, and organizing before you write many words. It is usually the most important step in the whole writing process, just as the most important part of a building is its foundation.

BEFORE WRITING, ASK YOURSELF: "WHY AM I WRITING THIS PIECE?"

ML 109 Student Activity: Pre-Writing Introduction

1. What is the best thing you can do before actually writing your piece? _____

2. During what part of the writing process should you do most of your thinking and organizing?

   _____

3. Do you write a lot of words during this time? _____

4. What does the book compare pre-writing to in a building? _____

5. Before writing you should ask yourself _____ you are writing this particular piece.

NAME _____ Language Arts Mini Lessons

Mini Lesson 110: Three Main Categories of Contests

How can learning this help you? There are three main types of writing contests: essays, short stories, and poetry. If you can research the type(s) of contests you want to enter, determine their deadlines, entry fees, etc., you will be able to plan your writing around them all. Don't limit yourself to just one category. Experiment and explore.

THE THREE MAIN CATEGORIES ARE:

  Essays

  Short Stories

  Poetry

ML 110 Student Activity: Three Main Categories of Contests

What are the three main types of writing contests?

1. _____

2. _____

3. _____

4. What is your favorite type of writing contest category? _____

5. What is your least favorite type of writing contest category? _____

Mini Lesson 111: Essay Outline

How can learning this help you? Essays can be both informative and argumentative. Most essay contests give students a theme to write about. A good theme in an argumentative essay contest is about a controversial issue that has good and bad points on all sides. A good judge will not evaluate your paper on whether they agree with you or not, but on how well you defend your stand and convincingly present your plan to overcome the controversial issue. You are wise to give convincing arguments with both logical and emotional points.

A TYPICAL ESSAY OUTLINE (ALSO IN THE APPENDIX)

If you learn to craft your essay around an outline like this sample, it will make your essay much more organized and clear.

INTRODUCTION

Catch the reader's interest.

Thesis statement: You may want to include a measurable objective in your thesis statement. The thesis statement is the heart of the essay. Keep referring back to it in your essay.

Briefly acknowledge counterarguments.

Minimize the counterarguments

BODY: EXPLAIN YOUR POINTS

First point

Second point

Third point

CONCLUSION: CONVINCE US THAT YOU'RE RIGHT

Summarize

Final statement

Call to action for an argumentative essay

(CONTINUED NEXT PAGE)

ML 111 Student Activity: Essay Outline

Choose your topic for the essay and then fill out this outline form about it.

A. Introduction

    1. Catch our interest: _____

    2. Thesis statement: _____

Include a measurable objective in your thesis statement. The thesis statement is the heart of the essay. Keep referring back to it in your essay.

    3. Briefly acknowledge counterarguments _____

    4. Minimize the counterarguments _____

B. Body: Explain your points

    5. First point: Problem _____

    6. Second point: Solution _____

    7. Third point: Benefits _____

C. Conclusion: Convince us you are right

    8. Summarize: _____

    _____

    9. Final statement: _____

    _____

    10. Call to action for an argumentative _____

    _____

NAME _____   Language Arts Mini Lessons

Mini Lesson 112: Trait 1 Ideas

How can learning this help you? Most short story and poetry contests do not give you a theme about which to write. Some, like the PTA Reflection Contest, do. Since there are many more opportunities to enter poetry contests than other writing contests, and since poems are shorter than other kinds of writing (and *supposedly* easier to write), this lesson explores poetry more than essays or short stories.

SOURCES FOR IDEAS

Another story

Event: current or historic

Theme

Person/character

Imagery: emotional and/or sensory

ML 112 Student Activity: Trait 1 Ideas

Write down at least one story or poem idea to write about from each of these add sources for ideas.

1. Another story _____

2. Event: current or historic _____

3. Theme _____

4. Person/character _____

5. Imagery: emotional and/or sensory _____

Mini Lesson 113: Trait 2–Organization / Outline

How can learning this help you? Outlining is a method of keeping your writing organized and prevents you from wandering down sub-plotlines that take you so far away from the real story that you can never get back! The outline will keep you focused on your end goal and help you fill in all the pieces.

NARRATIVE OUTLINE

Student Author Cameron P. Edwards chose a comparatively mundane occasion, a piano recital, instead of a historic event about which to write. Cameron used strong voice and excellent word choice. He also purposely put in some short, one- or two-word, lines to show his thoughts in disarray. Notice that the poem does not rhyme, but is free verse. This poem took First Place in his state and Eleventh Place in the nation in a contest.

I Just Came Along for the Ride

Cameron P. Edwards

Applause trickles in my ears
as I stand and shuffle
across my row
to the aisle.
I look from side to clapping side
into the faces of the judges
whose son or daughter
always wins, in their parentally approving minds.
After years of performance,
I've learned to ignore what they think
and remember that what I know
is all that really matters.
My blood pumps loudly in my ears
as I mumble my piece
and
composer
and my
thoughts

(CONTINUED NEXT PAGE)

become a

disarray,

so I take a deep Breath

staring down at the ivory keys

to think sensibly once again,

moving my eyes across the glistening white.

I reach up to tap my first note,

and then I'm off!

My fingers are racing over the keyboard

Flying over like they are afire.

I slow into a graceful swing,

pushing the louds, muffling the softs, piano, forte,

piano, forte

pouring heart and soul into the song

like it's all that really matters.

Then, before I know it,

I'm lifting my fingers from the keys,

standing up

from the bench,

and bowing.

The funny thing was:

The music played itself.

I just came along for the ride.

ORGANIZING A NARRATIVE OUTLINE

There must be two main parties trying to beat each other in the story.

Choose your protagonist (hero) and antagonist (villain).

Give the protagonist at least one admirable quality (courage, honesty, strength, wisdom, loyalty, beauty, etc.) that the reader can respect about them.

Show the admirable quality; don't just tell us about it.

Remember, the more the readers admire the protagonist, the more they care about them. The more they care about the protagonist, the more they care what happens to them. The more they care about what happens to the protagonist, the more they care about what happens in the story.

(CONTINUED NEXT PAGE)

ML 113 Student Activity: Trait 2 Organization / Outline

Fill out this form for the preceding poem, "I Just Came Along for the Ride."

Characters

1. Protagonist (hero) _____

2. Antagonist (villain) _____

3. Protagonist's main admirable trait _____

Setting

4. Where it happens _____

5. When it happens _____

NAME _____

Mini Lesson 114: Trait 2 Organization / Plot

How can learning this help you? The plot is critical for any type of writing. This *is* the story. It's made up of characters, settings, and many, many more elements you choose to include. You have your ideas. Now you can organize them into the best way to showcase your ideas.

NARRATIVE CHARACTER AND SETTING OUTLINE

Fill out this form for a brief outline of a poem you would like to write.

Characters

  Protagonist (hero) _____

  Antagonist (villain) _____

  Protagonist's main admirable trait _____

Setting

  Where it happens _____

  When it happens _____

NARRATIVE PLOT

You have your ideas. Now organize them into the best way to showcase them.

EXPOSITION

The exposition does three things: it briefly tells us who the characters are at the start of the story and how they got to be that way, it informs us about the fragile beginning balance, and it starts the action of the plot moving with the upsetting incident.

THE BEGINNING BALANCE

Life is bearable, perhaps even good, but there are hints of future trouble. Some stories skip the beginning balance and start right off with the upsetting incident. This also eventually tells us who the characters are at the beginning of the story and how they became that way.

UPSETTING INCIDENT

Something upsets the beginning balance so that life no longer seems bearable.

RISING ACTION

As the protagonist tries to restore the beginning balance, they encounter a series of crises that get progressively harder to overcome. As they work to overcome the crises and eventually tries to overcome the upsetting incident, they change for the better—wiser, stronger, more capable, etc.

(CONTINUED NEXT PAGE)

CLIMAX

Usually the protagonist wins and restores the beginning balance, so life, though now damaged, is bearable again. The climax is really important for both the protagonist and antagonist to "win." Sometimes the protagonist loses and fails to restore the beginning damage. Sometimes he/she even loses their life while trying. That is known as a tragedy.

RESOLUTION

Resolving things and tying up any loose ends. One possible thing is to show how your protagonist changed for the better during the conflict. Some stories end with the climax and have no resolution. If you have a resolution, it is good to make it as short as possible. Once the climax has been reached, it's hard to retain the reader's interest much longer.

ML 114 Student Activity #A: Organization / Plot

Fill out this form for a brief outline of a poem you would like to write.

Characters

1. Protagonist (hero) _____

2. Antagonist (villain) _____

3. Protagonist's main admirable trait _____

Setting

4. Where it happens _____

5. When it happens _____

ML 114 Student Activity #B: Narrative Plot

Fill out this more extensive outline for your poem you would like to write.

Plot

1. Exposition

   a. Beginning Balance _____

   b. Upsetting Incident _____

2. Rising Action _____

(CONTINUED NEXT PAGE)

NAME _____   Language Arts Mini Lessons

Crises

a. _____

b. _____

c. _____

3. Climax _____

4. Resolution (optional) _____

5. Trade outlines with a partner and tell each other two positive and two negative comments.

ML 114 Student Activity #C: Narrative Characters for Your Writing

Fill in the blanks below for an outline of one of your other narrative topics. Remember that this is just a brief outline. Write 20 words or less in total, and purposely use incomplete sentences and mostly nouns and verbs in this.

Characters

1. Protagonist (hero) _____

2. Antagonist (villain) _____

3. Protagonist's main admirable trait _____

Setting

4. Where it happens _____

5. When it happens _____

(CONTINUED NEXT PAGE)

NAME _____

ML 114 Student Activity #D: Narrative Plot for Your Writing

Create the plot outline for this new poem or story.

Plot

1. Exposition

    a. Beginning Balance _____

    b. Upsetting Incident _____

2. Rising Action _____

Crises

    a. _____

    b. _____

    c. _____

3. Climax _____

4. Resolution (optional) _____

5. Trade outlines with a partner and tell each other two positive and two negative comments.

You now have two outlines of work you can develop into a finished product.

Mini Lesson 115: Poetry Organization

How can learning this help you? If you want to be a great poet, the "less is more" rule really applies. Poetry is the most descriptive genre in the Narrative Mode, but it is also usually the shortest in length. There are many great poems that are only eight or less lines long.

POETRY IS THE MOST DESCRIPTIVE GENRE

Student author Hayley Halls used the organization of chronology of a child's day to tell her story of patience and loyalty. She also showed strong voice by sharing the little girl's feelings and thoughts.

Our Castle

Hayley Halls

I've been waiting for you all day today

Alone in my sandbox with nothing to play.

I see all the other kids running around with their friends

Playing games from imaginations that have no ends.

They've been having so much fun, and I wish I were in it,

But I know I can't

'cause you'll be here any minute.

We'll build dragons and princesses that live in big castles, and . . .

"Oh no," I think, as I see the sun set,

A day has gone by, and you still haven't come yet.

It's time for bed, so I slump inside.

My sadness and pain I cannot hide.

I take one last look over my shoulder

To see if you're there, though the day is now colder.

But all I can see is my footprints in the sand

Where maybe tomorrow our castles will stand.

(CONTINUED NEXT PAGE)

NAME _____

ML 115 Student Activity: Poetry Organization

1-3. Write 50 words or less describing an incident from the first half of your life. Use the poem Our Castle as your model. Try to base your rough draft on one of the narrative outlines you have already written.

_____

_____

_____

4. Focus on the organization of this very short piece.

5. Trade papers with each other and compare.

NAME _____   Language Arts Mini Lessons

Mini Lesson 116: Rough Draft

How can learning this help you? If you are beginning your rough draft, it is exactly that—rough. By leaving every third line blank, you have that line to write on when you revise. If you are typing your rough draft, double-space it, so you have room between lines to revise.

DON'T SWEAT THE SMALL STUFF—YET

Every time you're tempted to stop and check your draft for conventions, imagine you're driving down the freeway in a large semi-truck, and suddenly you have to stop. Think of all the work it takes to do that. After you finally stop, you have to slowly shift the gears higher and higher and higher until you're finally cruising again. That's what happens to your right-brained, creative thoughts and overall ideas when you stop to see if you inserted a comma or spelled a word correctly. It forces your large, flowing ideas to grind to a halt, then you have to somehow start them up again.

When resolving things and tying up any loose ends, one possible thing is to show how your protagonist changed for the better during the conflict. Some stories end with the climax and have no resolution. If you have a resolution, it is good to make it as short as possible. Once the climax has been reached, it's hard to retain the reader's interest much longer.

ML 116 Student Activity: Rough Draft

Leave every third line blank. Write your contest piece. If you're writing by hand, make sure your paper has an X at the beginning of every third line. If you're typing, double-space. Don't write in this X line now, but use it later for revision.

1. Did you leave every third line blank (X) for revision space? _____

2. Did you use the stream-of-consciousness method? _____

3. Did you follow your outline except for when you got better ideas? _____

4. Did you leave the small stuff to work on later? _____

5. Did you check your outline to see if you left anything out that you still want in? _____

Mini Lesson 117: Stream-of-Consciousness Writing

How can learning this help you? What is "stream-of-consciousness" writing? It is the fluid thoughts that develop in your characters' minds (or the narrator's mind) as the narrative progresses, almost as if you are inside their (the characters') heads thinking their thoughts. Some students think they can skip the rough draft and move from their outline to their final copy. No matter how able and experienced we are as writers, we can always improve what we have written.

LOOK FIVE LINES DOWN

Use the outline you just made as your "road map." Leave every third line blank for notes.

Follow your outline when it works; depart from it when you have better ideas. This is useful in narrative writing.

Write your overall thoughts down.

Do you get stressed out when you have to write something? Do you find that it's hard to remember all of the things you are supposed to include? When you're writing, do you get so worried about everything that you forget what you are trying to say? If you follow your outline and focus on your overall ideas, you may find that writing will become much easier.

"Don't sweat the small stuff yet." Use your creativity to develop your ideas. Remember, drafting is a right-brained activity. Use the stream-of-consciousness method to draft. Let your overall ideas flow through your mind and onto the paper. Don't stop to worry about any conventions like grammar, spelling, punctuation, etc. yet.

ML 117 Student Activity: Stream-of-Consciousness Writing

Referring to your outline, write your rough draft. Follow your outline except where it doesn't work or where you come up with a better idea. Don't worry about any grammar problems right now; just worry about following your stream-of-consciousness and get your main ideas down.

1-3. Write your rough draft based on your outline on a separate piece of paper.

4. Did you use the stream-of-consciousness method?

5. Write eight or more words describing how it worked for you.

_____

_____

_____

_____

Mini Lesson 118: Rough Draft Review

How can learning this help you? By now, you should be grasping why the rough draft with its outline and the stream-of-consciousness method are the best methods to writing a serious piece. Review what you have learned about rough drafting. It will save a bad piece of writing and enable you to create a good one instead.

ROUGH DRAFTING CAN BE A LIFE SAVER

ML 118 Student Activity: Rough Draft Review

1. Did you leave every third line blank (x) for revision space? _____

2. Did you use the stream-of-consciousness method? _____

3. Did you follow your outline except when you got better ideas? _____

4. Did you leave the small stuff to work on later? _____

5. Did you check your outline to see if you left anything out that you still want in? _____

Mini Lesson 119: Trait 3 Voice

How can learning this help you? What is "voice" in writing? Simply stated, it is the way *you choose* to be heard. Are you going to be scholarly, cynical, paranoid, funny, argumentative, kind, reflective, or just a normal guy or girl. The sky is the limit here but once you have chosen a voice, for you as the narrator, or for individual characters, you must stick with it in that particular piece of writing.

Student Author Aubree M. Davis explored the horrible thoughts and emotions of someone enduring a severe eating disorder. She shared the girl's feelings and thoughts, and we can almost feel the terrible emotions of this person. Aubree chose to write in first-person (I, me, we, us) which makes it more personal. It's as if the girl is sharing her secrets with us. This poem received First Place in the state in a contest.

USE THE TOOLS YOU HAVE BEEN TAUGHT—AND USE YOUR IMAGINATION!

Strange Eating Disorder

Aubree M. Davis

I feel eyes on me.

They're trying to see through my mask,

See that I'm empty inside,

See that I'm not happy and put together.

They're trying to see me eat things I don't deserve.

I always stand on the scale

seeing things I don't want to see.

Always too high; never too low.

Strange voices in my head saying, "You're fat,"

or, "You don't deserve this."

Why are they here? Is it true?

I believe them. I know they're right.

I need help.

(CONTINUED NEXT PAGE)

It has seemed like months now.

When I look at food, my mouth waters,

but my mind curses me for it.

It's not my fault.

It's not my fault that I'm dirty and ugly.

Everyone always tells me I'm so skinny,

They tell me that I make them sick.

I know they're jealous. Who wouldn't be?

My beautiful thick black hair is now stringy and falling out.

My pretty blue eyes are now bloodshot.

There are large bags under my eyes from no sleep.

My skin is very saggy.

My world is getting darker.

I feel so alone.

Maybe the easiest way out is to die.

I will let death eat me away,

No one ever knowing.

ML 119 Student Activity #A: Voice

Read through the poem "Strange Eating Disorder," and write down five places where the author Aubrey shows her protagonist's voice through her feelings and thoughts.

1. _____
2. _____
3. _____
4. _____
5. _____

(CONTINUED NEXT PAGE)

ML 119 Student Activity #B: Voice in Your Writing

Return to a narrative piece you've written. Find and/or add five times where your protagonist shows voice by sharing their thoughts and emotions, as well as by what they say and do.

1. _____

2. _____

3. _____

4. _____

5. _____

Mini Lesson 120: Revising Overall Content

How can learning this help you? When revising your overall content, read your work focusing on the first four traits: Idea Development, Organization, Voice, and Word Choice.

FOCUS ON THE FIRST FOUR TRAITS

Develop the ideas with originality and clarity. Check your overall idea and content as well as its development.

Make sure your organization is showcasing your ideas and content.

Evaluate your piece for how strong your voice is: your opinions, thoughts, and feelings.

Fill in your blank lines, margins, and spaces with revisions and improvements.

Re-read your piece, concentrating on strong, specific words and imagery. Especially evaluate your verbs—use active, specific ones.

Remember, you're trying to improve the big things in your rough draft such as clearer thoughts, better persuasion, stronger characters, and more intense conflicts.

ML 120 Student Activity #A: Revising Overall Content

Check your writing and answer the strong points and suggestions for improvement for these categories.

A. Ideas and Content: Strong points

1. _____
2. _____
3. _____

Suggestions for improvement

4. _____
5. _____

B. Organization: Strong points

1. _____
2. _____
3. _____

(CONTINUED NEXT PAGE)

NAME _____   Language Arts Mini Lessons

Suggestions for improvement

1. _____

2. _____

ML 120 Student Activity #B: Revising Voice

Check your writing and answer the strong points and suggestions for improving voice for these categories.

A. Ideas and Content: Strong points

1. _____

2. _____

3. _____

B. Suggestions for improvement

4. _____

5. _____

Mini Lesson 121: Trait 4 Word Choice

How can learning this help you? Word choice is critical because this is one of the best ways to keep your reader's attention, especially when you keep your variety of word usage big, interesting, and yes, fun.

Student author Kira Nicole Baker used great sense imagery to describe the event of the Christian Nativity. With a very effective use of minimal words, she gave a powerful description. Keeping it in third-person point of view gave distance to the magnitude of the event.

SENSE, OR SENSORY, IMAGERY IS VERY EFFECTIVE FOR A POWERFUL DESCRIPTION

Tonight

Kira Nicole Baker

The sound of a baby crying

is heard.

A light,

a bright star in the heavens,

largest and brightest of all

is seen.

The sweet smell of hay

and the odor of livestock is smelled.

The aroma of the shepherd's

dinner

under the midnight moon

and the flavor of the sweet grass

eaten by their sheep

is tasted.

(CONTINUED NEXT PAGE)

The spirit of love,

of joy,

of peace.

The spirit of God

is felt.

The sound of Herald Angels

singing

is heard.

Tonight,

this calm, cool,

unfaltering night;

tonight,

the Savior,

the Son of God;

tonight

the King is born.

ML 121 Student Activity #A: Word Choice

1-5. Read through the poem "Tonight," and mark five places where the author shows strong imagery and specific word choice.

_____

_____

_____

_____

(CONTINUED NEXT PAGE)

ML 121 Student Activity #B: Word Choice in Poetry

Return to the narrative piece you've written. Find and/or add five times where you show imagery and strong, specific word choices. If you are not writing a rhymed poem, check your writing for good visual and non-visual imagery.

A. Visual Imagery: Strong points

1. _____

2. _____

3. _____

Suggestions for improvement

4. _____

5. _____

B. Non-Visual Imagery: Strong points

6. _____

7. _____

8. _____

Suggestions for improvement

9. _____

10. _____

Mini Lesson 122: Editing Paragraphs and Sentences

How can learning this help you? Editing is about revision, correction, checking redundancies, misspellings, misuse of words, grammar, and the list goes on. Check your sentence fluency; also make sure each paragraph develops its topic, its whole topic, and nothing but its topic.

CHECK YOUR SENTENCE FLUENCY

Editing is done after you are done revising your paper. All of the large, flowing revisions of the first four traits of writing are complete, and you are now finally ready to "sweat the small stuff" that was discussed in the Rough Draft section. Editing is a left-brained activity.

To revert to the analogy on driving that was given in the Rough Draft lessons, you should now get off the freeway and out of your semi, climb onto a tractor, and slowly "drive" through your writing, carefully sifting through each word to look for every possible mistake.

Look for the types of mistakes in the last two writing traits: Sentence Fluency and Writing Conventions (see Trait 5 Sentence Fluency and Trait 6 Writing Conventions), including one topic per paragraph (or stanza for a poem), grammar, punctuation, spelling, and capitalization for more help on editing. Use the proofreading symbols in the Appendix.

EDITING PARAGRAPHS AND SENTENCES

Sentences are the base of writing, and paragraphs help us to organize our sentences into topics. (A stanza in poetry is the equivalent of a paragraph in prose.)

ML 122 Student Activity: Editing Paragraphs and Sentences

Study the piece of writing on which you are working. Try to improve the paragraphs/stanzas listed below in your piece. Each one covers the whole topic and nothing else. (Remember that a stanza in poetry is similar to a paragraph in prose.)

A. Paragraphs: Strong points

1. _____

2. _____

3. _____

Suggestions for improvement

4. _____

5. _____

(CONTINUED NEXT PAGE)

NAME _____   Language Arts Mini Lessons

B. Sentences: Complete? Variety?: Strong points

6. _____

7. _____

8. _____

Suggestions for improvement

9. _____

10. _____

NAME _____

Mini Lesson 123: Editing Usage and Punctuation

How can learning this help you? Usage and punctuation errors are some of the most noticeable mistakes we make. When you can master these, your piece will reflect a very finely edited result.

POOR PUNCTUATION IS AN EASY WAY TO ANNOY YOUR READER

ML 123 Student Activity: Editing Usage and Punctuation

Study the piece of writing you are working on. Try to improve the categories listed below in your piece.

A. Grammar Usage: Strong points

1. _____

2. _____

3. _____

Suggestions for improvement

4. _____

5. _____

B. Punctuation (remember especially pause = comma; stop = period): Strong points

6. _____

7. _____

8. _____

Suggestions for improvement

9. _____

10. _____

Mini Lesson 124: Editing Spelling and Capitalization

How can learning this help you? Of all the marvelous things Great Britain gave America, their language is not one of them. It's difficult because so many of our words have multiple meanings, spellings, and often pronunciation.

INCORRECT SPELLING AND CAPITALIZATION IS THE RESULT OF PURE LAZINESS

ML 124 Student Activity: Editing Spelling and Capitalization

Study the piece of writing on which you are working. Try to improve the categories listed below in your piece.

A. Spelling: Strong points

1. _____
2. _____
3. _____

Suggestions for improvement

4. _____
5. _____

B. Capitalization: Strong points

6. _____
7. _____
8. _____

Suggestions for improvement

9. _____
10. _____

Mini Lesson 125: Editing Rhyme and Rhythm

How can learning this help you? While rhyming and rhythm are not required for poetry, adhering to an arbitrary rule helps you think more creatively to communicate, often resulting in thought-provoking and beautiful language. Playing with a set of limits is one thing that makes writing poetry enjoyable and challenging! (Your teacher may not require rhyming and rhythm, but they may give you extra credit for it.)

RHYME AND RHYTHM CAN BE A LOT OF FUN

ML 125 Student Activity: Editing Rhyme and Rhythm

If you are writing a rhymed poem, check these things.

A. Rhyming: Strong points

1. _____
2. _____
3. _____

Suggestions for improvement

4. _____
5. _____

B. Rhythm ; Strong points

6. _____
7. _____
8. _____

Suggestions for improvement

9. _____
10. _____

Mini Lesson 126: Proofreading

How can learning this help you? As the author, here's what you should remember about a proofreader.

THE AUTHOR/PROOFREADER RELATIONSHIP

If someone is kind enough to give a suggestion, the least you can do is consider it. Don't think you're always right.

Appreciate the effort the person made to help you improve your paper.

Thank the proofreader for trying to help you with your paper.

However, remember that it is your paper. Use the suggestions you agree with, but don't feel obligated to use the ones with which you disagree.

If you're unclear about some of the suggestions, ask the proofreader about them in a friendly, inoffensive manner. Don't be afraid to ask.

ML 126 Student Activity: Proofreading

Words of advice for the author:

1. If someone is kind enough to give you a _____, the least you can do is consider it.

2. Don't think you're always _____.

3. _____ The effort the proofreader made to help you improve your paper.

4. Use the suggestions you _____ with, but not the ones with which you disagree.

5. If you're unclear about a suggestion, ask the proofreader about it in a _____ manner.

Mini Lesson 127: Proofreading Each Other's Papers

How can learning this help you? This may seem like a useless activity, but it has great value. When you can have other people read your writing, they catch things you might never see. They may also have suggestions of things to add that they, as readers, want to know more about, and they often catch mistakes our own eyes pass over since we have read the piece so many times! As a proofreader, what should you remember?

PROOFREADING ETIQUETTE

Remember that you are simply trying to help the author improve their paper.

Be sure to write positive comments as well as negative ones.

Write specific suggestions on ways to improve the writing, especially according to the Six Traits.

Don't just write what you think the author wants to hear. Tell them exactly what you feel needs to be improved.

Remember that the author will probably agree with some of your suggestions and disagree with others. It's their paper, and they have the right to have the final say.

ML 127 Student Activity: Proofreading Each Other's Papers

Words of advice for the proofreader:

1. As the proofreader, you are trying to _____ the author's paper.

2. Write _____ comments as well as negative ones.

3. Write suggestions for the paper according to the Six _____

4. Don't just tell the author what you think they want to _____

5. Who has the final say about disagreements on the paper? _____

NAME _____   Language Arts Mini Lessons

Mini Lesson 128: Proofreading Ideas and Organization

How can learning this help you? As you learn new things from other people's proofreading, you can use those things you learned in your future papers.

USE PROOFREADING TO HELP YOU!

ML 128 Student Activity: Proofreading Ideas and Organization

Study the piece of writing on which your partner is working while they work on your piece. Try to improve the categories listed below in their work.

A. Ideas: clear and original: Strong points

1. _____

2. _____

3. _____

Suggestions for improvement

4. _____

5. _____

B. Organization helps display the ideas: Strong points

6. _____

7. _____

8. _____

Suggestions for improvement

9. _____

10. _____

Mini Lesson 129: Proofreading–Voice and Word Choice

How can learning this help you? Student author Shannon Babb found original, specific words to describe the wonders of a cave. She also has good, consistent rhythm. Her strong imagery almost puts us inside the cave.

USE ORIGINAL, SPECIFIC WORDS TO DESCRIBE

Secret Castle

Shannon Babb

Shimmering diamonds

Crystalline pools

Waterfalls frozen in time

Ivory drapery

Sleek curtain walls

Chandeliers clinging to domes

Dragon teeth

Giant daggers

Shields of icy stone

Wondrous crystals

Deep hidden mines

Damp chilly caverns unknown

(CONTINUED NEXT PAGE)

NAME _____

ML 129 Student Activity: Proofreading Voice and Word Choice

Read through the poem "Secret Castle," and mark five places where the author shows strong imagery and specific word choice. Learn from proofreading other's papers to improve your voice and word choice. Study the piece of writing on which your partner is working. Try to improve the categories listed below in their piece.

A. Voice: shares the protagonist's feelings and thoughts: Strong points

1. _____

2. _____

3. _____

Suggestions for improvement

4. _____

5. _____

B. Word choice flavor and interest to the piece: Strong points

6. _____

7. _____

8. _____

Suggestions for improvement

9. _____

10. _____

NAME _____

Mini Lesson 130: Proofreading Paragraphs and Sentences

How can learning this help you? Many serious, professional writers meet in what is known as "writer's groups." This is where a half dozen or more writers get together, they each bring pages of their work (a copy for each author attending), and then exchange papers to take home and peruse, edit, suggest, critique, etc. for the next meeting of the writer's group. This is a very valuable way to proofread and be productive for others at the same time. This is one way professional writers help each other with their paragraphs and sentences.

COLLABORATING WITH OTHER WRITERS CAN HELP YOUR WRITING BECOME BETTER

ML 130 Student Activity: Proofreading Paragraphs and Sentences

Study the piece of writing on which your partner is working. Try to improve the categories listed below in their piece.

A. Paragraphs: each one covers a topic, a whole topic, and nothing else. A poetry paragraph is a stanza: Strong points

1. _____

2. _____

3. _____

Suggestions for improvement

4. _____

5. _____

B. Sentences: complete sentences and variety of structure. Strong points

6. _____

7. _____

8. _____

Suggestions for improvement

9. _____

10. _____

Mini Lesson 131: Proofreading Usage and Punctuation

How can learning this help you? Word usage and punctuation are huge factors in raising or lowering the reader's annoyance level with your writing. If you are constantly using the wrong word, the reader supplies the correct one in their mind and *you are the culprit* who forces them to do that. This is also true of poor punctuation. These are two more ways you can learn from proofreading someone else's paper to improve your own. You may also learn from proofreading other's papers to improve your usage and punctuation.

IMPROVE YOUR USAGE AND PUNCTUATION THROUGH PROOFREADING

ML 131 Student Activity: Proofreading Usage and Punctuation

Study the piece of writing on which your partner is working. Try to improve the categories listed below in their piece.

A. Usage: Strong points

1. _____

2. _____

3. _____

Suggestions for improvement

4. _____

5. _____

B. Punctuation: Strong points

6. _____

7. _____

8. _____

Suggestions for improvement

9. _____

10. _____

NAME _____

Language Arts Mini Lessons

Mini Lesson 132: Proofreading Spelling and Capitalization

How can learning this help you? Two of the easiest parts of writing—spelling and capitalization—can be a little tricky sometimes. Proofreading other's papers can improve *your* spelling and capitalization.

IMPROVE YOUR SPELLING AND CAPITALIZATION THROUGH PROOFREADING

ML 132 Student Activity: Proofreading Spelling and Capitalization

Study the piece of writing on which your partner is working. Try to improve the categories listed below in their piece.

A. Spelling: Strong points

1. _____

2. _____

3. _____

Suggestions for improvement

4. _____

5. _____

B. Capitalization: Strong points

6. _____

7. _____

8. _____

Suggestions for improvement

9. _____

10. _____

Mini Lesson 133: Trait 5 Sentence Fluency

How can learning this help you? Student author Blake Hallock used his excellent vocabulary, fine sentence fluency, and strong voice to create this terrifying midnight walk through a forest of fear. Blake also had fine rhyme and rhythm.

POWERFUL WORD CHOICES AND AN EXCELLENT VOCABULARY

See how powerful Blake's word choices make this poem. Since this is a rhymed poem, notice he never sacrifices meaning for the sake of a rhyme. Notice also how the rhythm never misses a beat.

Forest of Fear

Blake Hallock

O, blackened skies and frosted wind,

They curse me on this moonless night.

Furtive creatures, unseen terror,

My wide eyes darting, lacking light.

Unknown paths of dirt and stone,

Winding through the forest black,

Sounds of creatures, heavy footfalls,

Glances forward, glances back.

Howls of icy appetite,

Echo from the east and west,

From the beasts that crave the life-blood

of me, their loathed and hated guest.

Heavy breathing, frightened eyes,

I hurry at a quickened pace,

Lost, I peer into the forest,

Wiping dampness from my face.

(CONTINUED NEXT PAGE)

Hopeless wanderings, getting colder,

Pulling close my tunic tight,

Through blackened wind and frosted skies,

On this, a cursed and moonless night.

ML 133 Student Activity: Trait 5 Sentence Fluency

Choose five powerful words you discovered in Forest of Fear.:

1. _____

2. _____

3. _____

4. _____

5. _____

NAME _____   Language Arts Mini Lessons

Mini Lesson 134: Proofreading Rhyme and Rhythm

How can learning this help you? If you have written a rhymed poem, study Blake Hallock's fine poem, and from proofreading other's papers to improve *your own* rhyme and rhythm. Make sure you haven't sacrificed meaning for the sake of a rhyme, and make sure your rhythm is consistent.

NEVER SACRIFICE MEANING FOR THE SAKE OF A RHYME

If you haven't written a rhymed poem, study your piece and see where you can improve your word choice. Follow Blake's examples, like "Howls of icy appetite" and "Heavy breathing, frightened eyes."

ML 134 Student Activity: Proofreading Rhyme and Rhythm

Study the piece of writing on which your partner is working. Try to improve the categories listed below in their piece. If you are writing a rhymed poem, check these things for extra credit.

A. Rhyming: Strong points

1. _____
2. _____
3. _____

Suggestions for improvement

4. _____
5. _____

B. Rhythm: If you rhyme, you also need rhythm: Strong points (This is extra credit)

6. _____
7. _____
8. _____

Suggestions for improvement

9. _____
10. _____

Mini Lesson 135: Word Choice in Poetry

How can learning this help you? The words you choose can make magic, cause distress, bring hope, shatter hearts, and a myriad of other emotions. Emotion is the derivative of the ingenious use of strong, compelling

WORD CHOICE

ML 135 Student Activity: Word Choice in Poetry

If your partner is not writing a rhymed poem, check their writing for good visual and non-visual imagery.

A. Visual Imagery: Strong points

1. _____

2. _____

3. _____

Suggestions for improvement

4. _____

5. _____

B. Non-visual Imagery: Strong points

6. _____

7. _____

8. _____

Suggestions for improvement

9. _____

10. _____

Mini Lesson 136 Some of the Best Writing Contests

Students particularly like the Creative Communications poetry contests because such a large number of participants can win and be published.

Essay Contests	Eligible	Deadline	Maximum Length	Theme? Y/N	Entry Fee	Top Prize
Bennington College Young Writers Awards	10-12	11/1	1,500	No	No	$500
Hemingway Festival, University of Idaho	11-12	1/15	1,500	No	No	$500
NAACP	1-12	1/31	750	Yes	No	
PTA Reflections	K-12	Varies	2,000	Yes	No	Certificate
Scholastic Awards Art and Writing	7-12	Varies	Varies	Yes	No	$10,000
Voice of Democracy	9-12	10/31	3-5 min. rec.	Yes	No	$30,000
Young Authors Writing Competition, Columbia College	9-12	1/31		No	No	$300
Short Story Contests	**Eligible**	**Deadline**	**Maximum Length**	**Theme? Y/N**	**Entry Fee**	**Top Prize**
Bennington College Young Writers Awards	10-12	11/1	1,500	No	No	$500
Hemingway Festival, University of Idaho	11-12	1/15	1,500	No	No	$500
PTA Reflections	K-12	Varies	2,000	Yes		Certificate
Scholastic Awards	7-12	Varies	Varies	No	$7	$10,000
Thomas Wolfe Memorial Contest, Asheville, NC	4-12	10/__	800	Yes	No	$50
Poetry Contests	**Eligible**	**Deadline**	**Maximum Length**	**Theme? Y/N**	**Entry Fee**	**Top Prize**
Bennington College Young Writers Awards	10-12	11/1	3 poems	No	No	$500
Creative Communication	K-9	4/8, 8/27, 12/17	21 Lines	No	No	$25+ In Book
Hemingway Festival, University of Idaho	11-12	1/15	1-5 Poems	No	No	$500
PTA Reflections	K-12	Varies	2,000	Yes	No	Certificate
Rattle Young Poets Current Events	Written by 15, submitted by 18	Each Friday	Any length	Yes	No	$100
Rattle Young Poets Anthology	Written by 15, submitted by 18	Varies	1-4 poems any length	No	No	$200
Scholastic Awards	7-12	Varies	Varies	No	$7	$10,000

Chapter Seven: From Phrases to Paragraphs

What should you learn from this chapter? A sentence is the main unit of writing, but we all have to write other writing units, too. We write single words, phrases, clauses, sentences, and paragraphs. This chapter will help you with all of these.

The Lessons

Chapter Seven: From Phrases to Paragraphs 174
   Mini Lesson 137: Sentences and the Sentence Backbone 176
   Mini Lesson 138: Practice Using the Sentence Backbone 179
   Mini Lesson 139: Phrases and Clauses 180
   Mini Lesson 140: Prepositional Phrases 181
   Mini Lesson 141: Identifying Prepositional Phrases 183
   Mini Lesson 142: Creating Prepositional Phrases 184
   Mini Lesson 143: Prepositional Phrases 185
   Mini Lesson 144: Verbal Phrases 186
   Mini Lesson 145: Understanding Clauses 188
   Mini Lesson 146: Dependent Clauses with Commas 190
   Mini Lesson 147: FANBOYS Conjunctions 191
   Mini Lesson 148: Types of Complements 192
   Mini Lesson 149: Reviewing Sentence Parts 194
   Mini Lesson 150: Practice Sentence Parts 196
   Mini Lesson 151: Sentences with Errors 197
   Mini Lesson 152: Sentence Fragments 198
   Mini Lesson 153: Run-On Sentences 199
   Mini Lesson 154: Types of Sentences 200
   Mini Lesson 155: Complex Sentences 201
   Mini Lesson 156: Compound Sentences 202
   Mini Lesson 157: Sentence Combining 203
   Mini Lesson 158: Review Different Sentence Types 204
   Mini Lesson 159: Subject/Verb Agreement 206
   Mini Lesson 160: Paragraphs 208
   Mini Lesson 161: Topic Sentences in Paragraphs 209
   Mini Lesson 162: Practice Paragraphs 210
   Mini Lesson 163: Supporting Sentences in Paragraphs 211

Mini Lesson 164: Paragraph Principles 212
Mini Lesson 165: Sentences in Paragraphs.. 213
Mini Lesson 166: Summary Review for Paragraphs... 214
Mini Lesson 167: Dialogue Paragraphs 216
Mini Lesson 168: Punctuation in Dialogue Paragraphs 217
Mini Lesson 169: Focus on Layout.. 219
Mini Lesson 170: Improve Your Writing and Layout... 220

Mini Lesson 137: Sentences and the Sentence Backbone

How can learning this help you? Learning how to write correct sentences may be the most helpful concept you will ever learn about writing structure. Why? Sentences are the primary units of writing. A sentence is simply a group of words that expresses a complete thought. It must include a subject and verb (predicate). This chapter will help you to write complete sentences, as well as identify the different types of sentences.

THE SENTENCE BACKBONE IS CRITICAL FOR YOUR UNDERSTANDING OF GOOD WRITING

It is made up of a sentence in a paragraph with subjects, verbs, phrases (particularly prepositional phrases), and complements. Sentences may be very simple or very complex.

This preview of what makes up the Sentence Backbone will prepare you for the Mini Lessons to come on all aspects of building sentences and paragraphs, from short to long sentences and paragraphs that include all the building blocks like phrases, clauses, and more. These are the basic units of writing with the sentence being the primary unit.

THE SENTENCE BACKBONE

A sentence is simply a group of words that expresses a complete thought.

It must include a subject and verb (predicate).

The Sentence Backbone method may help you more than anything else to identify and write correct sentences and to understand good grammar. Another helpful practice is to first identify any prepositional phrases in the sentence and put parentheses around them.

That eliminates prepositional phrases from being any part of the sentence backbone.

THERE ARE THREE MAIN PARTS OF THE SENTENCE BACKBONE

SUBJECT

The subject is a noun or pronoun that tells what or who the sentence is about.

Example: The coach led the team.

To find the subject, ask, ". . . What or who is this sentence about?" (coach)

VERB

The verb (predicate) tells what the subject does.

Example: The coach led the team.

To find the verb (predicate), ask, "The subject what?" (led)

(CONTINUED NEXT PAGE)

NAME _____   Language Arts Mini Lessons

COMPLEMENT

The complement completes the action or meaning of the subject and verb. Sentences don't need to have complements, but probably about 75 percent of them do. To find the complement, if there is one, ask, "What or whom is after the subject and verb?" (team)

   Example: The coach led the team.

ML 137 Student Activity #A: Sentence Backbone

What are the three parts of the Sentence Backbone?

1. _____

2. _____

3. _____

Identify the backbone of each of the following sentences in the following way. Put parentheses around any prepositional phrase(s), S above the subject(s), V above the verb(s), and C above the complement(s), if there is a complement.

4. I want some pizza. _____

5. At the bowling alley, Deron rolled three strikes. _____

6. Jackie called her friend. _____

7. Jackie called for her friend. (Find and mark the difference between #6 and #7.) _____
   _____

8. In the summer we are lazy. _____

9. The tall kid won the basketball game. _____

10. The poor girl fell and dropped her books. _____

CONTINUED NEXT PAGE)

ML 137 Student Activity #B: Sentence Backbone

Write ten sentences with subjects, verbs, and complements.

Subject	Verb (Predicate)	Complement
The tall kid	won	the basketball game
What or *who* is this sentence about?	The subject *what*?	*What* or *whom* is after the subject and verb?
1.		
2.		
3.		
4.		
5.		
6.		
7.		
8.		
9.		
10.		

ML 137 Student Activity #C: Sentence Backbone

Put parentheses around any prepositional phrase(s), S above the subject(s), V above the verb(s), and C above the complement(s), if there is a complement. Many words aren't the subject, verb, or complement. For now, we will disregard them because we're only looking for the sentence backbone, which is the subject, verb, and complement.

1. The teacher is happy.
2. I watched Gordon wrestle last night.
3. Grandpa has a turkey on his farm.
4. Jenny really loves chocolate candy.
5. Rocco studied hard.
6. Hannah sings alto.
7. Our show choir concert is actually tonight.
8. I finally got an A in history!
9. Jeff and Christy got wet and cold in the rain.
10. Hank ran past a lineman and tackled their quarterback.

NAME _____   Language Arts Mini Lessons

Mini Lesson 138: Practice Using the Sentence Backbone

How can learning this help you? The sentence backbone is undeniably the most useful tool in all of grammar. Practice writing sentences that utilize this "backbone" by following these simple steps. First, identify any prepositional phrases in the sentence and put parentheses around them. That eliminates them from being any part of the sentence backbone.

THREE MAIN PARTS OF THE SENTENCE BACKBONE

To find the subject, ask, ". . . What or who is this sentence about?"

To find the verb (predicate) ask, ". . . The subject what?"

To find the complement, if there is one, ask "What or whom is after the subject and verb?"

ML 138 Student Activity: Practice Using the Sentence Backbone

Write the following sentences and identify their backbones in the following way. Put parentheses around the prepositional phrase(s), S above the subject(s), V above the verb(s), and C above the complement(s), if there is a complement.

1. Write a sentence with a subject, verb, and complement.

   _____

2. Write a sentence with a prepositional phrase at the end of the sentence.

   _____

3. Write a sentence that asks a question.

   _____

4. Write a sentence with two different subjects.

   _____

5. Write a sentence with two different verbs and complements.

NAME _____   Language Arts Mini Lessons

Mini Lesson 139: Phrases and Clauses

How can learning this help you? Learn to use phrases and clauses more effectively within the framework of correct sentences. There are two main types of phrases—prepositional phrases and verbal phrases. They each have sub-types as well.

TWO TYPES OF PHRASES: PREPOSITIONAL AND CLAUSES

A phrase is a group of related words that acts like a single part of speech. It doesn't need to have a verb.

Example: Chris ran onto the field. _____ Prepositional

Example: Chris loved to win. _____ Verbal

Example: Leaping in front, Chris intercepted the pass _____ Verbal

Example: Concentrating hard, Chris followed the receiver. _____ Verbal

A clause is a group of words with a subject and verb.

Example: Concentrating hard, Chris followed the receiver.

ML 139 Student Activity: Phrases and Clauses

Answer these five questions:

1. A _____ is a group of related words that acts like a single part of speech.

2. Does a phrase need a verb? _____

Underline the phrases in these sentences. The number in parentheses is how many phrases.

3. Encouraged, Ashley hurried toward the counseling office. (2 phrases)

4. Amanda won the election for vice president by a landslide. (2 phrases)

5. Grinning happily, Amanda strode onto the stage and to the podium. (3 phrases)

Mini Lesson 140: Prepositional Phrases

How can learning this help you? Prepositional phrases are groups of words that start with a preposition and end with their object. They may be used in many ways, and there are many prepositions to use!

SO MANY PREPOSITIONS; SO LITTLE TIME . . .

An easy way to find most prepositions that start prepositional phrases is to use a simple sentence: "The worm crawled _____ the apple." Any word that will fit into that blank and make sense can be a preposition. (There will be more information on this subject under Parts of Speech.)

>   Examples: around, by, down, over, through, up

All of those words fit into the blank in the sentence about the worm. About ninety percent of all prepositions will fit into that blank.

Of is the most commonly used preposition and, ironically, it doesn't make sense in the worm sentence. Other prepositions that don't make sense in the worm sentence include as, during, since, and than, but they may still be used as prepositions.

>   Example: She hasn't had any candy since (preposition) last Saturday.

Once you have found the preposition, an easy way to find the object of that preposition is to ask what or whom is after the preposition.

>   Example: "The worm crawled up the shiny red apple."
>   Up *what*? *The apple.*
>   *Apple* is the object of *Up*.

Prepositional phrases can be at the start, in the middle, or at the end of sentences.

Use the prepositional phrase, "on the penalty kick."

>   Example: On the penalty kick, Jan scored a goal. (start)
>   Example: Jan, on the penalty kick, scored a goal. (middle)
>   Example: Jan scored a goal on the penalty kick. (end)

You don't have to have *any* prepositional phrases in sentences, but you may have *several*.

>   Example: (By the middle) (of the morning), Jose finished his homework (for history). (3 phrases)

After disqualifying all of the prepositional phrases, it's much easier to find the subject, verb, and complement. (S is subject, V is verb, C is complement)

>   S V   C
>   Example: The girl set her book (on the table).

(CONTINUED NEXT PAGE)

ML 140 Student Activity: Prepositional Phrases

Create the following six sentences and write them in the chart below. Put your sentence in the chart that follows the ten sentences. Put any prepositional phrases into the appropriate column. Put S in the column if the prepositional phrase starts the sentence, M if it's in the middle, and E if it ends the sentence.

1. Write a sentence that asks a question.

2. Write a sentence that starts with a prepositional phrase.

3. Write a sentence that ends with a prepositional phrase.

4. Write a sentence with a prepositional phrase in the middle.

5. Write a sentence with no prepositional phrases.

6. Write a sentence with two prepositional phrases.

In these four sentences put the appropriate parts in the correct places in the chart below.

7. I will buy some popcorn in a minute.

8. The boy in the blue jacket rode his bike to school during the bad storm. (3 prepositional phrases)

9. At dawn, Ali went to the chicken coop for the eggs the chickens had laid. (3 prepositional phrases)

10. I rode the subway around town after school. (2 prepositional phrases)

Prepositional Phrase	Subject	Verb (Predicate)	Complement
(in the end) What is the prepositional phrase, if any?	the tall **kid** What or Who is this sentence about?	**won** The subject what?	the basketball **game** What or whom is after the Verb?
1.			
2.			
3.			
4.			
5.			
6.			
7.			
8.			
9.			
10.			

Mini Lesson 141: Identifying Prepositional Phrases

How can learning this help you? Prepositional phrases are usually *not* very important, but they often get mistaken for important things, so it is good to identify them at the first and put parentheses around them to disqualify them from being anything but a prepositional phrase.

THERE ARE A FEW TRICKS TO IDENTIFYING PREPOSITIONAL PHRASES

Prepositional phrases are not a part of the Sentence Backbone (subject, verb, complement), so when pointing one out, put parentheses around it to disqualify it.

Remember: Learn to find a preposition by seeing if it fits into the blank of the sentence, such as "The worm crawled _____ the apple."

If the word is a preposition, find its object. For instance, in the sentence, "The worm crawled through the apple," if the preposition is through, then ask, "Through what?" The answer is apple. Apple is the object of the preposition through. Consequently, the prepositional phrase starts with the preposition through and ends with its object, apple. The whole prepositional phrase is through the apple. If there are other words between the preposition and its object, they are part of the phrase, such as, "The worm crawled (through the shiny, rosy, red apple)."

ML 141 Student Activity: Identifying Prepositional Phrases

1. What sentence do you use to identify prepositional phrases in sentences?

_____

2. In the sentence, "Cole ran up the stairs," "up" is the preposition. What term is "stairs"? _____

Put parentheses around the prepositional phrases in the following three sentences.

3. In the morning Cheryl went to the kitchen and put jam on her toast. (3 prepositional phrases)

4. After school Jocelyn ran to the auditorium door and saw her name on the cast list. (3 prepositional phrases)

5. Dave put his hand on the wrench and loosened the nut on the bolt. (2 prepositional phrases)

NAME _____   Language Arts Mini Lessons

Mini Lesson 142: Creating Prepositional Phrases

How can learning this help you? Creating prepositional phrases can be fun. They are groups of words that start with the preposition, end with its object, and may have adjectives in between.

HAVE FUN WITH YOUR PREPOSITIONAL PHRASES

Many of your sentences will have complements in them. However, to keep the grading of this exercise consistent, disregard whether a sentence has a complement or not.

ML 142 Student Activity: Creating Prepositional Phrases

Put parentheses around the prepositional phrases in the sentence you create below.

1. To find the object of that preposition, ask _____ or who is the preposition about?

2-4. Create three sentences that end with a prepositional phrase.

_____

_____

_____

5-6. Create two sentences with a prepositional phrase in the middle.

_____

_____

7-8. Create two sentences that start with a prepositional phrase.

_____

_____

9-10. Create two sentences with two prepositional phrases in each sentence.

_____

_____

Mini Lesson 143: Prepositional Phrases

How can learning this help you? Prepositional phrases often describe other words in the sentence. There are two types of prepositional phrases: an adjective phrase or an adverb phrase. Identifying these two types of phrases is not very important, but it's interesting to note that you can construct a prepositional phrase with an adjective(s) or an adverb(s).

ADJECTIVE PHRASES

Adjective phrases are prepositional phrases used to modify/describe nouns or pronouns.

Example: John has a car with a sunroof. With a sunroof is a phrase that describes the noun car.

ADVERB PHRASES

Adverb phrases are prepositional phrases that modify/describe verbs, adjectives, or other adverbs.

Example: Heather moved to a farm. To a farm modifies the verb moved by telling where they moved.

ML 143 Student Activity: Types of Prepositional Phrases

1. What type of prepositional phrases are used to modify/describe nouns or pronouns? _____

2. What type of prepositional phrases are used to modify/describe verbs? _____

3. Does the following sentence have an adjective or adverb phrase? _____

    She ran to the corner.

4. Create a sentence with an adjective prepositional phrase. After creating the sentence, put parentheses around each prepositional phrase.

    _____

5. Create a sentence with an adverb prepositional phrase. After creating the sentence, put parentheses around each prepositional phrase.

    _____

Mini Lesson 144: Verbal Phrases

How can learning this help you? In the backwaters of English grammar, we find verbals and verbal phrases. The three types are infinitive, gerund, and participial phrases. They are types of verbs but are used as other parts of speech.

THREE TYPES OF VERBALS: INFINITIVE, GERUND, AND PARTICIPIAL PHRASES

Infinitive phrases usually begin with the word to and are followed by a verb.

Example: Cathy wants to win. (win is a verb, so to win is a prepositional phrase)
Example: Cathy ran to class. (class is not a verb, so to class is a prepositional phrase, not an infinitive phrase

Gerund phrases are verb forms ending in -ing that are used as nouns. Like nouns, gerunds and gerund phrases can function as subjects, direct objects, and objects of prepositions, etc.

Example: (Reading his book) relaxed Dave. (gerund phrase: Reading his book functions as the subject)
Example: She passed the test (by studying). (prepositional phrase)

Participial phrases are verb forms used as adjectives. They're verbs that end in *-ing, -d,* or *-ed*.

Example: I saw a spider (climbing its web) (Participial phrase)
Example: (Nearly exhausted), Shaun sat down (on a log). (Nearly exhausted is a participial phrase, and on a log is a prepositional phrase.)

ML 144 Student Activity #A: Verbal Phrases

Match the letter of the definitions with the correct phrase.

1. What is a prepositional phrase? _____

2. What is an infinitive phrase? _____

3. What is a participial phrase? _____

4. What is a gerund phrase? _____

5. What phrase is in this sentence? Running fast, she set a new record. _____

6. Verb form that begins with the word to which is followed by a verb _____

7. Groups of words that start with a preposition and end with its object _____

8. Verb form ending in -ing; used as a noun _____

9. Verb form ending in -d , -ed, or -ing; used as adjectives _____

10. What sentence does this book use to find a preposition? _____

(CONTINUED NEXT PAGE)

ML 144 Student Activity #B: More on Verbal Phrases

Follow the model phrases in the examples on page 180 and create your own sentences with them.

1. Create a sentence that has an adjective prepositional phrase. _____

_____

2. Create a sentence that has an adverb prepositional phrase. _____

_____

3. Create a sentence that has an infinitive verbal phrase. _____

_____

4. Create a sentence that has a gerund verbal phrase. _____

_____

5. Create a sentence that has a participial verbal phrase. _____

_____

Mini Lesson 145: Understanding Clauses

How can learning this help you? Clauses are groups of words that contain a subject and verb (predicate). There are two kinds of clauses: independent clauses and dependent clauses.

INDEPENDENT CLAUSES

Independent clauses can stand alone and make sense as complete sentences. An independent clause (see example) is "I want the shoes." It makes sense by itself.

    Example: Juan made the honor roll.
    Example: I want to be in the concert, but I have to practice.

Independent clauses may also be combined with other clauses.

Multiple clause sentences may be connected with the seven FANBOYS conjunctions: for, and, nor, but, or, yet, so. These conjunctions may often be used interchangeably. (More details in the FANBOYS Mini Lesson.)

    Example: Samantha lost the school election, *for/and/but/yet/so* she got a job in a grocery store.

DEPENDENT CLAUSES

Dependent (subordinate) clauses cannot stand alone as complete sentences. They depend on independent clauses to help them make sense. A dependent clause usually starts with a word like one of these: *after, although, as, because, if, since, that, until, when, which, while,* and *who.*

    Example: I want the shoes that Nathan has.

The dependent clause *"that Nathan has"* must depend on the independent clause, *"I want the shoes"* to make sense.

ML 145 Student Activity #A: Understanding Clauses

Write three sentences that each have an independent clause followed by a comma, a FANBOYS conjunction, and another independent clause. Circle the FANBOYS conjunction.

1. _____
2. _____
3. _____

Write two sentences that have an independent clause and a dependent clause. Underline the dependent clause.

4. _____
5. _____

(CONTINUED NEXT PAGE)

ML 145 Student Activity #B: More on Understanding Clauses

Review the information about clauses in the previous lesson.

Alone or with a partner, compose sentences with these types of clauses.

1. Compose a sentence with one independent clause and one dependent clause.

   _____

2. Create a sentence with two independent clauses and no dependent clauses.

   _____

3. Compose a sentence with one independent clause followed by one dependent clause.

   _____

4. Compose a sentence with one dependent clause followed by one independent clause.

   _____

5. Compare your clauses with another pair of students.

Mini Lesson 146: Dependent Clauses with Commas

How can learning this help you? Sentences that begin with an independent clause and finish with a dependent clause normally do not need a comma after the independent clause, but sentences that start with a dependent clause and finish with an independent clause usually do need a comma after the dependent clause.

RULE-OF-THUMB: WHERE YOU PAUSE, INSERT A COMMA. WHERE YOU STOP, INSERT A PERIOD.

Independent clause at the beginning; dependent clause at the end
  Example: I'll study (no comma needed) until I get too sleepy.
Dependent clause at the beginning; independent clause at the end
  Example: Because of my injury, (comma needed) I didn't play in the game.

ML 146 Student Activity #A: Dependent Clauses with Commas

1. Clauses are groups of words that contain a _____ and a verb (predicate).

2. Independent clauses can stand _____ and make sense as complete sentences.

3. Dependent clauses cannot stand _____ and make sense as a complete sentence.

Write down two of the conjunctions that start dependent clauses.

4. _____

5. _____

ML 146 Student Activity #B: Creating Dependents Clauses

Remember that to work in a sentence, a dependent clause must also have an independent clause with it. The independent clause must be able to stand alone.

Write three sentences that start with a dependent clause conjunction which leads us into a dependent clause.

1. _____

2. _____

3. _____

Write two sentences that end with a dependent clause.

4. _____

5. _____

NAME _____   Language Arts Mini Lessons

Mini Lesson 147: FANBOYS Conjunctions

How can learning this help you? As you probably know by now, these are the seven FANBOYS conjunctions: *for, and, nor, but, or, yet, so*. This book will be referring to them frequently.

IT HELPS IF YOU MEMORIZE THE FANBOYS CONJUNCTIONS

ML 147 Student Activity: FANBOYS Conjunctions

1-7. List and memorize the seven FANBOYS conjunctions below. This lesson will help embed them in your mind.

F _____

A _____

N _____

B _____

O _____

Y _____

S _____

In the following three sentences, underline all of the independent clauses once and the dependent clauses twice. Also, put a circle around any FANBOYS conjunctions, and put a box around any conjunctions that start dependent clauses.

8. My favorite holiday is Christmas, but I like Halloween a lot, too.

9. Although I really like Thanksgiving a lot, I enjoy Christmas even more.

10. I like the food best on Thanksgiving because you get both quality and quantity.

Mini Lesson 148: Types of Complements

How can learning this help you? Complements can be broken down into four types. However, knowing their types is less important than knowing how to *identify* them as complements.

FOUR TYPES OF COMPLEMENTS

Direct Objects. This complement does not describe the subject. Most complements are direct objects.

Example: The coach led the team. (Coach and team are different from each other.) Direct object.

Predicate Adjectives. This complement describes the subject.

Example: The coach is smart. (Smart describes the coach.)

Predicate Nouns. This complement (a noun) is the about same thing as the subject.

Example: The coach is a wise man. (Coach and man are about the same person.)

Predicate Pronoun. This complement (a pronoun) is the same thing as the subject. (Predicate pronouns are being used less nowadays.)

Example: The winning coach was he. (Coach and he are the same person. As odd as it may sound, he is correct, not him because he refers to the subject, the coach.)

Indirect objects are not a type of complement; however, they are a common part of our speech.

```
   S     V    IO    C(DO)
```
Example: Alex threw Rob the ball. Alex didn't throw Rob; he threw the ball. Ball is the direct object type of complement. Rob is the indirect object.

ML 148 Student Activity #A: Types of Complements

1. Which type of complement describes the subject in a sentence? _____

Which two types of complements are the same thing as the subject?

2. _____

3. _____

4. Which type of complement is different from the subject? _____

5. Which is the most common type of complement? _____

(CONTINUED NEXT PAGE)

NAME _____   Language Arts Mini Lessons

ML 148 Student Activity #B: More on Types of Complements

Creating your text helps you to learn what the concept is. Review the four different types of complements (direct objects, predicate nouns, predicate pronouns, and predicate adjectives), as well as indirect objects. Now, create a sentence for each of these.

1. Create a sentence with a direct object.

   _____

2. Create a sentence with a predicate noun.

   _____

3. Create a sentence with a predicate pronoun.

   _____

4. Create a sentence with a predicate adjective.

   _____

5. Create a sentence with an indirect object.

   _____

Mini Lesson 149: Reviewing Sentence Parts

How can learning this help you? Reviewing the Sentence Backbone and parts of sentences, such as various phrases, clauses, etc. will help you when writing your sentences.

THE SENTENCE BACKBONE WILL KEEP YOU ON TRACK WHEN WRITING

Before identifying the sentence backbone, remember how helpful it is to find any prepositional phrases and put parentheses around them to disqualify them from becoming part of the sentence backbone. This avoids confusion which might cause you to think the *object* of the preposition is the *subject* or *complement*, and it *can't* be.

A prepositional phrase is a group of words that starts with a preposition and ends with its object. They may be used in the beginning, middle, or end of sentences. Many sentences have more than one prepositional phrase in them.

To find a preposition, use the sentence "The worm crawled _____ the apple."

Some of the prepositions that work in the blank of the "The worm crawled _____ the apple" include *by, down, in, out, past, through, up,* and many others. Exceptions of prepositions that don't fit into that sentence include *of* (the most common preposition), *as, during, except,* and *like*.

To find the object of that preposition, ask ". . . the preposition *what*?" (The worm crawled up *what*? *The apple*.)

After disqualifying all of the prepositional phrases, it's much easier to find the subject, verb, and complement.

Example: (At the end) (of class), the girl (in the back) took her pencil (from the desk.)

ML 149 Student Activity #A: Types of Sentence Parts

Use these sentences and determine the Subject, Verb, Prepositional Phrase, and Complement. Use the table provided on the next page.

1. Over the river and through the woods, to Grandmother's house we go.

2. The little girl spilled her books onto the ground.

3. I love hot dogs around a campfire.

4. Did you see that shooting star in the sky?

5. In our tent it was cold when the sun finally rose.

(CONTINUED NEXT PAGE)

Prepositional Phrase	Subject	Verb (Predicate)	Complement
What is the prepositional phrase, if any?	What or Who is this sentence about?	The subject what?	What or whom is after the Verb?
1.			
2.			
3.			
4.			
5.			

ML 149 Student Activity #B: Sentences with Sentence Parts

Creating your sentences with requested sentence parts gives you a better understanding of what the parts are. Remember that a prepositional phrase is simply, "A group of words that starts with a preposition and ends with its object."

Create these sentences and put them into the chart above.

1. The football team won its first game by a touchdown.
2. Shauna and Darci got A's on their chemistry test.
3. Dozens of kids want to audition for the musical.
4. Because the school lunch ladies work so hard, we get delicious school lunches.
5. It's important to learn the punctuation rules.

ML 149 Student Activity #C: Sentences with Prepositional Phrases

1. Write a sentence that starts with a prepositional phrase.
   _____

2. Write a sentence that ends with a prepositional phrase.
   _____

3. Write a sentence with a prepositional phrase in the middle.
   _____

4. Write a sentence with two prepositional phrases.
   _____

5. Write a sentence with no prepositional phrases.
   _____

Mini Lesson 150: Practice Sentence Parts

How can learning this help you? After you identify prepositional phrases and eliminate them from being in the sentence backbone, then find the sentence backbone, you will understand complete sentences better. Remember, a subject and a verb are necessary to have a complete sentence. Complements or prepositional phrases are not required, but most sentences have them.

FIND THE SENTENCE BACKBONE, AND THE REST WILL FOLLOW

ML 150 Student Activity: Practice Sentence Parts

Mark the following sentences and identify their sentence backbones. Put parentheses around the prepositional phrase(s), S above the subject(s), and V above the verb(s). One of the sentences does not have a complement, but label the other four types of complements in the following way: DO is Direct Object, PA is Predicate Adjective, PN is Predicate Noun, and PP is Predicate Pronoun.

1. Ms. Peterson is a great teacher for our school.

2. The principal was he.

3. The basketball player ran down the court.

4. After lunch the lunch lady cleaned the counter.

5. That girl is so nice.

Mini Lesson 151: Sentences with Errors

How can learning this help you? When you purposely make errors and work together to correct them, you can see more clearly and define problems that your own eyes may have "skipped over."

MAKE ERRORS ON PURPOSE? *WHY?*

ML 151 Student Activity: Sentences with Errors

Get into pairs and compose five sentences. Have at least three errors in each sentence.

1. Usage: have at least one mistake in verbs or subject/verb agreement.

   _____

2. Usage: Use one or more incorrect personal pronouns (I/me, she/her).

   _____

3. Punctuation: Have at least one mistake in commas and/or apostrophes.

   _____

4. Spelling: Include at least one misspelled word.

   _____

5. Capitalization: Have one or more capitalization errors.

   _____

Trade your sentences with another pair of students and correct each other's errors.

Mini Lesson 152: Sentence Fragments

How can learning this help you? A sentence fragment is a group of words that does not express a complete thought or make a complete sentence, even though they are usually intended to. A sentence fragment is usually missing a subject or verb. If you wonder if some words are a complete sentence, ask yourself the three questions below.

HOW TO SOLVE A FRAGMENT PROBLEM

What is the subject?

What is the verb?

Do these words express a complete thought?

Using parentheses around prepositional phrases eliminates them from being a subject or verb.

Fragment		Sentence
The boy (in the choir).	No verb	The boy sang in the choir.
Ran (to the door).	No subject	She ran to the door.
(In the evening).	No subject or verb	It rained (in the evening).
The boulder be.	Subject and verb, but not a complete thought	

ML 152 Student Activity: Sentence Fragments

Put parentheses ( ) around the prepositional phrase(s), S above the subject(s), V above the verb(s), and C above any complement(s).

1. Did Dom remember the treats?

One of these four sentences is correct; three are fragments. Put CS for each complete sentence and F for each fragment. Also, tell what is missing in the fragments.

2. Brian in that classroom.

_____

3. She saw Nick at the movie.

_____

4. Slept at the end of class.

_____

5. A big gray bug.

_____

Mini Lesson 153: Run-On Sentences

How can learning this help you? Run-on sentences are two or more sentences that are written as one sentence. They are usually separated by a comma or no punctuation mark at all.

THREE WAYS TO CORRECT RUN-ON SENTENCES

Example: Kelly tasted the cake, it was good.

Make two sentences.	Kelly tasted the cake. It was good.
Insert a comma and a FANBOYS conjunction.	Kelly tasted the cake, and it was good.
Insert a semicolon.	Kelly tasted the cake; it was good.

ML 153 Student Activity: Run-On Sentences

Put parentheses ( ) around any prepositional phrase(s), S above the subject(s), V above the verb(s), and C above any complement(s). In the left margin mark CS if complete, F if a fragment, and RO if it's a run-on sentence.

1. Lots of winter activities in our school.

One of these four sentences is correct; two are run-on sentences, and one is a fragment. Put CS for the complete sentence, R for run-on sentences, and F for the fragment.

2. Basketball is really exciting, we have a good team with some tall players.

3. Did you know I'm in the musical, it goes on in February.

4. Our great wrestling team.

5. The choir and band concerts sounded beautiful.

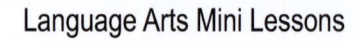

Mini Lesson 154: Types of Sentences

How can learning this help you? These sentences have one independent clause, so they don't usually need commas. However, they may have compound parts of sentences that look like other clauses. Put parentheses ( ) around the prepositional phrase(s), S above the subject(s), and V above the verb(s).

DISCOVER SIMPLE SENTENCES

Examples:

    S   V
Darrell works (at Target). [Simple sentence]

    S   S   V
Darrell and Kristy work (at Target). [Simple sentence with a compound subject]

    S   V   V
Mandy works and learns (at Target). [Simple sentence with a compound verb]

    S   V   V
Mandy works (at Target) and plays ball (in school).

ML 154 Student Activity: Types of Sentences

1. Write a simple sentence with a prepositional phrase at the beginning.

   _____

2. Write a simple sentence with a compound subject.

   _____

3. Write a simple sentence with a compound verb.

   _____

4. Write a simple sentence with a compound complement.

   _____

5. Write a simple sentence with an infinitive phrase (*to* plus a verb).

Mini Lesson 155: Complex Sentences

How can learning this help you? Learning the structure of complex sentences will help you know the difference between a complex sentence and a run-on sentence. These sentences consist of an independent clause and one or more dependent (subordinate) clauses. An independent clause can stand alone as a sentence, but a dependent clause has to lean on an independent clause for support. If you're still unclear, go back to the lesson on clauses.

STRUCTURE IS KEY

        Dependent   **Independent**
Example: Before the alarm rings, [Jess usually wakes up.]

        Dependent   **Independent**
Example: [Roger was really sad] because Amy moved.

ML 155 Student Activity: Complex Sentences

Put parentheses ( ) around any prepositional phrase(s), S above the subject(s), V above the verb(s), and C above any complement(s).

1. When Ingrid opened her locker, three books fell out.

Put SS if it's a simple sentence and C x S if it's a complex sentence.

2. A big, brown bug bit a big, brown bear.

3. Students were sad since the dance was canceled.

4. Andy and Mark were elected team captains.

5. As the sun set, the mountain air got cold.

NAME _____

Mini Lesson 156: Compound Sentences

How can learning this help you? Compound sentences consist of *two or more independent clauses*. They are linked with either a semicolon or a comma and one of the FANBOYS conjunctions: *for, and, nor, but, or, yet, so*.

      Dependent   **Independent**   **Independent**

Example: As the crowd cheered, Randy pitched the ball, *and/but/so* Emily hit a home run.

      Dependent   **Independent**   **Independent**

Example: Randy pitched the ball, *and/but/so* Emily hit a home run, as the crowd cheered.

      Independent   **Independent**

Example: Mrs. Peterson cast the play; *and/but/yet/so* the tall kid got a part.

ML 156 Student Activity: Compound Sentences

1. How many independent clauses do you need in a compound sentence? _____

2. What are the two ways to link together two independent clauses?

    a. _____

    b. _____

3. What is the name of the seven conjunctions that connect independent clauses? _____

Write seven compound sentences. Use a FANBOYS conjunction after a comma in the sentence: for, and, nor, but, or, yet, so. Write seven compound sentences. Use a FANBOYS conjunction in each sentence: for, and, nor, but, or, yet, so.

4. for: _____

5. and _____

6. nor _____

7. but _____

8. or _____

9. yet _____

10. so _____

Mini Lesson 157: Sentence Combining

How can learning this help you? Combining short, choppy sentences makes them more interesting and fluent.

WHEN COMBINING SENTENCES

Add only the *information* from the second sentence that is *missing* in the first sentence.

Example: Katie was afraid. She was afraid because it was dark.
Example: Katie was afraid because it was dark.

ML 157 Student Activity: Sentence Combining

Combine each of these pairs of sentences into one sentence.

1. Robert and Mary lived across the street. Their last name was Brown.

2. Richard, Lee, and Jan made the team. They were my friends.

3. I love June. School's out. The weather's good.

4. Lisa and Cindy were cheerleaders. They were also in the play.

With a partner or alone find or create these kinds of sentences or sentence parts:

5. A simple sentence

6. A complex sentence

7. A compound sentence

8. Two short sentences about the same topic; combine them into one sentence

9. A sentence fragment _____

10. A run-on sentence _____

Trade your sentences with a partner and check each other's work.

Mini Lesson 158: Review Different Sentence Types

How can learning this help you? How can learning this help you? When you remember the different sentence types, it will help you to use them correctly.

REVIEW DIFFERENT SENTENCE TYPES

ML 158 Student Activity #A: Review Different Sentence Types

Learning to find the sentence backbone is the second most helpful grammatical principle you may ever learn. Write the terms for these definitions.

1. A group of words that does not express a complete thought. _____

2. These consist of an independent clause and one or more dependent clauses. _____

3. These connect short, choppy sentences to make them more interesting and fluent. _____

4. The name for the main parts of the sentence—the subject, verb, and complement. _____

5. What are two or more sentences that are combined into one sentence called? _____
   _____

ML 158 Student Activity #B: More Sentence Review

Fill in the blanks with the correct terms about the sentence backbone.

1. A _____ is a group of words that expresses a complete thought and includes a subject and verb.

2. What do you ask to find the subject? _____

3. What do you ask to find the verb? _____

4. What do you ask to find the complement, if there is one? _____

5. What type of phrases should you find before identifying the sentence backbone? _____
   _____

(CONTINUED NEXT PAGE)

ML 158 Student Activity #C: Prepositional Term Review

Remember that, although prepositional phrases are not important in the structure of a sentence, it is very easy to get the object of the preposition mixed up with the subject or complement of the sentence. That's why we identify any prepositional phrases and put parentheses around them to disqualify them from being any part of the sentence backbone.

1. To find a preposition, use the sentence, "The _____."

2. A prepositional _____ is a group of words that _____

3. _____ starts with a preposition and ends with its _____ _____

4. What is the most common preposition? _____

5. What do you ask to find the object of the preposition? _____

NAME _____

Mini Lesson 159: Subject/Verb Agreement

How can learning this help you? Subject/Verb Agreement mistakes are not only *noticeable* in your *writing*, but they are one of the most noticeable problems in your *speaking*. If you don't know how to spell a word or when to insert a semicolon when you speak, people won't know it, but if you say, "We *was* going to the game," instead of "We *were* going to the game," most people will notice it.

SUBJECT/VERB AGREEMENT MISTAKES *NOT* TO MAKE

Singular or Plural Subjects

A verb must agree with its subject in number—singular or plural.

Singular Subjects

A singular subject requires a singular verb.

Example: Matt *studies* hard. *Matt* is the singular subject; *studies* is the singular verb.

Plural Subjects

A plural subject requires a plural verb.

Example: They study hard. *They* is the plural subject; *study* is the plural verb.

Compound Subjects

When compound subjects are joined by or, either/ or neither/nor, the verb agrees with the subject closer to it.

Example: *Neither* the boys *nor Ashley* (singular) *likes* spaghetti.

When compound subjects are joined by *and* or *both/and*, the *verb* is usually *plural*.

Example: I'll bet *both* Kara *and* Michelle *win* a trophy at the meet.

ML 159 Student Activity #A: Subject / Verb Agreement

Underline the word that shows the correct subject/verb agreement.

1. The car (run/runs) well.

2. The cars (run/runs) well.

3. Neither Rhett nor Yvonne (like/likes) the other team.

4. Many girls (excel/excels) in math and science.

5. Most of the group (enjoy/enjoys) fantasy novels.

Check your answers with a partner.

(CONTINUED NEXT PAGE)

ML 159 Student Activity #B: Subject / Verb Agreement

Being able to recognize and understand the singular and plural agreements between the subjects and verbs helps you with your writing and your speaking.

1. Subject/Verb agreement mistakes are noticeable in both your writing and your _____.

2. A singular subject requires a _____ verb.

3. A plural subject requires a _____ verb.

Underline the correct answer.

4. Neither Kris nor Ryan get/gets discouraged.

5. Both Ryan and his friends get/gets to go swimming.

Mini Lesson 160: Paragraphs

How can learning this help you? Paragraphs are the writing units that help you organize your sentences into basic topics. Each well-written paragraph is organized into its own mini-paper.

PARAGRAPHS ORGANIZE THE CONTENT

Paragraph. These are simply groups of sentences that are about the same topic. They are organized together to help the reader understand what they should understand about that topic before moving on to the next topic in the next paragraph. All of the paragraphs then link together about the same overall topic and compose a paper or story. For instance, if your paper's purpose is to describe a cabin in the woods, one paragraph might be about the scenery as you approach the cabin, another paragraph might be about what the outside of the cabin looks like, and other paragraphs might be about the sights, sounds, and smells inside the cabin.

Paragraph Length. Most paragraphs are typically four to ten sentences long. Any fewer sentences probably mean that the paragraph isn't fully developed; any more sentences may mean that it needs to be split in two because it's covering too much. Longer paragraphs often discourage the readers from finishing the paragraph. They need a break and a fresh start in a new paragraph.

Expository and Argumentative Paragraphs. These should generally be longer than four sentences, while narrative paragraphs are often fine being shorter. Of course, when you're using dialogue (conversation), begin a new paragraph each time you change speakers. Narrative paragraphs are sometimes as short as one word; i.e. "Yes," "Why?" "Because," etc.

ML 160 Student Activity: Paragraphs

This is a good practice to help you with paragraphs.

1. Imagine you are on trial for writing paragraphs correctly in a court of law.
2. Stand up.
3. Raise your right arm "to the square."
4. Repeat the following with your instructor.
5. Say the following overly dramatically.

> **In paragraphs, I do solemnly swear to develop the topic, the whole topic, and nothing but the topic.**

This practice can help you have each of your paragraphs develop the topic, the whole topic, and nothing but the topic.

Mini Lesson 161: Topic Sentences in Paragraphs

How can learning this help you? If you can write good topic sentences, it will be easier for you to write good paragraphs, because topic sentences are the key to the paragraphs.

EXCELLENT TOPIC SENTENCES MAKE IT EASIER TO WRITE GOOD PARAGRAPHS

The topic sentence states the main idea of the paragraph.

The topic sentence puts boundaries around the topic, letting it be broad enough, but not too broad.

The topic sentence usually introduces what the paragraph will be about.

About ninety percent of all topic sentences are the first sentences in the paragraphs. In the Mini Lesson example, the topic sentence is the first one.

If the topic sentence is second, the first sentence usually introduces the topic sentence.

ML 161 Student Activity: Topic Sentences in Paragraphs

Fill in the answers.

1. The topic sentence states the _____ of the paragraph.

2. The topic sentence usually _____ what the paragraph will be about.

3. About _____ percent of all topic sentences are the first sentences in the paragraphs.

4. Write down the first two words of the topic sentence in paragraph 1. _____

5. Write down the first two words of the topic sentence in paragraph 2. _____

Paragraph 1. The junior prom was the most wonderful evening of my entire life. I got a beautiful new pink gown, and my hair looked great. But the best part was my date, Ryan. I think he's the most handsome boy in the whole school. When we got to the dance, everyone said how beautiful I looked, and Ryan said he agreed with them. Ryan and I seemed to really dance well together, too. I felt like Cinderella at the ball. Like Cinderella's ball, our dance ended too quickly, and Ryan took me home, but he asked me for another date. I'll never forget the junior prom as long as I live.

Paragraph 2. Of all the exciting evenings I've spent until now, one stands out the most by far. The junior prom was the most wonderful evening of my entire life. I got a beautiful new pink gown, and my hair looked great. But the best part was my date, Ryan. I think he's the most handsome boy in the whole school. When we got to the dance, everyone said how beautiful I looked, and Ryan said he agreed with them. Ryan and I seemed to really dance well together, too. I felt like Cinderella at the ball. Like Cinderella's ball, our dance ended too quickly, and Ryan took me home, but he asked me for another date. I'll never forget the junior prom as long as I live.

NAME _____ Language Arts Mini Lessons

Mini Lesson 162: Practice Paragraphs

How can learning this help you? The legendary college basketball coach Bobby Knight said, "Practice doesn't make perfect; only perfect practice makes perfect." That is why it is so important to practice writing and grammar skills.

"PERFECT PRACTICE DETERMINES A PERFECT RESULT"

ML 162 Student Activity: Practice Paragraphs

Work alone or together with a partner.

Find and write down the topic sentence in three different paragraphs.

1. _____

2. _____

3. _____

4. Find a topic sentence that is the first sentence of a paragraph.

_____

5. Find a topic sentence that is not the first sentence of the paragraph.

_____

NAME _____   Language Arts Mini Lessons

Mini Lesson 163: Supporting Sentences in Paragraphs

How can learning this help you? When you are writing a paragraph, develop one topic, the whole topic, and nothing but that topic. Supporting sentences explain, expand, or prove a topic sentence correct. They do this by giving specific details, facts, examples, or reasons.

DEVELOP ONE TOPIC, THE WHOLE TOPIC, AND NOTHING BUT THAT TOPIC

ML 163 Student Activity: Supporting Sentences in Paragraphs

1. Write a paragraph about a favorite holiday.

_____
_____
_____
_____

2. Have a topic sentence and at least three supporting sentences.

_____
_____
_____
_____

3. Make sure the supporting sentences explain, expand, or prove a topic sentence correct.

_____
_____
_____
_____

4. Underline the topic sentence.

_____

5. Trade papers with a classmate and review and comment.

_____
_____

Mini Lesson 164: Paragraph Principles

How can learning this help you? Learning paragraph principles, such as focusing on the topic, the topic sentence (usually the first sentence), and the concluding sentence is imperative. But the concluding sentence is critical because, in a well-written paragraph, it brings the paragraph to a close. It summarizes, ties thoughts together about the paragraph's topic, and/or gives the reader food for thought.

THE CONCLUDING SENTENCE SUMS IT ALL UP

ML 164 Student Activity: Paragraph Principles

1. _____ are the units that help you organize your sentences into basic topics.

2. Each well-written _____ is organized into its own mini paper.

3. The topic sentence states the main idea of the _____.

4. The topic sentence also _____ us to the paragraph's topic.

5. The topic sentence puts boundaries around the _____, letting it be broad enough, but not too broad.

6. About ninety percent of all topic sentences are the _____ sentences in paragraphs.

7. If the first sentence is not the topic sentence, then it usually is the _____ sentence.

8. When you are writing a _____, develop one topic, the whole topic, and nothing but that topic.

9. _____ sentences explain and expand the meaning of the topic sentence.

10. The _____ sentence brings the paragraph to a close.

Mini Lesson 165: Sentences in Paragraphs

How can learning this help you? We learn how to write good paragraphs by writing topic sentences, supporting sentences, and conclusions. Let's review using a short piece for our lesson.

REVIEW ON WRITING GOOD PARAGRAPHS

ML 165 Student Activity: Sentences in Paragraphs

Answer the following questions from the paragraph below.

1. Write the first two words of the topic sentence of the paragraph below. _____

Write the first two words of the two supporting sentences that don't really fit into the paragraph's topic.

2. _____

3. _____

4. Write the first two words of the concluding sentence. _____, _____

5. Compare your answers with a partner.

    Nate liked the recognition of being one of the best athletes in the school, and he felt very confident in his sports abilities. However, he was really nervous about taking the drama class his friends had talked him into. His friends were good in both sports and drama. Nate didn't read very well, and he was afraid the other students would laugh at him. Classes for the first three weeks were mostly boring, but twice he had to read a part from a play in front of the other students, and he was embarrassed. He was glad that lunch came after the class because he could look forward to it. Then they had auditions for a play. On a dare, Nate tried out. He got a small part that had some really funny lines in it. When they performed the play. Nate did really well. He decided that drama was a fun class after all.

Mini Lesson 166: Summary Review for Paragraphs

How can learning this help you? Remember to raise your right arm to the square and repeat, "In paragraphs, I do solemnly swear to develop the topic, the whole topic, and nothing but the topic."

IDENTIFYING PARAGRAPH PARTS

ML 166 Student Activity #A: Summary Review for Paragraphs

Work alone or together with a partner and read five paragraphs in a computer article, magazine, or book, and find three sentences in them that are off-topic, which means they don't belong in that paragraph because they are not really about the topic. Write the off-topic sentences down.

1. _____
2. _____
3. _____

Find two good concluding sentences to paragraphs.

4. _____
5. _____

ML 166 Student Activity #B: Write a Well-Constructed Paragraph

1. Write a 5 to 10 sentence paragraph on something you like about your community. It could be the people, government, sports, arts programs, public library, or a park, etc.

_____
_____
_____
_____
_____
_____
_____

2. Write a topic sentence that introduces the topic and sets parameters around it.

_____

(CONTINUED NEXT PAGE)

3. Create 3 or more supporting sentences that support and develop the topic.

_____

_____

_____

4. Make sure you don't have any off-topic sentences in your paragraph.

_____

_____

_____

_____

5. Finish with a concluding sentence that summarizes and ties together the topic.

_____

_____

_____

_____

ML 166 Student Activity #C: Proofread Each Other's Paragraphs

Get into groups of three or four students.

1. Pass your paragraph to the person on your left.

2. Read and critique the paragraph passed to you based on the first four traits (ideas, organization, voice, and word choice).

3. Pass the paper you just evaluated to the left. Take the next paper.

4. Read and critique the new paragraph passed to you for sentence fluency and writing conventions: grammar, capitalization, punctuation, and spelling.

5. After each paragraph has been critiqued once by someone in your group, discuss each paper aloud, emphasizing what was good about the topic sentence, supporting sentences, and concluding sentences in each paragraph.

NAME _____   Language Arts Mini Lessons

Mini Lesson 167: Dialogue Paragraphs

How can learning this help you? A key exception to this is in dialogue or conversation. In a typical conversation people often speak in long paragraphs, but they also often speak in one sentence or even one word. To help the reader of our written passage keep track of who is speaking, we should start a new paragraph each time we change speakers.

DIALOGUE OR CONVERSATION

Some complete dialogue paragraphs might be as short as, "Yes," or, "I will." If a different character speaks next, start a new paragraph.

ML 167 Student Activity: Dialogue Paragraphs

1-2. Write a three- to six-paragraph (very) short story about three people in line for school lunch. Have at least one paragraph that is only one word long; have at least one paragraph that is at least three sentences long.

_____
_____
_____

3. Have at least three sentences that have dialogue in them.

_____
_____
_____

4. Have at least one sentence that is only one word long, like, "Yes."

_____
_____

5. Have at least one paragraph that has three sentences in it.

_____
_____
_____
_____

Mini Lesson 168: Punctuation in Dialogue Paragraphs

How can learning this help you? When you correctly punctuate dialogue or conversation, the reader can understand who is speaking with no confusion. There are a few major things to remember when punctuating dialogue.

PUNCTUATING DIALOGUE

Put *double* quotation marks (" ") around anything that a person/character says.

Read your passage to yourself. When you hesitate, insert a *comma*, and when you stop, insert a *period*.

ML 168 Student Activity #A: Punctuation in Dialogue Paragraphs

Read the passage to yourself. When you hesitate, insert a comma, and when you stop, insert a period. (As said before, this instruction is the single most helpful principle.)

Put (double) quotation marks around anything that a person/character says.

Usually, put a comma after the word that precedes a direct quote.

Capitalize the first word of every direct quote.

Put a comma after the last word before the direct quote unless that word ends a sentence and needs an end mark.

At the end of the quote, put a comma or end mark before you put the final quotation marks.

    Ashley ate another bite of her hamburger and complained, "My little brother is so weird."

    "Why?" asked Ron.

    "He puts ketchup on everything!" she admitted.

    "Everything?"

    "Everything!" she groaned, slurping the remaining soda in her cup. "I mean everything. For breakfast he not only puts it on his eggs, but also on his French toast."

    "Ugh," said Ron. "I can see putting jam on French toast instead of syrup, but ketchup? That doesn't sound good at all."

    Ashley picked up an onion ring. "He says that some people put ketchup on eggs," she said, "and he says French toast is just like an egg on toast." She plopped the onion ring into her mouth without bothering to close it.

(CONTINUED NEXT PAGE)

ML 168 Student Activity #B: Punctuation in Dialogue Paragraphs

Punctuate the continuation of the story below. There are brackets [ ] inserted around each number to help you see where to start and stop.

There are a total of 38 punctuation marks needed in the following short lesson on dialogue. Remember to insert punctuation like periods, commas, and apostrophes in addition to the ones needed around the dialogue.

1. Put (double) quotation marks around anything that a person/character says.

2. Usually put a comma after the word that precedes a direct quote.

3. Capitalize the first word of every direct quote.

4. Put a comma after the last word before the direct quote unless that word ends a sentence and needs an end mark.

5. At the end of the quote, put a comma or end mark before you put the final quotation marks.

1. [Ron put his half-eaten hamburger onto the tray and shoved it away   That sounds terrible he said I can see why you think hes weird He picked up his cup to drink out of it]

2. [That's not the worst of it though responded Ashley

Oh no groaned Ron as he put his undrunk cup of soda onto his tray]

3. [Ashley wiped off her mouth with her napkin then blew her nose on it   My brother not only puts ketchup on his fried chicken he also puts it on his chocolate cake]

4. [I have to go said Ron as he hurriedly dumped his trays contents into the trash and started quickly out the door]

5. [What are we doing in biology next hour asked Ashley

Ron swallowed hard then said Dissecting dead frogs]

NAME _____   Language Arts Mini Lessons

Mini Lesson 169: Focus on Layout

How can learning this help you? Layout is also important since neatness and appearance on the page have as much to do with understandable text as any other convention. Layout includes neatness, illustrations, the font, graphic organizers like numbers or bullets, and the general appearance of the page.

NEATNESS, ILLUSTRATIONS, FONTS, NUMBERS, AND BULLETS ALL ADD TO THE LAYOUT

ML 169 Student Activity: Focus on Layout

Look through two of your assignments for different classes and focus on the layout.

Are your first and last name printed neatly? _____

Is the assignment title and other information clearly labeled? _____

Is your handwriting clear enough for the teacher to easily read it? _____

Get with a partner and see how each of you did.

Be willing to share your work with the class, if called upon.

NAME _____

Mini Lesson 170: Improve Your Writing and Layout

How can learning this help you? The two main purposes of writing conventions are clarity and consistency. If we all capitalize consistently and correctly, implement usage correctly, punctuate correctly, and spell the words the same (correct for the usage) way, it will make it much easier for our readers to understand and comprehend. Learn to see and correct errors in your papers, as well as the papers of others.

CLARITY AND CONSISTENCY

Learn proofreading symbols and how to use them (see Appendix). These simplify corrections and give everyone the same group of correction symbols to work from.

Analyze examples of good and poor conventions and layout, and discuss the differences.

Keep practicing by revising and editing other's writing. The more you edit one another's work, the better you become at it. The more you help others, the better you become at analyzing and editing the conventions and layout in your writing.

ML 170 Student Activity: Improve Your Writing and Layout

1-2. What are the two purposes of writing conventions?

_____

_____

3. You should learn to spot and identify the _____ in your own papers and in others.

4-5. As you improve your editing, you'll help the writing of:

_____

_____

Chapter Eight: Parts of Speech

Why is this chapter important for you? Convention errors not only make writing unclear for readers, but they also are the most easily noticed by them. Not nearly as many of your readers will notice a poorly developed idea or a weak word choice as they will notice a misspelled word or a missed comma. The parts of speech may not be as important as the parts of a sentence, but they still have important rules to help clarify things.

The Lessons

Chapter Eight: Parts of Speech	221
Mini Lesson 171: Identifying Parts of Speech	222
Mini Lesson 172: Using Parts of Speech in Sentences	223
Mini Lesson 173: Nouns	224
Mini Lesson 174: Pronouns	226
Mini Lesson 175: Pronoun Contractions	228
Mini Lesson 176: Indefinite Pronouns	229
Mini Lesson 177: Plural Indefinite Pronouns	230
Mini Lesson 178: Vague Indefinite Pronouns	231
Mini Lesson 179: Proper Adjectives	232
Mini Lesson 180: Verbs and Auxiliary Verbs	233
Mini Lesson 181: Verb Tenses	235
Mini Lesson 182: Adverbs	237
Mini Lesson 183: Adverbs and Adverb Contractions	238
Mini Lesson 184: Conjunctive Adverbs	240
Mini Lesson 185: Adjectives and Adverbs	241
Mini Lesson 186: Synonyms and Substitutes for *Said*	242
Mini Lesson 187: Prepositions	243
Mini Lesson 188: Preposition or Adverb	245
Mini Lesson 189: Coordinating and Correlative Conjunctions	246
Mini Lesson 190: Interjections	248
Mini Lesson 191: Identifying the Parts of Speech	249
Mini Lesson 192: Review the Parts of Speech	250
Mini Lesson 193: Review Pronouns, Nouns, Adjectives, Interjections	251
Mini Lesson 194: Review Verbs, Adverbs, Prepositions, Conjunctions	252

NAME _____ Language Arts Mini Lessons

Mini Lesson 171: Identifying Parts of Speech

How can learning this help you? The grammar experts have realized that it's not effective for students to spend a large amount of time on parts of speech like the previous generations did, but it's still important to understand the main points about them. There are eight parts of speech.

THE EIGHT PARTS OF SPEECH

ML 171 Student Activity: Identifying Parts of Speech

Try to write down the correct part of speech about which each of these questions is asking.

1. Is the word describing a verb, adjective, or another adverb? _____

2. Does the word connect words or groups of words? _____

3. Is the word naming a person, place, thing, or idea? _____

4. Is the word expressing strong emotion or surprise? _____

5. Is the word describing a noun or pronoun? _____

Term	Definition	Example
Noun	A person, place, thing, or idea	
Pronoun	Takes the place of a noun	
Adjective	Describes a noun or pronoun	
Verb	Shows action or state of being	
Adverb	Describes a verb, adjective, or other adverb	
Preposition	Connects nouns and pronouns with other words in the sentence (The worm crawled _____ the apple.)	
Conjunction	Connects words or groups of words	

NAME _____

Language Arts Mini Lessons

Mini Lesson 172: Using Parts of Speech in Sentences

How can learning this help you? The better you learn the eight parts of speech (noun, verb, adjective, adverb, pronoun, preposition, conjunction, and interjection), the more correctly you will be able to use them in sentences.

USE THE EIGHT PARTS OF SPEECH CORRECTLY

ML 172 Student Activity: Using Parts of Speech in Sentences

Write down the correct part of speech about which each of these questions is asking.

1. Does the word take the place of a noun? _____

2. Does the word show action or state of being? _____

Get with a partner and write a sentence that has at least one word that is the part of speech that is listed in parentheses; i.e. (Noun) Melina went to class. Melina and class are both nouns.

Underline the word(s) that is the part of speech you want.

3. (Noun) _____

4. (Verb) _____

5. (Pronoun) _____

6. (Preposition) _____

7. (Conjunction) _____

8. (Interjection) _____

9. (Adjective) _____

10. (Adverb) _____

Trade papers with another pair of students and answer the questions on their paper.

Mini Lesson 173: Nouns

How can learning this help you? Nouns are what the sentence—or a part of it—is about. Nouns (and pronouns) function as the subject, the complement, and the object of the preposition in the sentence. If the noun is proper—or specific—it needs to be capitalized.

NOUNS

Ask: Is the word naming a person, place, thing, or idea?

Example: *Ken* saw two cute *girls* in the *hall*.
Example: I have *faith* in the *United States*.

Proper nouns are specific nouns, like names or titles and should be capitalized. Most nouns are common nouns and don't need to be capitalized.

ML 173 Student Activity #A: Nouns

Write down the five nouns in order from this sentence.

Greg says that a person who claims that little things don't matter has never tried to sleep with a mosquito in his tent.

1. _____
2. _____
3. _____
4. _____
5. _____

ML 173 Student Activity #B: More Nouns

Write down the five nouns in this sentence in the left column. Write the part of the sentence they function as in the right column.

The old woman and little boy sat on the porch and discussed religion until dark.

Nouns	Sentence Function
1. _____	_____
2. _____	_____
3. _____	_____
4. _____	_____
5. _____	_____

(CONTINUED NEXT PAGE)

NAME _____   Language Arts Mini Lessons

ML 173 Student Activity #C: Common Nouns and Proper Nouns

A common noun is a person, place, thing, or idea which is not capitalized. A proper noun is a specific person, place, thing, or idea and is capitalized.

Type	Common Noun	Proper Noun
Person	Teacher	Ms. Robinson
Place	school	Carbon High School
Thing	a canyon	Grand Canyon
Idea	patriotism	Pledge of Allegiance

From the following sentence, write down the two common nouns in the left column, and write the three proper nouns in the right column.

The school was Lakeridge Middle School, and the teacher was excellent.

1. _____   3. _____
2. _____   4. _____
5. _____

Mini Lesson 174: Pronouns

How can learning this help you? Pronouns are a substitute for a noun. They can make sentences more interesting.

PRONOUNS

Is the word taking the place of a noun?

Example: If Rachel gives Daniel a book, the pronouns would be like this:
"The book is my (Rachel's) present to you (Daniel)."

Subjective and Objective Case in Personal Pronouns

The subjective case represents the subject and usually goes *before* the verb; the objective case represents the complement or the object of the preposition and usually goes *after* the verb.

Person	Subjective	Objective	Possessive
First-person	I	me	my
	we	us	our
Second-person	you	you	your
Third-person	she	her	her
	he	him	his
	it	it	its
	they	them	their

When should you use a subjective or objective case in the sentences below? Temporarily delete the other word to see which is correct.

He/him went to the concert. Example: Brittany and *he/him* went to the concert. *He* is the correct answer.

We/Us like to play football.

Example: *We/Us* boys like to play football. *We* is the correct answer.

I/me went shopping.

Example: Cheryl went shopping with *I/me*? *Me* is the correct answer.

Always say or write the other person's name before the *I/me*. Never say, "*Me/I and . . .*"

Sometimes a word like *her* can be used as either an adjective—She brought *her* purse, or as a pronoun—That was *her*. If *her* is used to describe something—That was *her* father, *her* describes the noun *father* so it is an adjective.

(CONTINUED NEXT PAGE)

ML 174 Student Activity: Pronouns

Write down the pronouns in these sentences. The numbers in parentheses tell the number of pronouns in each sentence.

1. I want her to help me with his poster. (3)

_____

2. Why did you want her to help you? (3)

_____

3. Jackson won her first medal when she tripped and fell. (1)

_____

4. Did Brian bring the book for her, or did he give it to Jane and him? (4)

_____

5. I don't like it when she acts mean to them. (4)

_____

Mini Lesson 175: Pronoun Contractions

How can learning this help you? Pronoun contractions are made by combining two words but leaving out one or more letters. An apostrophe is used to show where the letters are deleted, for example, *it's, they're,* and *who's.* The problem is that there are personal pronouns almost like them. A good way to tell the difference is to divide the word in question into two words and see if the two words make sense.

DIVIDE THE WORD IN QUESTION INTO TWO WORDS

If you can divide the word into two words, then you need the apostrophe.

Example	Example Sentence	Can the word be divided into two words? Yes or No
it/it's	The cat hurt its/it's leg.	Can you say: it is? NO
your/you're	I think your/you're done.	Can you say: "I think you are (you're) done." You are. YES
who's/whose	Who's book is this?	Can you say: "Whose book is this?" Who is? NO
who is (who's)	Do you know who's/whose here?	Can you say: Who is? YES

ML 175 Student Activity: Pronoun Contractions

Circle the correct usage of the word.

1. Its/It's beginning to look a lot like Christmas.

2. The horse likes its/it's oats.

3. Whose/Who's woods these are is a good question.

4. Nick said your/you're answer is correct.

5. Maggie said your/you're taste is impeccable.

Mini Lesson 176: Indefinite Pronouns

How can learning this help you? Indefinite pronouns do not refer to a definite person, place, thing, or idea, so they are called indefinite pronouns. The singular indefinite pronouns include words like each, either, everybody, everyone, everything, somebody, and someone.

INDEFINITE PRONOUNS ARE SINGULAR

It seems odd to call words such as *everybody* singular since they must have more than one, but grammatically, they are singular. Indefinite pronouns are usually singular and need singular verbs. If the indefinite pronouns are plural, they need plural verbs.

Singular Pronoun   **Verb**

Everybody   *is*   here.

ML 176 Student Activity: Indefinite Pronouns

Write five sentences, each with a different singular indefinite pronoun in it.

1. _____

_____

2. _____

_____

3. _____

_____

4. _____

_____

5. _____

_____

Mini Lesson 177: Plural Indefinite Pronouns

How can learning this help you? Since there are plural indefinite pronouns, we need to also identify them. Plural indefinite pronouns include both, few, many, several. They need plural verbs.

PLURAL PRONOUNS NEED PLURAL VERBS

Pronoun	Verb	
Several	grow	here.

ML 177 Student Activity: Plural Indefinite Pronouns

Write five sentences, each with a different plural indefinite pronoun in it.

1. _____

2. _____

3. _____

4. _____

5. _____

Mini Lesson 178: Vague Indefinite Pronouns

How can learning this help you? A few indefinite pronouns may be used as either singular or plural, depending on their usage in the sentence.

SOME INDEFINITE PRONOUNS CAN BE EITHER SINGULAR OR PLURAL

All, any, most, none, and *some* may be singular or plural. The number of these pronouns is decided by the words around them, like the objects of the prepositions.

Example: *Most* (of the *boys*) *are* tired. *Boys* is plural, so *are* is used.
Most (of the *concert*) *was* good. *Concert* is singular, so *was* is used.

ML 178 Student Activity #A: Vague Indefinite Pronouns

Circle the correct answer.

1. *Your/You're* going to get an A in that class.

2. Everybody is going to get his or *her/their* turn.

3. We hope that some of us *are/is* on the team.

Fill in the blanks.

4-5. Indefinite pronouns are usually _____ and need _____ verbs.

ML 178 Student Activity #B: Vague Indefinite Pronouns

List five examples of vague indefinite pronouns that can be either singular or plural.

1. _____

2. _____

3. _____

4. _____

5. _____

Mini Lesson 179: Proper Adjectives

How can learning this help you? Is the word describing a noun or pronoun? Does it answer what kind, which one(s), how many, or how much? If so, it is an adjective whose function is to modify or describe nouns and pronouns and make them more specific and interesting. The example sentences show how adjectives (Adj) are used. The arrow (>) is pointing to the word the adjective describes

ADJECTIVES MODIFY OR DESCRIBE NOUNS AND PRONOUNS

Does the word describe a noun or pronoun? Does it answer what kind, which one(s), how many, or how much?

        Adj Adj N V Adj   Adj   N Adj   N

Example: The > stray > dog seems nice.   The stray > dog, nice > dog

        Adj   Pro   V Adj N   Adj   Pro   Adj N

Example: Almost everyone ran four miles. almost > everyone, four > miles

The words *a, an,* and *the* are the three most commonly used adjectives. They are called *articles*. Words like *his, hers,* and *my* show possession and function as *possessive* adjectives.

A proper noun is a specific person, place, or thing and is capitalized

    Example: Ms. Ortiz
    Example: Mount Rushmore.

A proper adjective is a specific type of adjective and is capitalized.

    Example: Swedish meatballs
    Example: Utah snow

ML 179 Student Activity: Proper Adjectives

Write Adj above all of the adjectives, N above all of the nouns, and Pro above all of the pronouns. Draw an arrow (>) from each adjective to the word it describes. The number of adjectives in the sentence equals the number in parentheses. Use a curved line with an arrow on the end to point from each adjective to its noun. Where there are multiple adjectives, use a longer line with an arrow at the end of it.

1. The rusty old car was once a shiny new classic. (6)
2. He wants some red roses for his sad girlfriend. (4)
3. Johnny's brown and black dog is an Airedale. (4)
4. Did you see that large flock of Canadian geese fly over us? (3)
5. Amy had a pretty, red scarf over her long, curly, blonde hair. (7)

Mini Lesson 180: Verbs and Auxiliary Verbs

How can learning this help you? Verbs are the engines of sentences. They show action or state of being. The more specific and active your verb choice, the more interesting your writing can to be. Does the word show either action or a state of being? If it shows either, it is a verb.

23 AUXILIARY (HELPING) VERBS

These 23 auxiliary verbs are extremely helpful to memorize; that's because they don't *seem* like verbs since they don't show action. However, they are very commonly used verbs, and you probably won't be able to identify them as verbs if you don't have them memorized. They can help a regular verb, or they can stand alone as the only verb. Often there is more than one auxiliary verb in a sentence.

Example: Kelsey has talked to Tyler before. (*has* supports the regular verb talked)
Example: We are almost home! (*are* is the only verb in the sentence.)

These verbs don't have to be in this order, but it helps when memorizing them.

Four Groups of Two				8 verbs
A	C	Sh	W	
am	can	shall	will	
are	could	should	would	
Five Groups of Three				15 verbs
B	D	H	M	I-W
be	do	has	may	is
been	does	have	might	was
being	did	had	must	were

(CONTINUED NEXT PAGE

ML 180 Student Activity #A: Verbs and Auxiliary Verbs

Create a sentence using an auxiliary verb to support a regular verb. Put parentheses ( ) around any prepositional phrases, mark S above the subject, V above both the auxiliary verb and the main verb(s), and C above any Complement.

1. _____

   _____

Create two sentences using an auxiliary verb to support a regular verb. Put V above both verbs.

2. _____

   _____

3. _____

   _____

Create two sentences using an auxiliary verb as the only verb. Put parentheses ( ) around any prepositional phrases, S above the subject, V above the verb(s), and C above any complement.

4. _____
5. _____

ML 180 Student Activity #B: Auxiliary Verbs

23 AUXILIARY VERBS

Memorize the 23 Auxiliary Verbs and fill out the following chart.

Four Groups of Two				8 verbs
A	C	Sh	W	
Five Groups of Three				**15 verbs**
B	D	H	M	I-W

Mini Lesson 181: Verb Tenses

How can learning this help you? Nearly all stories are written in the past tense. It's the easiest and safest way to keep your tenses straight. It simply keeps saying that these events already happened. You may also write stories in the present tense. Present tense gives stories a sense of urgency, as if the action is happening right then; however, it can be troublesome when switching to the past tense.

THE SIX VERB TENSES

Six verb tenses are used to show different time periods. Using the sample verb *walk*. Notice how most of them add one or more auxiliary verbs such as like, have, had, and will have.

Present tense	I walk, she walks.
Past tense	I walked.
Future tense	I will walk tomorrow.
Present perfect tense	I have /he has walked.
Past perfect tense	I had walked.
Future perfect tense	I will have walked.

Adding -ing to a verb, such as walking, makes it the progressive form.

TENSE AND ASPECT CHART (USING THE VERB *SEE* AS THE EXAMPLE)

Tense and Aspect	Verb: to see	First-person Singular	Complement
Verb Category	Past	Present	Future
Simple	I saw	I see	I will see
Progressive	I was seeing	I am seeing	I will be seeing
Perfect	I had seen	I have seen	I will have seen
Perfect Progressive	I had been seeing	I have been seeing	I will have been seeing

ML 181 Student Activity #A: Verb Tenses

Write down which verb tense each of these sentences is.

1. By 1 p.m. the dentist will have finished putting the filling in my tooth. _____

2. I will leave the dentist's office much happier than when I entered. _____

3. If I had set the appointment earlier, I would be done by now. _____

4. I walked into the dentist's office at precisely 12:15. _____

5. My tooth has ached for the last time today. _____

(CONTINUED NEXT PAGE)

ML 181 Student Activity #B: Review Verb Tenses

Write down all the verbs in the following sentence and identify the correct verb tense.

1. Circle the verbs in this sentence. Include the three auxiliary verbs.

    Did Angela say she would buy milk, or should we buy some?

    _____

2. Circle the verbs in the following sentence. Include the auxiliary verbs.

    Ricardo has moved here from Peru, and he will be going to school now.

3. Circle the verb(s) and tell what tense they are in the following sentences.

    Danny and Jody walked down the path together. What is the tense? _____

    They had won the game by half-time. What is the tense? _____

    By next term, most or all of you will have passed this class. What is the tense?

    _____

4. Richard has tried hard in sports. What is the tense?_____

5. Put parentheses ( ) around any prepositional phrase(s), S above the subject(s), V above the verb(s), and C above any complement(s) in the sentence below.

    In 1959, Kennedy and Nixon appeared and debated on TV at the first presidential debates.

Mini Lesson 182: Adverbs

How can learning this help you? An adverb describes a verb, adjective, or another adverb. It answers the questions *how, when, where,* or *to what extent.* Common adverbs are *here, there,* and *where*. They often start sentences and seem like the subject, but they aren't.

ADVERBS ARE DESCRIBERS

          Adj Adj Adj   N   V   Adv Adv Adv Adj Adv V   Adv   Adv
Example: The rather old clock ran slightly fast. *rather > old, fast > ran, slightly > fast*

Many of the most common adverbs answer the question *when*.

    Example: *always, usually, often, sometimes, seldom,* and *never* answer *when*.

Words ending in *-ly*. Many adverbs end in *-ly*.

    Example: *accurately, cautiously, quickly,* and *speedily.*

Words ending in *-ly* are usually used as adverbs, but sometimes they're used as adjectives.

Verb/adverb contractions are made by combining two words, but omitting one or more letters. An apostrophe is used to show where the letters are deleted. Verb/adverb contractions are combinations of an auxiliary verb and the adverb *not*.

    Example: *can't, didn't, doesn't, hasn't, shouldn't* and *won't*

ML 182 Student Activity: Adverbs

Circle the adverbs in each sentence.

1. We usually have pizza on Fridays, but it doesn't always happen. (2)

2. The usually happy Danny seemed quite sad when he and Leslie lost their debate. (3)

3. In the rather chilly morning, the heavy dew was not pleasant. (2)

4. I can't wait until the prom when we can really dance. (3)

5. Jane really seldom or never gets a grade lower than an A. (3)

NAME _____

Mini Lesson 183: Adverbs and Adverb Contractions

How can learning this help you? Is the word describing a verb, adjective, or another adverb? Does it answer the questions *how, when, where,* or *to what extent*? If so, it's an adverb.

WHAT WORD DOES EACH DESCRIBE?

        Adj Adv   Adj N   N V Adv   V Adv

Example: My extremely > old trombone > case was really < beaten <up.

Many of the most common adverbs answer the question *when*.

Example: Always, usually, often, sometimes, seldom, and never answer when.

Many adverbs end in *ly*.

Example: Accurate*ly*, cautious*ly*, quick*ly*, and speedi*ly*.

Words ending in *ly* are usually used as adverbs, but sometimes they're used as adjectives.

VERB/ADVERB CONTRACTIONS

These are made by combining two words, but omitting one or more letters. An apostrophe is used to show where the letters are deleted. Verb/adverb contractions are combinations of an auxiliary verb and the adverb *not*.

Example: ca*n't*, did*n't*, does*n't*, has*n't*, should*n't*, and wo*n't*.

Here, there, and *where* are common adverbs. They often start sentences and seem like the subject, but they aren't.

Example: Here's the missing piece to the puzzle.

The sentence—and therefore the subject—is about the *piece*, not *Here's*.

MISPRONOUNCED CONTRACTIONS

Here, there, and *where* have contractions that are often mispronounced. A common mistake even people with generally good grammar make is using the singular contraction for the plural contraction. Which is correct?

Example: Where's the musicians? (musicians is plural, so the correct contraction is *Where're the musicians?*

Example: There's lots of stars tonight. (lots is plural, so the correct contraction is *There're lots of stars tonight.*

Word	Singular Contraction	Plural Contraction
here	here's	here're
there	there's	there're
where	where's	where're

(CONTINUED NEXT PAGE

ML 183 Student Activity: Adverbs and Contractions

Write Adj over each adjective and Adv over every adverb. Draw an arrow < > from each adverb or adjective to the word it describes.

1. There she goes!

2. Where has my little dog gone?

3. Here's/Here're the flowers with the sweet fragrance.

4. There's/There're gold in those hills.

5. Where's/Where're the cookies?

NAME _____

Mini Lesson 184: Conjunctive Adverbs

How can learning this help you? A conjunctive adverb is sometimes used to separate the clauses of a compound sentence. The conjunctive adverbs include *besides, consequently, however, moreover, nevertheless, then,* and *therefore*. When you use one of these to separate two independent clauses, put a semicolon before the conjunctive adverb and a comma after.

PUT A SEMICOLON BEFORE THE CONJUNCTIVE ADVERB AND A COMMA AFTER

Notice how many conjunctive adverbs can be used in this sentence.

Example: They all ordered hamburgers; *consequently/however/nevertheless/moreover/therefore*, they spent all of their money.

Use a semicolon before conjunctions like *however, therefore, nevertheless*, etc. Put a comma after them.

ML 184 Student Activity: Conjunctive Adverbs

In this sentences, delete the FANBOYS conjunction and insert a conjunctive adverb. Punctuate them.

1. On Christmas Eve the kids were excited so they had a hard time sitting still at the program.

_____

_____

2. The kids barely touched their turkey dinner, but they ate their raisin pudding.

Write down three conjunctive adverbs that could be used after eating.

_____

_____

3. The two youngest kids were too excited to sleep, so Annie told them stories until they slept.

Write down three conjunctive adverbs that could be used after sleep.

_____

4. Create a sentence with a conjunctive adverb in it. Punctuate it correctly.

_____

_____

5. Create a sentence with a semicolon in it. Punctuate it correctly.

_____

_____

NAME _____   Language Arts Mini Lessons

Mini Lesson 185: Adjectives and Adverbs

How can learning this help you? Both adjectives and adverbs describe words: adjectives describe nouns and pronouns, and adverbs describe verbs, adjectives, and other adverbs. Adjectives tell *what* and *how many*, and adverbs tell *how, when, where,* or *to what extent*. Adverbs *tell how, when, where,* or *to what extent*.

WHAT IS THE DIFFERENCE BETWEEN ADJECTIVES AND ADVERBS?

ML 185 Student Activity: Adjectives and Adverbs

1. From the following sentence, write down the seven adjectives and one adverb, plus the words they modify.

   At the rickety old dock, they sat and dangled their hot, dusty feet in the water.

   Adjectives: 1._____ 2._____ 3._____
   4._____ 5._____ 6._____ 7._____
   Adverbs: 1._____

2. From the following sentence, write down the three adjectives and the two adverbs, plus the words they modify.

   The sickly old man was really exhausted.

   Adjectives: 1._____ 2._____ 3._____
   Adverbs: 1._____ 2._____

3. Write down the four adverbs, plus the words they modify.

   Bill slowly rested his old bones on the creaky piano bench and lifted his fingers to the ivory keys.

   Adverbs: 1._____ 2._____ 3._____ 4._____

4. Write down each of the four adjectives and three adverbs, plus the words they modify.

   Did you really know that the adjectives actually describe those nouns and pronouns?

   Adjectives: 1._____ 2._____ 3._____ 4._____
   Adverbs: 1._____ 2._____ 3._____

5. Write down the six adjectives and two adverbs, plus the words they modify.

   Al carefully put the small golden stones into his bag and eagerly dug in the black dirt for more.

   Adjectives: 1._____ 2._____ 3._____
   4._____ 5._____ 6._____
   Adverbs: 1._____ 2._____

Mini Lesson 186: Synonyms and Substitutes for *Said*

How can learning this help you? Have you ever been writing dialogue, looked over it, and saw that you had used the word *said* in nearly every sentence? It's hard not to. There are other words you can use for variety. Here is a list of synonyms for *said*. You can usually find several of these words to substitute for *said*.

ML 186 Student Activity: Synonyms and Substitutes for *Said*

Write five sentences, each with one of these synonyms for *said* in it.

Synonyms	and	Substitutes	for *Said*
add	announce	answer	claim
declare	disclose	divulge	estimate
express	guess	imply	maintain
mention	pronounce	relate	remark
reply	report	respond	reveal
speak	suggest	tell	utter

1. _____

2. _____

3. _____

4. _____

5. _____

Mini Lesson 187: Prepositions

How can learning this help you? Prepositions can be tricky, and serious writers need to understand their proper usage. Learn how to use them well and accurately.

PREPOSITIONS

A preposition connects words or word groups to the rest of the sentence.

Example: The car was stuck in the dark, oozing mud. (*Mud* is the object of the preposition *in*.) Prepositional phrases often answer where or when.

Example: The girl on the diving board is the lifeguard. (Where is she? On the diving board.) An easy way to find most prepositions that start prepositional phrases is to use a simple sentence: "The worm crawled _____ the apple." Any word that will fit into that blank and make sense can be a preposition.

Examples: *around, by, down, over, through, up*

All of those words fit into the blank in the sentence about the worm. About ninety percent of all prepositions will fit into that blank.

Of is the most commonly used preposition and, ironically, it doesn't make sense in the worm sentence. Other prepositions that don't make sense in the worm sentence include *as, during, since,* and *than,* but they may still be used as prepositions.

Example: She hasn't had any candy since (preposition) last Saturday.

Once you have found the preposition, an easy way to find the object of that preposition is to ask what or whom is after the preposition.

Example: "The worm crawled up the apple." Up what? *The apple. Apple* is the object of *up.*

ML 187 Student Activity #A: Prepositions

Fill in the blanks with the correct terms about the sentence backbone.

1. To find a preposition, use the sentence, "The_____."

2. What is the most common preposition? _____

3. A prepositional _____ is a group of words that starts with a preposition and ends with its object.

Put parentheses ( ) around the prepositional phrases in these next two sentences.

4. The girl in the white dress is the bride for the next wedding. (2)

5. By the afternoon I'm ready for a nice, long nap. (2)

(CONTINUED NEXT PAGE)

ML 187 Student Activity #B: Preposition Review

Practice makes perfect. Put parentheses ( ) around any prepositional phrases and Adv above any adverbs. Draw an arrow (<) (>) from any adverb to the word it describes.

1. The players quickly ran down the court and shot the ball.

2. The players quickly ran down and shot the ball.

Circle the correct answer.

3. Here's/Here're the name of the winner.

4. I know there're/there's several games to play.

5. Oh, where're/where's the lids to those jars?

Mini Lesson 188: Preposition or Adverb

How can learning this help you? Sometimes the same word can be a preposition or an adverb. The way to distinguish them is to see if the word has an object. If it does, it's a preposition; if it doesn't, it's an adverb.

USE A PREPOSITION OR AN ADVERB

Example: Angela slowly climbed up the stairs.

Up *what*? Stairs. *Stairs* is the object of the preposition *up*.

Example: Angela slowly climbed up.

Up *what*? There's no object, so *up* is an adverb.

ML 188 Student Activity: Preposition or Adverb

Put parentheses ( ) around the prepositional phrases and put Adv above the adverbs. Circle the correct answer.

1. Cameron and Lauren went out the door

2. Cameron and Lauren went out

3. Lauren sat down and studied.

4. Cameron went down the stairs and studied.

5. The table tipped over and broke.

Mini Lesson 189: Coordinating and Correlative Conjunctions

How can learning this help you? Conjunctions are connectors, so ask yourself, "Does the word connect words or groups of words?" If it does, it's a conjunction.

CONJUNCTIONS ARE CONNECTORS

Example: Buy some eggs and milk.
Example: Science is my favorite subject, but I also like math.

Coordinating (FANBOYS) conjunctions separate independent clauses. Insert one of these seven FANBOYS conjunctions after the comma for independent clauses.

   F is for   A is and   N is nor   B is but   O is or   Y is yet   S is so

Use a comma before one of these conjunctions *if* it has a clause (subject and verb) both *before* and *after* that conjunction.

Example: I beat you in tennis, *so/and* you owe me a hamburger.

Use a semicolon *before* conjunctions like *however, therefore, nevertheless, i.e.,* etc. Put a comma *after* them.

CONJUNCTIONS FOR DEPENDENT CLAUSES

Some of the common conjunctions that start dependent clauses include *after, although, because, before, if, than, when, where,* and *whether.*

Don't use a comma if the dependent clause follows an independent clause.

Example: You beat me in tennis *because the wind kept blowing my ball back at me.*

Do use a comma after the dependent clause if it starts the sentence and is followed by an independent clause.

Example: *Because the wind kept blowing my ball back at me*, you beat me in tennis.

These coordinating FANBOYS conjunctions also connect words:

Example: Jackie and Brad are here.
Example: She was confident, yet humble.

CORRELATIVE CONJUNCTIONS

This type of conjunction is a *correlative* conjunction. It uses two words in pairs.

   both . . . and   not only . . . but (also)   either . . . or
   whether . . . or   neither . . . nor

Example: Either I do the assignment or I get an F.

(CONTINUED NEXT PAGE)

ML 189 Student Activity #A: Coordinating and Correlative Conjunctions

Create three sentences that use a FANBOYS conjunction that is in the parentheses.

1. (so) _____

_____

2. (or) _____

_____

3. (for) _____

_____

Create sentences that use the correlative conjunctions that are in the parentheses.

4.. (both . . . and) _____

_____

5. (whether . . . or) _____

_____

ML 189 Student Activity #B: Coordinating and Correlative Conjunctions

Practice the conjunctions—FANBOYS and others—so you use them correctly.

1. Use one of the FANBOYS conjunctions to complete this sentence. Write the word before the needed comma, insert the comma, then write an appropriate FANBOYS conjunction.

   Melissa plays the flute _____ Dora plays the trombone.

2. Insert a conjunction (not a FANBOYS conjunction) to combine this dependent and independent clause. *If* a comma is needed, write the word it follows, then put the comma after that word.

   _____ the party was over Samuel took Jocelyn to her home.

3. Insert a conjunction to combine this independent and dependent clause. If a comma is needed, write the word it follows, then put the comma after it.

   Samuel took Jocelyn to her home _____ the party was over.

4. Insert a conjunction to combine this independent and dependent clause. If a comma is needed, write the word it follows, then put the comma after it.

   Jeffrey licked his ice cream cone _____ rode his bike home.

5. Use a FANBOYS conjunction and comma in this sentence.

   Gina sighed and looked sadly at the stage _____ she wished the play wasn't over.

Mini Lesson 190: Interjections

How can learning this help you? Interjections are used to show strong emotion or surprise. They can stand alone and not be part of a sentence, especially when expressing strong feeling. Ask if the word is expressing strong emotion or surprise.

HOW TO SHOW EMOTION OR SURPRISE

Example: Ouch! That skillet is hot.
Example: Oh, she didn't miss a note in that piece.

Notice that one of the above sentences has a comma after the interjection, and the other one, which shows strong emotion, has an exclamation point.

ML 190 Student Activity: Interjections

Write down the interjection and the appropriate punctuation and capitalization from each sentence.

1. Hah whether you like it or not I'm going home.

2. Why he would be happy to be in your study group.

3. Wow that was a great dunk.

4. I can't believe she would say that. My gosh

5. Oh she didn't think you were serious.

Mini Lesson 191: Identifying the Parts of Speech

How can learning this help you? If you can define a part of speech, you can probably use it correctly.

IF YOU CAN IDENTIFY IT, THEN YOU CAN USE IT

ML 191 Student Activity: Identifying the Parts of Speech

Follow the directions to complete each sentence.

1. There are four prepositional phrases in the following sentence. Put parentheses ( ) around each of them.

    In the middle of the night, our cat climbed up onto the old piano and walked across the keys.

2. There are four prepositional phrases in the following sentence. Put parentheses ( ) around each of them.

    "Over the river and through the woods to Grandmother's house we go."

3. Circle the correct pronouns for this sentence.

    Dale and she/her gave tickets to Susan and I/me.

4. Circle the correct pronouns for this sentence.

    The coach and they/them said we/us players should win the game.

5. Circle the correct pronoun for this sentence.

    Emily and me/I saw a great movie.

Mini Lesson 192: Review the Parts of Speech

How can learning this help you? Review the eight parts of speech which are nouns, pronouns, adjectives, verbs, adverbs, prepositions, conjunctions, and interjections.

TIME TO REVIEW

ML 192 Check for Understanding: Review the Parts of Speech

See if you can answer which part of speech each definition describes.

1. Does the word tell of either an action or a state of being? _____

2. Does the word show relationships between words or groups of words? _____

3. Is the word taking the place of a noun? _____

Answer the following questions.

4. What sentence does the book use to find prepositions? _____

5. What is the past perfect tense for the verb study? _____

Mini Lesson 193: Review Pronouns, Nouns, Adjectives, Interjections

How can learning this help you? Nouns and pronouns are the two parts of speech that normally become the subject or the complement of a sentence, and the adjective describes them. Knowing this helps you write correct sentences.

REVIEW

ML 193 Student Activity: Review Nouns, Pronouns, Adjectives, Interjec-

Get with a partner and write four questions that will help someone identify and learn these four parts of speech: nouns, pronouns, adjectives, and interjections.

1. _____

2. _____

3. _____

4. _____

5. Trade papers with another student and answer the questions on their paper.

Mini Lesson 194: Review Verbs, Adverbs, Prepositions, Conjunctions

How can learning this help you? Verbs show the action or state of being of the sentence, so they are like the engine that runs the car. Adverbs describe verbs, as well as describing adjectives and other adverbs. Prepositions connect nouns and pronouns with other words in the sentence.

ML 194 Student Activity #A: Verbs, Adverbs, Prepositions, Conjunctions

In the chart, next to each part of speech, write a sentence that uses that part of speech and underline the word(s) of that part of speech.

Term	Definition	Example
Verb	Shows action or state of being	
Adverb	Describes a verb, adjective, or other adverb	
Preposition	Connects nouns and pronouns with other words in the sentence (The worm crawled _____ the apple.)	

ML 194 Student Activity #B: Applying the Parts of Speech

Find at least one example of all eight parts of speech in each of the following two sentences. Write N over nouns, P over pronouns, Adj over adjectives, V over verbs, Adv over adverbs, Prep over prepositions, CON over conjunctions, and I over interjections.

Ah. The little dog and I slowly trotted over the bridge.

1. _____ 2. _____ 3. _____

4. _____ 5. _____

The dog saw a squirrel and quickly chased it up an old oak tree. Wow!

6. _____ 7. _____ 8. _____

9. _____ 10. _____

Chapter Nine: Writing Mechanics

Why is this chapter important for you? Writing mechanics involve applying rules such as capitalization, punctuation, and correct spelling to your writing. Good grammar and good mechanics are essential if you want to clearly communicate your ideas. This chapter will convey the essential parts of writing mechanics to help you accomplish that.

The Lessons

Chapter Nine: Writing Mechanics	253
Mini Lesson 195: Capitalization	254
Mini Lesson 196: Capitalizing Titles	255
Mini Lesson 197: Do Not Capitalize	256
Mini Lesson 198: Practice Capitalization	257
Mini Lesson 199: Punctuation Introduction	258
Mini Lesson 200: Commas	259
Mini Lesson 201: Practice with Commas	261
Mini Lesson 202: Comma Splices	262
Mini Lesson 203: Semicolons	264
Mini Lesson 204: Colons	266
Mini Lesson 205: End Marks	267
Mini Lesson 206: Apostrophes—Singular, Plural, or Possessive	268
Mini Lesson 207: Apostrophes/Contractions vs Possessive Pronouns	270
Mini Lesson 208: Dashes, Commas, and Parentheses	271
Mini Lesson 209: Hyphens	272
Mini Lesson 210: Quotation Marks in Dialogue	273
Mini Lesson 211: Quotation Marks / Underlining / Italics	274
Mini Lesson 212: Commas and Periods Review	275
Mini Lesson 213: Punctuation Review	276
Mini Lesson 214: Making Errors on Purpose	277

Mini Lesson 195: Capitalization

How can learning this help you? There are *general* reasons for capitalization but some may surprise you.

DO CAPITALIZE

The words North, South, East, West when they refer to a place or an area: "I'm from the *South*!"

The pronoun *I* and its contractions *I've, I'm, I'll, I'd*

Weekdays and months

The first word in a sentence or line of poetry

Nationalities, races, and religions

Proper nouns and their abbreviations: *Martin Luther King Jr., Ms. Garcia*

Nouns of historical importance

School courses that are languages or have a Roman numeral after them

Proper adjectives: "The *Greek* plays are fascinating."

ML 195 Student Activity: Capitalization

With a partner, find words in the following sentences with capitalization mistakes. Write them correctly.

1. I'm traveling north, but I'm from the west.

2. I enjoyed mt. rushmore, but my favorite place to see was bryce canyon national park.

3. are we supposed to meet at mcdonalds or burger king?

4. Most american students do well in english and math.

5. Do you take chemistry II or geometry?

6. We just finished studying the elizabethan period and shakespeare.

7. When I asked to see a doctor, they sent me to doctor gomez.

8. Have you read the lord of the rings series?

9. I talk with my mom about school, and I talk with dad about finances and sports.

10. Is march a winter or spring month?

Mini Lesson 196: Capitalizing Titles

How can learning this help you? Capitalization is used to start sentences and to emphasize important words so readers notice them. Here are the basic capitalization rules.

CAPITALIZATION: SOMETIMES YOU DO, SOMETIMES YOU DON'T

Capitalize titles of people if they are named.

> Example: Did you see the doctor?
> Example: Did you see Doctor Lee?

Capitalize titles of businesses and organized groups

Capitalize titles of relatives when they are used as names.

> Example: I asked Uncle Paul for some money.
> Example: I asked Mom for some money.

Capitalize titles of works of literature and art.

> Example: Gone With the Wind was an excellent book by Margaret Mitchell.
> Example: Leonardo da Vinci was responsible for the exquisite Mona Lisa.

ML 196 Student Activity: Capitalizing Titles

Write each underlined word. Capitalize the ones that need it.

1. dan likes the sherriff. _____

2. al likes sherriff jablonski. _____

3. she works for torrez construction. _____

4. anne is a member of the methodist church. _____

5. did you like the musical beauty and the beast? _____

Mini Lesson 197: Do Not Capitalize

How can learning this help you? There are times you don't capitalize. These are important to learn.

DO NOT CAPITALIZE

The words *north, south, east, west* when they refer to a direction: "Go west, young man."

The word *earth* if the word *the* comes before it

Seasons: *winter, spring, summer, fall*

If the noun (like *aunt*) is preceded by a possessive pronoun like *my* or *his*

ML 197 Student Activity: Do Not Capitalize

Write each underlined word. Capitalize the ones that need it.

1. Titles that take the place of the person's name. "I asked mom for money, but not my dad.

   _____

2. Seasons: winter, spring, summer, fall.

   _____

3. North, south, east, west when they refer to a place. "I'm from the east!"

   _____

4. North, south, east, west when they refer to the direction: "Go west, young man."

   _____

5. School courses that are languages or have Roman numerals after them like french and algebra II.

   _____

NAME _____

Language Arts Mini Lessons

Mini Lesson 198: Practice Capitalization

How can learning this help you? It cannot be said enough: practice makes perfect. It is good to become familiar with these rules. Some of the rules might not seem to make sense, so the best thing to do is to memorize them.

PRACTICE MAKES PERFECT

ML 198 Student Activity: Practice Capitalization

Create three of your own sentences with at least two capitalization errors in each sentence.

1. _____

2. _____

3. _____

4. Trade papers with a partner and correct the mistakes.

5. Write down anything new you learned about capitalization.

_____

_____

_____

_____

NAME _____

Mini Lesson 199: Punctuation Introduction

How can learning this help you? Punctuation helps you break up sentences, sentence parts, and words. It helps give meaning to your writing. Study these rules to improve your punctuation skills.

KEY PUNCTUATION RULES

Read your piece to yourself.

When you pause, insert a comma,

When you stop, insert a period.

ML 199 Student Activity: Punctuation Introduction

1. Write a sentence with at least one comma in it.

   _____

2. Write a sentence with at least one question mark in it.

   _____

3. Write a sentence with at least one semicolon in it.

   _____

4. Write a sentence with at least one pair of quotation marks in it.

   _____

5. Write a sentence with at least one hyphen in it.

   _____

Mini Lesson 200: Commas

How can learning this help you? Commas are a common but weak form of punctuation. They are like pawns in a chess game. They may not be powerful, but they *are* needed.

USE COMMAS IN THE FOLLOWING WAYS

After a clause

> Example: *When I eat too much pizza*, I get a headache.

To separate three or more items in a series

To separate independent clauses (see FANBOYS under Parts of Speech: Conjunctions)

After introductory elements

After a mild interjection

> Example: *Oh*, I didn't see you there.

After a prepositional phrase that has four or more words

> Example: *On warm nights*, we drank soda.

After two or more introductory prepositional phrases

> Example: *In the kitchen of my home*, I'll have lunch.

Around an appositive

> Example: Mr. Hutchings, *the basketball coach*, likes to fish in Minnesota.

With nouns of direct address

> Example: I want to go study, *Mom*.

To set off dates

> Example: On *Wednesday, July 11, 2020*, we wrote this.

To set off addresses

> Example: *1120 North Don Street, Kirksville, Missouri*, is his address.

(CONTINUED NEXT PAGE)

ML 200 Student Activity #A: Commas

1. Which punctuation mark is common but weak, like a pawn in chess?_____

2. What is a rule when punctuating your writing?

   "When you _____ insert a _____. When you _____ insert a _____.

3. Use a comma to separate three or more items in a _____.

4. Use a comma to separate _____ clauses.

5. Use a comma after an introductory prepositional phrase that has _____ or more words.

ML 200 Student Activity #B: Commas

These rules will help you be right about 80% of the time: Read your piece to yourself and, when you pause, insert a comma. When you stop, insert a period.

1. Use a comma after _____ or more introductory prepositional phrases.

2. Use a comma to set off nouns of _____ address.

3. Use a pair of commas around an _____.

4. Use a _____ to set off dates.

5. Use a _____to set off addresses.

Mini Lesson 201: Practice with Commas

How can learning this help you? If you memorize the following statement and follow it in your writing, you will probably be right 80% of the time. *Read your piece aloud to yourself.* When you *pause*, insert a comma, and when you *stop*, insert a period.

ML 201 Student Activity #A: Practice with Commas

Insert commas where needed in the following sentences.

1. On the warm nights we drank soda.

2. Mr. Hutchings the basketball coach likes to fish in Minnesota.

3. Mom I want to go study.

4. I had pepperoni sausage cheese and mushrooms on my pizza.

5. At the end of the day you should feel good about your efforts.

ML 201 Student Activity #B: More Practice with Commas

Insert commas where needed in the following sentences.

1. Oh I don't know about that.

2. On December 25 2020 I got a pair of skis for Christmas.

3. We lived at 355 East University Avenue Mesa Arizona for a year.

4. When my alarm goes off I'll have to get up.

5. We studied hard for the test and we all got good grades.

Mini Lesson 202: Comma Splices

How can learning this help you? Don't use a comma to connect (or splice) two sentences; it's not strong enough, and it becomes a run-on sentence. There are three ways to correct run-on sentences.

CORRECTING RUN-ON SENTENCES

Incorrect comma splice
Example: Lone Peak High scored three touchdowns, they won the game.
  (Correct) Lone Peak High scored three touchdowns, so they won the game.
  (Correct) Lone Peak High scored three touchdowns; they won the game.
  (Correct) Lone Peak High scored three touchdowns. They won the game.

Remember the seven FANBOYS conjunctions that may be used following a comma to separate clauses: *for, and, nor, but, or, yet, so.*

ML 202 Student Activity #A: Comma Splices

Each of these is a run-on sentence with a comma splice. Make each of them stronger. Use different punctuation each time.

1. Mr. Payne was an excellent teacher, Ms. Peterson was also really good.

___

2. I didn't study for the test, it was harder than I expected.

___

3. I'm sure I missed number 3 badly, what was the correct answer?

___

4. The principal was smart, he called the boy's parents.

___

5. The trombones played great, they must have practiced a lot.

___

(CONTINUED NEXT PAGE)

ML 202 Student Activity #B: Comma Splices

Use the proper punctuation and capitalization for each of these run-on sentences. Use different punctuation each time.

1. That party should win the election they have the best candidates

_____

2. I like that candidate she is really nice

_____

3. Heather liked his speech it made the most sense

_____

4. I will be glad when the election is over it's really distracting

_____

5. In school elections it's a popularity contest ability doesn't matter as much

_____

Mini Lesson 203: Semicolons

How can learning this help you? Semicolons are the least necessary punctuation mark in the English language. You can almost always substitute a different punctuation mark for a semicolon. Use one to separate two independent clauses without using a FANBOYS conjunction.

SEMICOLONS CAN BE REPLACED BY COMMAS MANY TIMES

Example: Randy plays the tuba, yet he also runs track.

Example: Randy plays the tuba; he also runs track.

The one place a semicolon is needed is when using a conjunctive adverb to separate the clauses of a compound sentence. The conjunctive adverbs include *besides, consequently, however, moreover, nevertheless, then,* and *therefore*. When you use one of these to separate two independent clauses, put a semicolon before the conjunctive adverb and a comma after it.

Example: Maria did well in tryouts; therefore, she got the part she hoped for.

Use a semicolon before conjunctions like *however, therefore, nevertheless,* etc. Put a comma after them

Memorize the seven FANBOYS conjunctions.

ML 203 Student Activity #A: Semicolons

1. In this sentence, delete the FANBOYS conjunction and insert a semicolon.

    Doug got an A in math, and his parents almost fainted.

2. In this sentence delete the semicolon and insert a FANBOYS conjunction.

    Michelle was sad she forgot her lunch money; fortunately, she had a granola bar in her locker.

3. Write down three conjunctive adverbs that could be used after *prom*.

    On Friday Jill accepted Roberto's invitation to the prom; he still had to rent a tuxedo.

4. Create a sentence with a conjunctive adverb in it. Punctuate it correctly.

5. Create a sentence with a semicolon in it. Punctuate it correctly.

(CONTINUED NEXT PAGE)

NAME _____   Language Arts Mini Lessons

ML 203 Student Activity #B: Semicolons

Use semicolons between clauses to take the place of FANBOYS conjunctions (*for, and, nor, but or, yet, so*) Use different punctuation each time.

    Example: Alex studied hard; Bartholomew did too.

Before interruption words (conjunctive adverbs)

    Example: For example, consequently, however, nevertheless, otherwise, therefore, etc.

Insert semicolons and other punctuation and capitalization as needed.

1. we decided to go sleigh riding it looked fun

_____

2. it was freezing we were glad we wore warm coats

_____

3. I went down first it was scary

_____

4. i turned the first corner and fell off i rolled over and over

_____

5. we soon got some hot chocolate it tasted so good

_____

NAME _____   Language Arts Mini Lessons

Mini Lesson 204: Colons

How can learning this help you? Colons are used on three different occasions. They are clear and quite easy to remember.

COLONS ARE USED IN THREE WAYS

Time

    Example: 10:24 a.m.

Business letter greetings

    Example: Dear Ms. Jones:

Formal lists

    Example: "We have the following: a book, a pen, and some paper."

Not for informal lists

    Example: "We have a book, a pen, and some paper."

ML 204 Student Activity: Colons

Insert colons and other punctuation and capitalization as needed.

1. school starts at 745 a.m.

_____

2. at my locker Jackie took off the following things a scarf, a coat and her gloves

_____

3. in class Carlos started his business letter dear ms. Hansen i have a suggestion

_____

4. at lunch I had some pizza, soda, and a cookie

_____

5. the last bell rang at 245 we went outside to get onto the bus

_____

Mini Lesson 205: End Marks

How can learning this help you? End marks include four kinds of punctuation: periods, question marks, exclamation marks, and quotation marks.

THERE ARE FOUR KINDS OF END MARKS

Use a period after a statement or request.

Use a question mark after a question.

Use an exclamation point after words showing strong emotion or a command.

Use quotation marks before and after a direct quotation.

ML 205 Student Activity: End Marks

Insert the correct punctuation: semicolons, colons, quotations marks, and end marks.

1. Dear Ms. Sandoval

2. I want some pizza however I just brushed my teeth

3. Katie yelled Hold onto my dog

4. Lee made a basket that tall kid also did

5. He brought his study materials a pen some paper and the textbook

Mini Lesson 206: Apostrophes–Singular, Plural, or Possessive

How can learning this help you? Nouns usually don't *possess* anything. However, when a noun, singular or plural, *does* possess something, it needs an apostrophe to show that possession.

APOSTROPHES WITH SINGULAR NOUNS

Most singular nouns do not end in *s*. When a singular noun possesses something, the apostrophe precedes the *s* (*'s*). The singular possessive of dog is *dog's*.

Example: The dog's collar is brown. (One dog possesses a collar, so it is *'s*.)

APOSTROPHES WITH POSSESSIVE NOUNS

Nouns usually don't possess anything. However, when a noun, whether singular or plural, does possess something, it needs an apostrophe to show that possession.

APOSTROPHES WITH PLURAL NOUNS

If a plural noun does not possess anything, no apostrophe is needed. The dogs don't possess anything, so no apostrophe is needed.

Example: The dogs ran through the garden.

APOSTROPHES WITH PLURAL NOUNS ENDING IN AN *S*

About 95 % of all plural nouns end in *s*. When these nouns become possessive, the apostrophe follows the s (*s'*).

APOSTROPHES WITH PLURAL POSSESSIVE

Example: The *dogs'* food dish was full. (*s'* shows that more than one dog possessed the food dish)

APOSTROPHES WITH PLURAL POSSESSIVE NOUNS NOT ENDING IN AN *S*

Only about 5 percent of the plural nouns don't end in *s*. Examples are women, firemen, alumni, and criteria.

APOSTROPHES WITH PLURAL POSSESSIVE OF *WOMEN* IS *WOMEN'S*

Example: Have you joined the women's club? (*'s* shows that several women possess a club)

(CONTINUED NEXT PAGE)

ML 206 Student Activity: Apostrophes–Singular, Plural, or Possessive

Circle the correct possessive pronoun.

1. The red cars/car's/cars' tire is low.

2. The cars/car's/cars' lined up for the race.

3. Both cars/car's/cars' windshield wipers were replaced.

4. All of the firemens/fireman's/firemen's helmets were delivered.

5. The alumnis/alumni's/alumnis' banquet was fun.

Mini Lesson 207: Apostrophes/Contractions vs Possessive Pronouns

How can learning this help you? When considering apostrophes with contractions and possessive pronouns, there are several pairs of similar words that are troublesome. Here are some examples.

CONTRACTIONS VERSUS POSSESSIVE

Contractions	Two Words	Possessive Pronouns
it's	it is	its
they're	they are	their
who's	who is	whose
you're	you are	your

If you can break the word-in-question into two words (like *who is*), insert an apostrophe; if you can't, don't add one.

Example: "Who's (who is) coming to dinner?" Contraction. Use an apostrophe.
Example: "I wonder whose book this is." Possessive pronoun. Don't use an apostrophe.

ML 207 Student Activity: Apostrophes/Contractions vs Possessive Pronouns

Circle the correct possessive pronoun.

1. I think its/it's getting dark.

2. The plot's poor villain was its/it's weakness.

3. I heard that their/they're going to win.

4. Whose/Who's coat this is, I wonder.

5. I believe your/you're up to bat next.

Mini Lesson 208: Dashes, Commas, and Parentheses

How can learning this help you? There are three types of punctuation marks that are used to set sentence sections apart: commas, parentheses, and dashes. These separators help emphasize key information you want your readers to notice and are used in similar ways. They all separate *groups of words*. Dashes are used with long explanations that interrupt the thought—two connecting hyphens make a dash or an *em dash*. Commas are used to indicate a pause, and parentheses are used to add a short amount of information outside of the content.

DASHES INTERRUPT THOUGHTS OR DIALOGUE

Example: Kris—the section leader of the outstanding flute section—is a gifted musician.

On a computer most word processing software will allow you to make the long (or *em*) dash by leaving a space, hitting the hyphen twice, leaving another space, and typing the next word. The two hyphens will then combine to make one long dash when you do type the next word after the dash.

ML 208 Student Activity: Dashes, Commas, and Parentheses

In each sentence, decide whether the words between the asterisks need dashes, commas, or parentheses and rewrite the portion of the sentence between the asterisks..

1. Independence day *July Fourth* is a highlight of the summer.

2. There are parades* complete with bands, soldiers, floats, and dignitaries* moving down the street.

3. Many people go camping *or at least picnicking* to get into America's great outdoors.

4. Others like their outdoors *complete with covered patio, lawn furniture, grill, and refrigerator* to be their backyard.

5. The evening's fireworks *which light up the sky with a million bright colors, designs, and sounds* are a perfect finale.

Mini Lesson 209: Hyphens

How can learning this help you? Hyphens separate *words*. There is no space before or after a hyphen.

HYPHENS ARE SEPARATORS

Divide a word by syllables at the end of a line.

When writing a span of numbers . . .

    Example: 21-99

When writing fractions in words . . .

    Example: three-fourths

Separate the parts of some compound words.

    Example: son-in-law
    Example: sons-in-law
    Example: bills-of-sale

ML 209 Student Activity: Hyphens

Insert hyphens or dashes where needed in these sentences. Since a dash takes up more than one space, draw it above the space between the words where it will go, and make it about as long as two typed spaces.

1. The Lakers won two thirds of their games.

   _____

2. Her mother in law was helpful.

   _____

3. Kelly who is excellent on the trumpet is first chair in the band.

   _____

4. I attended Roosevelt Elementary school from grades K 5.

   _____

5. Apples picked from the tree are amazing.

   _____

NAME _____   Language Arts Mini Lessons

Mini Lesson 210: Quotation Marks in Dialogue

How can learning this help you? Quotation marks inform the reader that a speaker or writer's exact words are being given. Quotes may be used at the beginning, middle, or end of a paragraph. Learn how to punctuate each one.

USING QUOTATION MARKS IN DIALOGUE

Example First: "Brady swam the fastest, so he should take first in State," said Coach Miller.
Example Middle: Coach Miller said, "Brady swam the fastest," so he thought Brady should take first in State.
Example End: Coach Miller said, "Brady swam the fastest, so he should take first in State."

Notice how the commas and quotation marks are placed in the middle sentence and how the word *so* is not capitalized. That's because it's the continuation of the sentence, "Brady swam the fastest."

ML 210 Student Activity: Quotation Marks in Dialogue

Punctuate and capitalize these sentences. Underline the letters that need to be capitalized.

1. guess what yelled sylvester i got a part in the play

_____

2. nicole answered sadly i'm glad for you but i didn't get one

_____

3. Did angie get a part asked sylvester

_____

4. roberto looked at the list wow she got the lead

_____

5. you all did well said mr brown it was hard to choose the best

_____

Mini Lesson 211: Quotation Marks / Underlining / Italics

How can learning this help you? Put quotation marks around titles of short literary works that can be part of a collection of long literary works. *Underline* (if you're writing by hand) or *italicize* (if you're typing) the titles of long literary works.

EXAMPLES OF USING QUOTATION MARKS, UNDERLINING, AND ITALICS

Short	Long
"Article"	Magazine
"TV Episode"	TV Series
"Chapter:	Novel
"Short Story" or "Poem"	Anthology
"Short Movie"	Long Movie

ML 211 Student Activity: Quotation Marks / Underlining / Italics

1. Does the typed title of a long movie need underlining, italics, or quotation marks? _____

2. Does the typed title of a short movie need underlining, italics, or quotation marks? _____

3. Write and punctuate the title of a short story.

   _____

4. Write and punctuate the title of a TV episode.

   _____

5. Write and punctuate the typed title of a novel.

   _____

Mini Lesson 212: Commas and Periods Review

How can learning this help you? Use a comma after a prepositional phrase that has four or more words in it or after two prepositional phrases. In addresses, use commas between the street address and the city, after the city, and after the zip code if the sentence continues. Do *not* use a comma alone to separate clauses.

KEY COMMA AND PERIOD RULES

Read the piece to yourself.

When you pause, insert a comma.

When you stop, insert a period.

ML 212 Student Activity: Commas and Periods Review

1. What is the rule used to decide if you need a comma or period?

   _____

2. What is one of the two times you use a comma after a prepositional phrase? _____

3. Insert commas in the complete address: 123 Elm Street Dayton Ohio 54321

   _____

4. Do you use a semicolon or a comma alone to separate two clauses? _____

5. Use a _____ between clauses to take the place of a conjunction and comma or a period.

6. Do you place the apostrophe before or after the *s* in a plural possessive noun that ends in *s*? _____

7. Where do you place the apostrophe in a plural noun that doesn't possess anything? _____

8. What is one way you use colons besides to separate the hour and minute when telling time?

   _____

9. Does a hyphen or dash separate groups of words and have a space before and after it? _____

10. Do you use quotation marks or italics when you type the title of a short story or poem? _____

Mini Lesson 213: Punctuation Review

How can learning this help you? Do you remember the parts on punctuation that you almost understood, but then forgot? This review may help reinforce the answers for you.

REVIEW

ML 213 Student Activity #A: Apostrophe and Colon Review

Insert the correct punctuation where needed.

1. (Apostrophes) The dogs tail is wagging.

2. (Apostrophes) After the sled dogs harnesses got tangled, the Eskimo girls tried to help them.

3. (Apostrophes) The womens department is on the second and third floors.

4. (Apostrophes) The racehorse hurt its leg.

5. (Colons) By 945 we need to have these things an apple, two pears, and three plums.

ML 213 Student Activity #B: Comma Review

Answer #1 and insert the correct punctuation where needed in #2-#5.

1. (Commas and periods) Read the piece to yourself. When you _____, insert a comma, and when you _____, insert a period.

2. (Commas) Michael Jordan Kobe Bryant and Larry Bird were all great basketball players.

3. (Commas) You need to practice your clarinet or you can't play your solo at the festival.

4. (Commas) After the history class I spoke with my teacher about the test I failed.

5. (Commas) On January 25 2021 the Schneiders were married.

ML 213 Student Activity #C: Semicolon, Dash, Quotation, etc. Review

1. (Quotation Marks / Underlining Semicolons) We attended the musical Phantom of the Opera it was good.

2. (Hyphens/ Dashes) The Tigers won two thirds of their games a big improvement from before.

3. (Quotation Marks / Underlining) Do you like the poem The Road Not Taken by Robert Frost?

4. Quotation Marks/Underlining) I enjoyed the article called Trouble in the Mideast that was in Time Magazine.

5. (Semicolons and Commas) The hikers were up before dawn however the storm stopped them from reaching the summit.

Mini Lesson 214: Making Errors on Purpose

How can learning this help you? When we purposely make errors in our writing, it helps us understand those errors and how to fix them. When we fix other people's errors, that also helps us to see the mistakes and figure out the correct answers.

REVIEW

ML 214 Student Activity: Making Errors on Purpose

With a partner, compose five sentences with two or more punctuation errors in each. Try to misuse different punctuation marks in each sentence. Your choices are periods, question marks, exclamation marks, commas, semicolons, colons, quotation marks, apostrophes, dashes, and hyphens. Put parentheses ( ) around the number of errors in each sentence you create.

1. _____

2. _____

3. _____

4. _____

5. _____

Exchange sentences with another student and correct the mistakes you find in theirs.

Chapter Ten: Literary Elements

Why is this chapter important for you? Learn to identify the different elements in a story while reading it. This can help you understand the story and its structure better and will also be of immense help when you write. These elements will help you enjoy, comprehend, and write fictional literature better, beginning with Characterization.

The Lessons

Chapter Ten: Literary Elements 278
    Mini Lesson 215: Characterization 279
    Mini Lesson 216: Conflict 280
    Mini Lesson 217: Plot Exposition 281
    Mini Lesson 218: Plot Rising Action 282
    Mini Lesson 219: Plot Crises 283
    Mini Lesson 220: Plot Climax and Resolution 284
    Mini Lesson 221: Dialogue and Point of View 285
    Mini Lesson 222: Setting and Imagery 287
    Mini Lesson 223: Finding Story Elements 288

Mini Lesson 215: Characterization

How can learning this help you? When writing a narrative, there are many aspects of the work that need to be incorporated that have to do with characterization. The qualities or the perception of the characters (animate or inanimate) are critical to creating the "picture in the mind" of the reader; things like a physical description, their thoughts, if they have them, how they react in the narrative, their speech patterns, and more.

CHARACTERIZATION IN LITERARY ELEMENTS

The protagonist—usually the hero—is the character who tries the hardest to repair the beginning balance once it is upset, while the antagonist tries the hardest to keep it upset. Most of the time there is one protagonist, even if they have helpers. There can sometimes be more than one antagonist, such as a group of people who are equally against the protagonist. If the reader cares about the protagonist, they will care about what happens to them; consequently, they will care about what happens in the story.

There are three ways for the writer to help us care more about the protagonist.

1. Give them an admirable quality so the reader can then admire them.
2. Share their feelings and thoughts.
3. Show how the protagonist changes during the story.

The antagonist, usually the villain, is generally evil, but sometimes they simply have opposing objectives from the protagonist. This is especially true in comedies. If the writer just tries to make the antagonist evil without showing the purpose, it will be unbelievable.

ML 215 Student Activity: Characterization

What are two of the three ways the author can help the readers care about the protagonist?

1-2. _____

_____

3. Sometimes the _____ isn't evil, but just opposes the protagonist.

4. Who tries hardest to repair the upsetting incident? _____

5. Who tries hardest to keep the upsetting incident upset? _____

NAME _____

Mini Lesson 216: Conflict

How can learning this help you? Conflict is what makes the narrative come alive. When there trouble is brewing, the reader is captured and excited about the outcome.

TYPES OF CONFLICT

Since conflict is the source of fiction, here are the types of conflict.

Internal or person against themselves

External or person against everyone and everything else

1. Person against person
2. Person against society (social norms of people in the story)
3. Person against nature (animals, plants, or elements)
4. Person against fate (luck, chance)
5. Person against the gods or the supernatural (as in Greek and Roman theater and horror stories).

ML 216 Student Activity: Conflict

What are the two main types of conflict?

1. _____

2. _____

List three of the types of external conflict

3. _____

4. _____

5. _____

Mini Lesson 217: Plot Exposition

How can learning this help you? The exposition introduces the situation, as well as who the main characters are and how they got to be the way they are at the story's start. It's best to only give too much exposition; just what is needed at the time, and then mix some action into it, or readers get bored.

EXPOSITION HAS TWO PARTS: THE BEGINNING BALANCE AND THE UPSETTING INCIDENT

Beginning balance

Life is bearable, but there is foreshadowing, or a hint, of bad things to come.

Upsetting incident

Something happens that makes life no longer bearable.

The protagonist is the character who tries the hardest to make things bearable again.

ML 217 Student Activity: Plot Exposition

What are the two parts of exposition?

1. _____

2. _____

3. Fiction is based on _____

To use a story and plot we all know, let's use the children's story of "Goldilocks and the Three Bears."

4. What is the beginning balance? _____

5. What is the upsetting incident? _____

Mini Lesson 218: Plot Rising Action

How can learning this help you? Fiction is based on conflict. The rising action is the part of the story, or main conflict, that starts after the upsetting incident and goes until the conflict reaches a climax where the protagonist either wins or loses. The rising action is typically about 75 percent of the story. During the rising action, the protagonist tries to repair the upsetting incident while the antagonist tries to keep it upset.

RISING ACTION CREATES THE DRAMA AND ANXIETY LEADING TO THE CLIMAX

ML 218 Student Activity: Plot Rising Action

1. _____ is based on conflict.

2. What is the part of the story called that is between the upsetting incident and the climax?
_____

3. About what percent of the story is the rising action? _____

4. Who tries hardest to repair the beginning balance? _____

5. Who tries hardest to permanently destroy the beginning balance? _____

NAME _____   Language Arts Mini Lessons

Mini Lesson 219: Plot Crises

How can learning this help you? Crises is the plural form of crisis. Within the rising action, or main conflict, typically there are two to five crises (crucial or decisive events). Overcoming crises typically makes the protagonist wiser, stronger, or better in some way, but each new crisis is usually harder for the protagonist to get through than the previous one.

DRAMA VS COMEDY

In dramas, the reader really wants the protagonist and their friends to win and restore the beginning balance. However, in comedies the main conflict doesn't seem very serious to the reader, so they don't care who wins. Therefore, they can distance themselves from the problems and laugh at the characters trying so desperately to overcome them.

ML 219 Student Activity: Plot Crises

1. Does the main conflict seem serious to the readers in drama or is it in comedy? _____

2. Does the audience care more who wins in the drama or the comedy? _____

3. What is the plural word for crisis? _____

4. How many crises should the main rising action of most stories have? _____ to _____

5. Is each new crisis usually harder or easier for the protagonist to overcome? _____

Mini Lesson 220: Plot Climax and Resolution

How can learning this help you? Summing up the story is critical and can make or break the success of the piece. Have you ever gone to a movie and been thoroughly displeased with the ending? It ruined the whole movie for you, didn't it? It's the same with writing.

CLIMAX, CHANGE, RESOLUTION

Climax: This is when the protagonist wins or loses. It's really important to them to win. It's *also* important for the antagonist to win. The writer should show that importance in the protagonist's feelings and thoughts.

Change: Somewhere around the end of the story, the writer should show how the protagonist has changed, usually as a result of the conflict. Award-winning writer Lois Lowry stated, "When the protagonist arrives at his destination, it has changed, as has the protagonist. Change is the central ingredient of each story."

Resolution: During this brief period at the end, any unfinished business is finished, so that everything fits together. Many times the protagonist's change is brought about because of the conflict. The author may also subtly add some brief, philosophical message. Often there is no resolution. If one is used, having too little is almost always better than too much.

ML 220 Student Activity: Plot Climax and Resolution

1. _____ is the central ingredient of each story.

2. Is it important for the protagonist to succeed in overcoming the upsetting incident? _____

3. What is the purpose of the resolution? _____

4. The _____ is when the protagonist permanently wins or loses.

5. The _____ is when any unfinished business is finished.

Mini Lesson 221: Dialogue and Point of View

How can learning this help you? Dialogue, or conversation, is what people say to each other (external) or to themselves (internal). Point of view is the eyes and mind through which we see the story.

DIALOGUE CREATES INTEREST; POINT OF VIEW SHOWS EVENTS AND CHARACTERS

Development of the plot

Development of the characters

Creation of an emotion or response for the audience such as laughter, sadness, or anger

POINT OF VIEW IS THE VANTAGE POINT TO SHOW EVENTS AND CHARACTERS

There are four types of point of view:

First-person (I, me, we)

Second-person (you, your)

Third-person limited (he, she, it, they)

Third-person omniscient (all-seeing, like a camera)

First-person shows the narrator's feelings and thoughts

> Example: "Fearfully, I crept into the dark tunnel." First-person tells what *I* or *we* thought and felt, and it involves us, the readers, more, so we become closer to the narrator. However, the reader can only see things from the narrator's view and know what the narrator knows.

Second-person—*you*. It is very hard to write successfully from the second-person point of view.

Third-person limited is like first-person except it is about *he, she,* and *they* instead of *I, me,* and *we*. Like first-person, it involves us more because it can include a person's thoughts and feelings, but it can only see inside what that one person can see.

Third-person omniscient (all-knowing and all-seeing) shows many different people and scenes that first-person and third-person limited can't show, and it can include a person's thoughts and feelings like first-person can, but not as effectively. It also gives more distance between the writing and the reader, which is good in many narratives.

(CONTINUED NEXT PAGE)

ML 221 Student Activity: Dialogue and Point of View

What are two of the three things that effective dialogue should do?

1-2. _____

_____

3. Which point of view shows the narrator's feelings and thoughts, but no one else's? _____

4. Which point of view shows many different people and scenes? It can't include a person's thoughts and feelings as well as first-person can. _____

5. Which point of view involves the reader like first-person, except it is about *him, her,* and *them* instead of *I* and *me*? _____

Mini Lesson 222: Setting and Imagery

How can learning this help you? Where and when a story takes place is critical to developing interest in the story. The more vivid and clear the setting is, the more the reader gets involved. Make a clear, specific description of the setting, but don't add unnecessary details, especially during unimportant parts. This will detract from the plot or character development.

SETTING AND IMAGERY INVOLVE THE SENSES

> "The process of gathering meaning from life always begins with the senses, and then passes on to feelings (emotional imagery), ideas, thoughts, and finally, judgments."
>
> Suzan Lake, veteran teacher

The more specific the images, the more interesting the readers will find the writing. Strong images generate strong feelings and thoughts in the readers. Remember that there are two types of imagery.

Sense imagery: *sight, sound, touch, taste, and smell*

Emotional imagery: *fear, joy, sadness, anger*, etc. These trigger memories of emotions we have felt in our own lives and involve us more in the text.

ML 222 Student Activity: Setting and Imagery

1. What is the literary element that describes when and where a story takes place? _____

2. Should you develop the setting more during important or unimportant parts of the plot? _____

What are two of the five types of sense imagery?

3-4. _____

_____

5. What is one of the types of emotional imagery? _____

Number	See	Hear	Touch	Smell	Taste
1					
2					
3					
Number	Joy	Excitement	Anger	Fear	Discouragement
4					
5					

Mini Lesson 223: Finding Story Elements

How can learning this help you? Why should you spend your time reading a children's story? This popular children's story that everyone knows was purposely chosen so you can look past the story and focus on the literary elements.

Each number in parentheses represents a literary element. Choose which element. Refer to the chart at the end of the story.

Little Red Riding Hood

Once upon a time near a deep, dark forest, a sweet little girl lived with her mother and father. Because the little girl had pretty red hair and a cape with a red hood on it, they called her Little Red Riding Hood. (1)

One afternoon her mother called her and said, "Little Red, Grandma is sick, and I have a basket of goodies for her. Would you take them to her?"

(2) "Of course," said Red, smiling. She was happy to take the goodies to Grandma's, and she was also happy because she would be able to play in the woods.

Red's mother interrupted her thoughts. "Now, don't dawdle, Red. Hurry to Grandma's and hurry back, so you're home before dark." Then her mother bent down close to Red and added, "Besides, I hear that the Big, Bad Wolf is loose again in the forest!"

Red's eyes went as wide as two fried eggs, and she gasped. "The B-Big, B-B-Bad W-W-W-Wolf? Oh, no!"

Sighing, Little Red's mother comfortingly said, "Now Honey, you'll be okay. I wouldn't send you if I thought there was any danger."

(3) Taking the basket of goodies, Little Red ran out the door and down the path into the woods.

She started fast, but she forgot about the Big Bad Wolf and started picking some roses and wildflowers for Grandma.

Little Red had just bent down to pick a beautiful red rose when a large shadow came over her. She slowly turned around to see what could cast such a giant shadow over her.

(4) She saw a large, hairy beast with long, jagged teeth and large, yellow eyes staring down at her.

(CONTINUED NEXT PAGE)

She gulped and then asked, "Who are you?"

(5) The beast sneered and said, "I'm the Big Bad Wolf," and he tipped his hat. Then he tilted his head back and howled.

The little girl didn't think he was too scary, so she asked, "Should I be afraid of you?"

He laughed and asked, "Say, where are you going, young lady?"

(6) "To my Grandma's house. I'm taking her these goodies. My grandma lives over the river and through the rest of the woods." She pointed in the direction.

"Oh, do you mean the grandma who lives in a little red house with a white picket fence?" he asked.

"Yes. That's the very one," answered the excited girl.

The Big Bad Wolf started to make a plan; a mean, evil plan. "Say, little girl. Did you know that a flood damaged the bridge down there? You have to go another way now and take the bridge over by that hill.

Little Red smiled, picked up her basket, and started off in the direction the Big Bad Wolf had pointed. "Thank you so much, Mr. Wolf."

"Don't mention it," he called after her, licking his lips in anticipation. Then he dashed off the right way, the faster way, over the river and through the rest of the woods, to Grandma's house.

It took Red a lot longer the way she went, but at dusk, she finally arrived at Grandma's house. She tapped on the door and heard a weird-sounding voice say, "Come in."

Little Red walked in, set the basket on the table, and walked over to Grandma's bed. In the dusk, there was someone in Grandma's nightgown and nightcap, but it surely didn't look like Grandma.

Red said, "Grandma, what a big nose you have."

"All the better to smell you with, my dear," answered the voice.

Red looked at the large, yellow eyes. They looked strangely familiar. "Grandma, what big eyes you have."

"All the better to see you with, my dear," came the voice.

Little Red came even closer and peered at the huge, drooling teeth. "Grandma, what big teeth you have!" said the little girl.

CONTINUED NEXT PAGE)

"All the better to eat you with!" yelled the Big Bad Wolf as he jumped out of bed and sprang after the screaming Little Red Riding Hood.

(7) Fortunately, the front door burst open, and the sheriff came in with his gun out and aimed at the Big Bad Wolf. "Freeze, Wolfy!' he yelled.

The Big Bad Wolf stopped, and the sheriff put him in paw-cuffs.

(8) "How did you know where to find me, Sheriff?" growled the Big Bad Wolf.

"I didn't know," answered the sheriff, "so I've just been following you ever since you got out of prison three days ago."

The Big Bad Wolf was angry. "Didn't you have any more faith in me than that?"

"Yes, I did, but you didn't have enough faith in yourself," he retorted. "I even bet the warden my favorite horse that you'd be good. It looks like I've lost my horse, thanks to you."

Little Red Riding Hood then interrupted and asked the Big Bad Wolf, 'Where's Grandma? What have you done with my grandma?"

Just then there was a bumping noise from inside the closet. Little Red rushed to the closet and flung open the door. There was Grandma, tied up and gagged but otherwise fine. After she was loose, Grandma said, "The Big Bad Wolf tied me up and gagged me, but when he left me, I hopped into the closet and hid so that he wouldn't find me."

"I am so glad you are okay, Grandma," said Red. Then she marched up to the wolf, pointed her finger at his face, and said, "And because of you, Mr. Wolf, I'll be much more careful around strangers."

As the sheriff led the Big Bad Wolf out the door, Grandma said, "Thanks to you bringing this basket of goodies, Red, you and I are the ones who will do the eating!"

MINI LESSON #223 WILL REFER TO "LITTLE RED RIDING HOOD"

(CONTINUED NEXT PAGE)

ML 223 Student Activity #A: Finding Story Elements

After you read "Little Red Riding Hood," match the terms from the story.

1. _____   a. admirable trait of protagonist
2. _____   b. antagonist
3. _____   c. beginning balance
4. _____   d. change for protagonist
5. _____   e. climax
6. _____   f. protagonist
7. _____   g. resolution
8. _____   h. rising Action
9. _____   i. upsetting incident
10. What was the point of view? _____

ML 223 Student Activity #B: Writing with Story Elements

1. Write a different ending for the story you just read. Make the ending 50 to 100 words long.

   _____

2. Write a 50 to 100 word part of the story and change the point of view; if it's written in first-person, change it to third-person omniscient, or from third to first-person, etc.

   _____

3. Dramatize (create a play) and adapt a short section of the story, either with others or alone.

   _____

4. Compose a poem or song about the whole story or a key dramatic section of it.

   _____

5. Analyze the story according to Goethe's three principles. (50-100 words)

   _____

(CONTINUED NEXT PAGE)

NAME _____

ML 223 Student Activity #C: Finding Story Elements

What is the artist/author trying to do? / How well are they doing it? Is it worth doing?

After you read "Little Red Riding Hood," use this chart and fill in at least 10 examples of sensory and emotional imagery.

Number	See	Hear	Touch	Smell	Taste
1					
2					
3					
Number	Joy	Excitement	Anger	Fear	Discouragement
4					
5					

Chapter Eleven: PAIR and KWL Compared

The Lessons

Chapter Eleven: PAIR and KWL Compared 293
    Mini Lesson 224: Compare PAIR with KWL 294
    Mini Lesson 225: PAIR Prior Understanding / General Comprehension 295
    Mini Lesson 226: PAIR Anticipating / General Comprehension 296
    Mini Lesson 227: Inputting / General Comprehension 298
    Mini Lesson 228: Relating / General Comprehension 299
    Mini Lesson 229: Prior Understanding in Expository Text 300
    Mini Lesson 230: Anticipating in Expository Text 302
    Mini Lesson 231: Inputting in Expository Text 303
    Mini Lesson 232: Relating in Expository Text 304
    Mini Lesson 233: Prior Understanding in Argumentative Text 305
    Mini Lesson 234: Anticipating in Argumentative Text 307
    Mini Lesson 235: Inputting in Argumentative Text 308
    Mini Lesson 236: Relating in Argumentative Text 309
    Mini Lesson 237: Prior Understanding in Narrative Text 310
    Mini Lesson 238: Anticipating in Narrative Text 312
    Mini Lesson 239: Inputting in Narrative Text 313
    Mini Lesson 240: Relating in Narrative Text 315
    Mini Lesson 241: Comprehension Application 316
    Mini Lesson 242: Text Organization Patterns 317

NAME _____

Mini Lesson 224: Compare PAIR with KWL

Why is this chapter important for you? PAIR (Prior Understanding-Anticipating- Inputting-Relating) is a simple way to pair you—the learner—with the material you are studying. If you can't comprehend what you try to input—read, hear, or view—it's a frustrating waste of time for you, and you can't learn what you need to. KWL (Know-Want to Learn/Know-Learned) is an alternative tool to do the same.

WHAT IS PAIR?

PAIR is a variation of the popular KWL comprehension process.

Here are the two comprehension processes side-by-side.

KWL Know-Want to Learn/ Know-Learned	Inputting Reading, Viewing, Hearing	PAIR P for Prior Understanding A for Anticipating I for Inputting R for Relating
What do you KNOW about a topic?	Before Inputting	What is your PRIOR understanding about the topic?
What do you WANT to know about it?	Before Inputting	What do you ANTICIPATE learning about it from your reading?
What did you LEARN about it while studying it?	During and after Inputting	What can you INPUT from studying it?

ML 224 Check Understanding: Compare PAIR with KWL

What do the letters K, W, and L stand for in this reading comprehension?

1. K _____

2. W _____

3. L _____

4-5. What do the letters PAIR represent in this reading comprehension chapter? _____

_____

Mini Lesson 225: PAIR Prior Understanding / General Comprehension

How can learning this help you? Focus on yourself and what you already understand of the topic you are reading about.

PRIOR UNDERSTANDING

What's your prior understanding of the topic?

What's your own prior knowledge (if any) with the topic?

What's your prior experience (if any) with the topic?

What's your prior attitude (if any) toward the topic?

What's your prior attitude (if any) about the author?

ML 225 Check Understanding: Prior Understanding / General Comprehension

Answer these four questions about this topic.

1. What's your own prior knowledge (if any) about the Heimlich maneuver?

   _____

2. What's your own prior experience (if any) with the Heimlich maneuver?

   _____

3. What's your prior attitude (if any) toward the Heimlich maneuver?

   _____

4. What's your prior knowledge (if any) about the author of the Heimlich maneuver?

   _____

5. Get with a partner and compare your prior understanding of the Heimlich maneuver.

   _____

296 NAME _____   Language Arts Mini Lessons

Mini Lesson 226: PAIR Anticipating / General Comprehension

How can learning this help you? Think about what you anticipate learning by reading the article "Gorilla Uses Heimlich Maneuver to Save Man" by Laurel Bowie.

WHAT DO YOU ANTICIPATE LEARNING ABOUT THE TOPIC?

Dr. Herman Heimlich, a famed thoracic surgeon in Chicago, said he created his Heimlich maneuver to save patients from choking to death because they got something lodged in their throat after a successful surgery on their throat.

After reading the article on the next page,—the introduction and first part of it—what are your expectations? If this is expository (nonfiction), you may wish to skim through the beginning and ending of the passage, any bolded words and phrases, and any illustrations and their captions.

What are your predictions about the article?

What questions do you want/need to find answers to in this article?

How will you best find those answers?

ML 226 Check Understanding: PAIR Anticipating / General Comprehension

MINI LESSONS #226-#228 REFER TO "GORILLA USES HEIMLICH MANEUVER TO SAVE MAN."

What are two of your predictions about the article?

1. _____

2. _____

What are two questions you want/need to find answers to in this article?

3. _____

4. _____

5. How can you best find those answers? _____

_____

(CONTINUED NEXT PAGE)

Gorilla Uses Heimlich Maneuver to Save Man
Laurel Bowie Newspaper Correspondent, 1990

"Claudius has been my pal for 15 years, and he isn't about to let anything happen to me," the grateful trainer told reporters. "He's smarter than most people—and if he wasn't, I'd probably be dead right now. He came up behind me and wrapped those big, hairy arms around my waist, and with one jerk that bone came out clean as a whistle."

The bizarre story began as Tino, 52, and some big-top buddies were eating lunch on the circus grounds outside Rome, Italy.

"I was munching on some chicken and got a chunk of bone stuck in my windpipe, and the next thing I knew I was turning blue," still-trembling Tino recalled. "It was the scariest thing that's ever happened to me. I just couldn't breathe and really thought I was going to die. My eyes were bugging out and I was pointing at my throat, trying to get somebody to help me. But they all thought I was joking around and nobody made a move. "Thank God Claudius was there."

The amazing ape was playing near the entrance to the mess tent when he realized his beloved master was in trouble and raced to the rescue. As the others watched in wonder, quick-thinking Claudius came up behind terrified Tino and applied a textbook Heimlich maneuver on his dying friend.

"It was simply unbelievable," said high-wire walker Rene Kieffer, who witnessed the gorilla's mind-blowing heroics. "A trained doctor couldn't have done it better.

"I knew that animal was sharp, but I never imagined he'd know how to do something like that." But the tickled trainer insists he wasn't surprised by his gentle gorilla's incredible feat.

"Claudius is the smartest animal I've ever seen," he said, giving his beastly buddy a hug. "He's learned everything I've ever tried to teach him. He can juggle and play the piano and ride a bike and even run a movie projector.

"He can think better than most humans. Two weeks ago they showed us how to do the Heimlich maneuver at our crew's regular safety meeting and Claudius watched the whole thing. And when I got in trouble, he was the only one who was smart enough to save my life.

Mini Lesson 227: Inputting / General Comprehension

How can learning this help you? You've done the "before reading" work by doing the Prior Understanding and Anticipating. Now you can determine what you are trying to Input or comprehend from Reading, listening to, or viewing this article.

COMPREHENSION FROM READING AND LISTENING

As you read "Gorilla Uses Heimlich Maneuver to Save Man," look for answers to possible questions on the main idea, vocabulary, sequence, details, cause and effect, and inference.

Pay special attention to headings, bolded words, topic sentences, etc.

Take notes.

Fill out the first 4 of the 5 W's plus H (*who, what, when, where, why, and how*).

Make inferences, or educated guesses, from hints in the text.

Check the correctness of your predictions.

Try to find the answers to your questions.

ML 227 Check Understanding: Inputting / General Comprehension

As you read "Gorilla Uses Heimlich Maneuver to Save Man," answer these questions.

1. When does this happen? _____

2. Where does this happen? _____

3. What happens? _____

4. What is the Main idea _____

5. How does this happen? _____

NAME _____

Mini Lesson 228: Relating / General Comprehension

How can learning this help you? One general comprehension tip is to relate all of your new knowledge, opinions, and feelings to your prior understanding of the topic. As you relate this article to your life and learning, using your new knowledge, opinions, and feelings from your prior understanding of the topic, you will find ways to apply this new understanding and knowledge for your personal benefit.

RELATING THE TEXT TO YOURSELF AND YOUR LEARNING

ML 228 Check Understanding #A: Relating / General Comprehension

On a separate sheet of paper, answer what you can about "Gorilla Uses Heimlich to Save Man."

1. Check the correctness of your predictions you wrote before reading.

2. See if you found the answers to your questions you wrote before reading.

3. Summarize what you just read.

4. Find the main idea. Write it in a single sentence.

5. What can you relate to your life and learning from this literature?

PAIR works whether the information is expository (explanatory), argumentative (persuasive), or narrative (story). It helps you remember what you already know about the topic, anticipate what you will learn about it, organize the information you learn, and relate it to your life and learning.

ML 228 Check Understanding #B: Relating / General Comprehension

Ask the 5 W's: especially Why?

1. Why does this happen?_____

2. What (if anything) would you do differently if you could change something?_____

_____

3. What (if anything) is the theme, or author's message, about life and/or people?_____

_____

4. Was there any part of the article where you became distracted?_____

5. How can you learn more about the topic, author, etc.?_____

THERE WILL BE A QUIZ ON THE ARTICLE: "GORILLA USES HEIMLICH MANEUVER TO SAVE MAN."

Mini Lesson 229: Prior Understanding in Expository Text

How can learning this help you? PAIR works whether the information is expository (explanatory), argumentative (persuasive), or narrative (story). It helps to remember what you already know about the topic, anticipate what you will learn about it, organize the information you learn, and relate it to your life and learning.

Focus on yourself and what you already understand about the topic about which you are reading.

PRIOR UNDERSTANDING

What's your prior understanding of the topic?

Focus on yourself and what you already understand about this topic.

What's your prior knowledge (if any) of the topic?

What's your prior experience (if any) of the topic?

What's your prior attitude (if any) toward the topic?

What's your prior attitude (if any) about the author?

LESSONS #229-#233 REFER TO "HOW DO BRASS INSTRUMENTS MAKE THEIR SOUNDS?" ON PAGE 308.

ML 229 Check Understanding: Prior Understanding in Expository Text

Answer these four questions about this topic.

1. What's your prior knowledge (if any) about brass instruments? _____

2. What's your prior experience (if any) about brass instruments? _____

3. What's your prior attitude (if any) about brass instruments? _____

4. What's your prior knowledge (if any) about the author? _____

5. Get with a partner and compare your prior understanding about brass instruments? _____

(CONTINUED NEXT PAGE)

How Do Brass Instruments Change Their Pitch?

Have you ever wondered how brass instruments change their pitch between high and low notes? There are two ways brass instruments can change their pitch. Adjust the opening between their buzzing lips. If they're a valve horn, like most of the brass instruments, they usually hold down one or more of their three keys. If they're a trombone and have a slide, they slide to one of seven positions.

Every time trombones go down one position, they go down half a note. The first position is with the slide closed against the main part of the horn. The second position is about two inches down. The third position is where the slide is almost to the bell (the large round end where the sound comes out). The fourth position is an inch past the bell. The fifth position is about three inches past the bell. The sixth position is most of the way down. The seventh position is almost at the end where the inner slide has a line that is slightly thickened.

What keys are used for the concert B Flat Scale?

Horn Type	How Change	B Flat	C	D	E Flat	F	G	A	B Flat
Key Horn	Keys Down	0	1 & 3	1 & 2	1	0	1 & 2	2	0
Slide Horn	Slide Position	1	6	4	3	1	4	2	1

NAME _____

Mini Lesson 230: Anticipating in Expository Text

How can learning this help you? Learn to anticipate information about the topic.

ANTICIPATING

After skimming through the title, introduction, and first part of this literature, what are your expectations? If this is expository (nonfiction), you may wish to skim through the beginning and ending of the passage, any bolded words and phrases, and any illustrations and their captions.

What are your predictions about the literature?

What questions do you want/need to find answers to in this literature?

How will you best find those answers?

ML 230 Check Understanding: #A Anticipating in Expository Text

What are two of your predictions about the article "How Do Brass Instruments Change Their Pitch?" (on the next page).

1. _____

2. _____

_____

What are two questions you want/need to find answers to in this article?

3. _____

4. _____

_____

5. How can you best find those answers? _____

_____

Mini Lesson 231: Inputting in Expository Text

How can learning this help you? You've done the "before reading," now you can determine what you are trying to input or comprehend from reading, listening to, or viewing this article on video.

COMPREHENSION FROM READING AND LISTENING

As you read "How Do Brass Instruments Make Their Sounds," look for answers to possible questions on the main idea, vocabulary, sequence, details, cause and effect, and inference.

Pay special attention to headings, bolded words, topic sentences, etc.

Take notes.

Fill out the first 4 of the 5 W's plus H. (*Who, What, When, Where, Why,* and *How*)

Make inferences, or educated guesses, from hints in the text.

Check the correctness of your predictions.

Try to find the answers to your questions.

ML 231 Check Understanding: Inputting in Expository Text

As you read "How Do Brass Instruments Make Their Sounds," answer these questions.

1. When does this happen? _____

2. Where does this happen? _____

3. What happens? _____

4. Who does this happen to? _____

5. How does this happen? _____

Mini Lesson 232: Relating in Expository Text

How can learning this help you? As you relate this article to your life and learning, using your new knowledge, opinions, and feelings from your prior understanding of the topic, you will find ways to apply this new understanding and knowledge for your benefit.

As you read "How Do Brass Instruments Change Their Pitch?" look for answers to possible questions on the main idea, vocabulary, sequence, details, cause and effect, and inference that relate to you.

Pay special attention to headings, bolded words, topic sentences, etc.

Take notes.

Make inferences, or educated guesses, from hints in the text.

Check the correctness of your predictions.

Try to find the answers to your questions.

ML 232 Check Understanding #A: Relating in Expository Text

Answer what you can about "How Do Brass Instruments Make Their Sounds?"

1. Check the correctness of your predictions you wrote before reading.

2. See if you found the answers to your questions you wrote before reading.

3. Summarize what you just read.

4. Find the main idea. Write it in a single sentence.

5. What can you relate to your life and learning from this literature?

ML 232 Check Understanding #B: Relating in Expository Text

Ask the 5 W's: especially Why?

1. Why does this happen? _____

2. What (if anything) would you do differently if you could change something? _____

3. What (if anything) is the theme, or author's message, about life and/or people? _____

4. Was there any part of the article where you got distracted? _____

5. How can you learn more about the topic, author, etc.? _____

THERE WILL BE A QUIZ ON "HOW DO BRASS INSTRUMENTS CHANGE THEIR PITCH?"

NAME _____

Language Arts Mini Lessons

Mini Lesson 233: Prior Understanding in Argumentative Text

How can learning this help you? Focus on yourself and what you already understand about the topic about which you are reading.

FOCUS ON YOUR PRIOR UNDERSTANDING OF THE TOPIC

What's your prior understanding of the topic?

Focus on yourself and what you already understand about this topic.

What's your prior knowledge (if any) of the topic, great male athletes?

What's your prior experience (if any) of the topic, great male athletes?

What's your prior attitude (if any) toward the topic, great male athletes?

What's your prior attitude (if any) about the author, great male athletes?

MINI LESSONS #233-236 REFERENCE THE ARTICLE "THE GREATEST MALE ATHLETE" ON PAGE 313.

ML 233 Check Understanding: Prior Understanding in Agrumentative Text

Answer these four questions about this topic.

1. What's your prior knowledge (if any) about the great male athletes?

   _____

2. What's your prior experience (if any) with the topic, great male athletes?

   _____

3. What's your prior attitude (if any) toward the topic, great male athletes?

   _____

4. What's your prior knowledge (if any) about the author, Neil Johnson?

   _____

5. Get with a partner and compare your prior understanding of the best athlete in team sports.

(CONTINUED NEXT PAGE)

America's Greatest Male Team Sport Athlete

Of all of the famous male American athletes in team sports, several stand out as the greatest. If you had one vote for this, who would you pick? There are many great ones to consider, such as Michael Jordan in basketball, Tom Brady at football, and Wayne Gretzky in hockey. Admittedly, these players have been phenomenal. Each had a great work ethic and were devoted students of their game. However, when you consider the players' overall skills and versatility plus the impact on their game and how it is played, there can only be one answer: the Bambino: George Herman "Babe" Ruth.

Babe Ruth was released from reform school to play baseball. He started as a pitcher and helped the Boston Red Sox win three world championships. He won 23 and 24 games in his two best years. However, he wanted to become an everyday player, so he quit pitching and became an outfielder. Players didn't hit many home runs then. The American League record was only 16. In Ruth's first year as an everyday player, he set a new record of 29. He was then traded to the New York Yankees where they had a shorter right-field fence, and he hit the incredible number of 54 home runs followed by an even better 59. A few years later he raised the record another notch to 60, and that record stood for 34 years.

Ruth's home runs changed the game. Not that many people attended the games until then. More home runs meant more runs scored, which made the game more exciting and drew many more fans. Baseball became "America's Pastime" thanks to Babe's home runs.

Babe's great, versatile skills, excelling first as a pitcher and then a hitter, and because of how he changed the game, it increased fan interest and attendance. We have to choose Babe as America's greatest male athlete.

NAME _____

Mini Lesson 234: Anticipating in Argumentative Text

How can learning this help you? After skimming the article, note the title, introduction, and first part of it. What are your expectations? If the article is expository (nonfiction), you may wish to skim through the beginning and ending of the passage, note any bolded words and phrases, and any illustrations and their captions.

WHAT DO YOU ANTICIPATE LEARNING ABOUT THE TOPIC?

What are your predictions about the literature?

What questions do you want/need to find answers to in this literature?

How will you best find those answers?

ML 234 Check Understanding: Anticipating in Argumentative Text

What are two of your predictions about the article?

1. _____

2. _____

What are two questions you want/need to find answers to in this article?

3. _____

4. _____

5. How can you best find those answers? _____

NAME _____

Mini Lesson 235: Inputting in Argumentative Text

How can learning this help you? You've done the before reading work by doing the Prior Understanding and Anticipating. Determine what you are trying to input or comprehend from reading, listening to, or viewing this article. As you read, look for answers to possible questions on the main idea, vocabulary, sequence, details, cause and effect, and inference.

Pay special attention to headings, bolded words, topic sentences, etc.

Take notes.

Make inferences, or educated guesses, from hints in the text.

Check the correctness of your predictions.

Try to find the answers to your questions.

ML 235 Check Understanding: Inputting in Argumentative Text

As you read this article, answer these questions.

1. When does this happen? _____

2. Where does this happen? _____

3. What happens? _____
_____

4. What is the main idea?
_____

5. How does this happen?
_____

Mini Lesson 236: Relating in Argumentative Text

How can learning this help you? You can relate this article to your own life and learning using your new knowledge, opinions, and feelings from your prior understanding of the topic.

RELATE TO WHAT YOU ARE ARGUING

Check the correctness of your predictions you wrote before reading.

See if you found the answers to your questions you wrote before reading.

Find the main idea. Write it in a single sentence.

Summarize what you just read.

Pay special attention to headings, bolded words, topic sentences, etc.

Take notes and make inferences or educated guesses from hints in the text.

Look for text organization patterns.

Make connections by connecting the text with yourself, your learning, and your world.

Monitor your comprehension and realize when you misunderstand or are distracted.

ML 236 Check Understanding: PAIR Relating in Argumentative Text

Answer what you can about "America's Greatest Male Athlete in Team Sports."

1. Check the correctness of your _____

2. Try to find the answers to your _____

3. Pay special attention to _____ and _____ words.

4. Take _____

5. Make _____, or educated guesses from hints in the text.

6. Look for text organization _____

7. Connect your text with _____, your learning, and your world

8. _____ your comprehension.

9. Realize when you misunderstand or are _____

10. Share your responses with a _____

THERE WILL BE A QUIZ ON "AMERICA'S GREATEST MALE ATHLETE IN TEAM SPORTS."

NAME _____   Language Arts Mini Lessons

Mini Lesson 237: Prior Understanding in Narrative Text

How can learning this help you? Focus on yourself and what you already understand about the topic about which you are reading.

PRIOR UNDERSTANDING

Focus on yourself and what you already understand about this topic.

What's your prior knowledge (if any) about the topic, forgive and forget?

What's your prior experience (if any) with the topic, forgive and forget?

What's your prior attitude (if any) toward the topic, forgive and forget?

What's your prior knowledge (if any) about the author?

MINI LESSONS #237-#240 REFERENCE "FORGETTING AND FORGIVING" ON PAGE 318.

ML 237 Check Understanding: Prior Understanding in Narrative Text

Answer these four questions about this topic.

1. What's your prior knowledge (if any) about the topic, forgive and forget?
   _____

2. What's your prior experience (if any) with the topic, forgive and forget?
   _____

3. What's your prior attitude (if any) toward the topic, forgive and forget?
   _____

4. What's your prior knowledge (if any) about the author, Neil Johnson?
   _____

5. Get with a partner and compare your prior understanding about forgetting and forgiving someone's mistakes.

(CONTINUED NEXT PAGE)

Forget About It

Lauren and Nicole, two kids who had been best friends for years, went to a school counselor for help. Nicole had done something that upset Lauren. They had argued about it and eventually started to yell at each other in the lunchroom. After an administrator broke up the argument, he sent them to the counselor's office.

After Lauren explained what Nicole had done, she was fully expecting the counselor to agree with her. Instead, the wise man asked her, "Do you want this friendship to work or not?"

Lauren looked at the counselor and replied, "Of course I do, but . . ."

"Then forget about it," interrupted the counselor. He then added, "Forget about what Nicole did."

Lauren stared at the counselor in shock then he started to re-explain.

The counselor stopped Lauren again by asking her, "Do you want this friendship to work or not?"

"Yes, but . . ."

"Then forget about it."

Lauren stared incredulously at the counselor. Exasperated, she started to explain for the third time.

For the third time, the counselor stopped Lauren and again patiently asked her, "Do you want this friendship to work or not?"

With a loud voice, Lauren started to tell the counselor again when she suddenly understood. She thought for a minute, and then in a quieter, humble voice, she stated, "Oh. So you're saying that if you—we—want this friendship to work, then whatever wrong thing we do, the other person should forget about it?

"Uh-huh," smiled the counselor.

A few weeks later, Lauren was recounting this experience to another friend. After Lauren was done, the friend asked Lauren what her friend Nicole had done that upset her so much, to which Lauren replied sincerely, "I don't know. I honestly forgot." She then added, "Actually, that taught me to forget about a lot of things because they just don't matter. It's helped our friendship, too.

NAME _____

Mini Lesson 238: Anticipating in Narrative Text

How can learning this help you? After skimming through the title, introduction, and first part of this literature, what are your expectations? If this is expository (nonfiction), you may wish to skim through the beginning and ending of the passage, any bolded words and phrases, and any illustrations and their captions.

WHAT DO YOU ANTICIPATE LEARNING ABOUT THE TOPIC?

What are your predictions about the literature?

What questions do you want/need to find answers to in this literature?

How will you best find those answers?

ML 238 Check Understanding: Anticipating in Narrative Text

What are two of your predictions about the article?

1. _____

2. _____

What are two questions you want/need to find answers to in this article?

3. _____

4. _____

5. How can you best find those answers? _____

_____

THERE WILL BE A QUIZ ON "FORGET ABOUT IT"

Mini Lesson 239: Inputting in Narrative Text

How can learning this help you? What are you trying to input or comprehend from reading, listening, or viewing this article? The *5 W's + H—who, what, when, where, and why and how—*can help you with narrative literature which is text in the form of a story. Now determine what you are trying to input or comprehend from reading, listening to, or viewing this article.

COMPREHENSION FROM READING AND LISTENING

As you read "Forget About It," look for answers to possible questions on the main idea, vocabulary, sequence, details, cause and effect, and inference.

Pay special attention to headings, bolded words, topic sentences, etc.

Take notes.

Fill out the first 4 of the 5 W's plus H. (who, what, when, where, why, and how)

Make inferences, or educated guesses, from hints in the text.

Check the correctness of your predictions.

Try to find the answers to your questions.

- Who/what is this about?
- Who/what is the protagonist or hero?
- What is their most admirable quality?
- What major change or realization, if any, do they go through?
- Who/what is the antagonist or villain?
- What is their most despicable quality?
- What makes us hate them?
- What do they do to upset everything?
- When does this happen?
- Where does this happen?
- What happens or what is the plot?

What is the exposition? This introduces us to the situation, as well as who the main characters are and how they got to be the way they are at the story's start.

What is the beginning balance: things aren't perfect, but they're bearable.

(CONTINUED NEXT PAGE)

NAME _____

What is the upsetting incident: things are no longer bearable. The protagonist is the one who tries hardest to make things bearable again.

What is the rising action? (The struggle between the protagonist restoring the beginning balance and the antagonist destroying it.)

What is the climax: when either the protagonist restores the beginning balance or the antagonist permanently destroys it)?

What is the resolution? Resolve any unfinished business.

ML 239 Check Understanding: Inputting in Narrative Text

As you read "Forget About It," answer these questions.

1. When does this happen? _____

2. Where does this happen? _____

3. What happens? _____

4. Who did it happen to? _____

5. How does this happen? _____

Mini Lesson 240: Relating in Narrative Text

How can learning this help you? You can relate this article to your own life and learning using your new knowledge, opinions, and feelings to your prior understanding of the topic.

FOR THE NARRATIVE MODE YOU MUST ASK THE 5TH W—WHY

Why do they do what they do?

Why does the protagonist do what they do?

Why does the antagonist do what they do?

What (if anything) would you do differently if you were the protagonist?

What (if anything) is the theme, or author's message about life and/or people?

What, from this literature, can you relate to your life and learning?

Get into groups of 3 to 5 people and discuss the story.

ML 240 Check Understanding: Relating in Narrative Text

Answer what you can about "Forget About It."

1. Why does this happen? _____

2. Why does the protagonist do what they do? _____

3. Why does the antagonist do what they do? _____

4. What (if anything) would you do differently if you were the protagonist? _____

5. What (if anything) is the theme, or author's message about life and/or people? _____

6. What from this story can you relate to your life and learning? _____

7. How can you learn more about the topic, author, etc.? _____

8. Does this passage of writing give me any other questions or thoughts? _____

9. Get into groups of 3 to 5 students and share what you wrote. _____

10. Share some of your group's responses with the class.

Mini Lesson 241: Comprehension Application

How can learning this help you? How many times have you heard this? "A picture's worth a thousand words." Graphic organizers and mnemonics are frequently beneficial in helping you comprehend your text. Often you can create your own graphic organizer or mnemonic to help you understand or remember a key concept.

PICTURES, CHARTS, ETC. CAN HELP YOU COMPREHEND YOUR WRITING

Graphic organizers are charts and illustrations that help you and your readers comprehend the concepts and their relationships to each other in reading material. A cluster, or web, is a type of graphic organizer. So is a Venn diagram.

Mnemonics are words in which the first letter represents another term.

Example: A phone number is given in the letters of a company.

This book's trademarked term *PAIR* helps to remember the four steps of the Reading Comprehension process: Prior Understanding, Anticipating, Inputting, and Relating.

HOMES is a mnemonic to remember the Great Lakes: Huron, Ontario, Michigan, Erie, and Superior.

ML 241 Check Understanding: Comprehension Application

1. Alone or with a partner, create a graphic organizer to help you compare two literary works or authors.

Your organizer may be as simple as a Venn diagram or something more complex.

2. Alone or with a partner, identify a mnemonic you have used before or create a new one. Write it down.

You may not use HOMES or PAIR.

Mini Lesson 242: Text Organization Patterns

How can learning this help you? Text organization will not only help you organize your thoughts and comprehension when reading, but it will help you find and reference what you have already read for future use.

TEN TYPES OF TEXT ORGANIZATIONS

Cause and Effect. Life and literature are often made up of a series of events. Each event frequently causes one or more effects. Each effect in turn often causes one or more other effects. It's like the ripple effect of a stone being tossed into a pond.

Compare and Contrast. Any two things have similarities and differences. To compare and contrast them, you need to discover how they're alike and how they're different. A Venn diagram uses circles to show relationships between things or groups of things. The circles that overlap have things in common, while the circles that do not overlap do not share those traits. These diagrams help to visually represent the similarities and differences between two ideas or concepts.

Description. This provides information about a place, time, event, concept, object, or person, etc. The more description, the easier for the reader to comprehend.

Sense imagery helps us imagine things. The five senses are see, hear, touch, taste, and smell.

Emotional imagery helps us feel things emotionally. Some of these feelings are joy, sadness, anger, etc.

Fact or Opinion. A fact is something that can be proven, while an opinion cannot. To say a certain movie was the best movie of the year is an opinion because people have different opinions on what was best. However, to say a certain movie won the Academy Award that year is a fact because it can be proven.

Inference. Inference combines what the reader already knows about something with what the text says about it to help the reader make an educated guess about the meaning.

Problem or Solution. Define the problem(s) in an issue, then analyze possible solution(s). After that, list the benefits received when overcoming the problem(s) with those solutions.

Question and Answer. Often a writer will ask a question to get the readers thinking. Then they answer the question. This is an especially effective learning tool in nonfiction writing.

Sequence or Chronology. Sequence is an arrangement of events, usually in the order of beginning to ending.

(CONTINUED NEXT PAGE)

NAME _____   Language Arts Mini Lessons

ML 242 Check Understanding #A: Text Organization Patterns

Fill in the blank with the matching type of text organization.

1. Define the problem(s) in an issue, then analyze possible solution(s). _____

_____

2. An arrangement of events, usually in the order of beginning to ending. _____

_____

3. Any two things have similarities and differences. To understand the difference, you need to discover how they're alike and how they're different.

_____

_____

4. Combines what the reader already knows about something with what the text says about it to help the reader make an educated guess about the meaning.

_____

5. Life and literature are often made up of a series of events which frequently cause one or more effects.

_____

(CONTINUED NEXT PAGE)

ML 242 Check Understanding #B: Text Organization Patterns

1-8. Get into small groups of 3 to 5 people. Together, write down two examples of each of these types of text organizations in the chart. Fill out your chart with the group even though you may think of the examples together.

Since each of the eight categories have two answer blanks, .5 points are earned for each answer for a total of 8 points. Question 9 and 10 are worth one point each for a total of ten points.

Text Organization Pattern	Title	Source Type	Date	Page
1. Cause and Effect				
Cause and Effect				
2. Compare and Contrast				
Compare and Contrast				
3. Description				
Description				
4. Fact or Opinion				
Fact or Opinion				
5. Inference				
Inference				
6. Problem or Solution				
Problem or Solution				
7. Question and Answer				
Question and Answer				
8. Sequence or Chronological				

Tell which of the eight different text organization patterns apply to the following two sentences.

9. Lee is the best athlete in our class. _____

10. Danny quite drinking soda every day, and he lost five pounds. _____

Chapter Twelve: Expanding Your Vocabulary

Why is this chapter important for you? Learning new words and their usage is critical for any serious writer, but also for those who just use new words day-to-day. And it's fun to learn new words! Impress your friends and family with your wide range of words and see how much praise you get.

The Lessons

Chapter Twelve: Expanding Your Vocabulary 320
    Mini Lesson 243: Introduction to Spelling 321
    Mini Lesson 244: Spelling Rules and Patterns 322
    Mini Lesson 245: Misspelled Words Due to *Schwa* 323
    Mini Lesson 246: Identify the *Schwa (ise/ize)* Sound 324
    Mini Lesson 247: Spelling Review 325
    Mini Lesson 248: Spelling Rules Review 326
    Mini Lesson 249: Reading Vocabulary / Context 328
    Mini Lesson 250: Using Context Clues 329
    Mini Lesson 251: Prefixes 330
    Mini Lesson 252: Prefixes and Suffixes 331
    Mini Lesson 253: Suffixes 332
    Mini Lesson 254: Word Relationships 334

Mini Lesson 243: Introduction to Spelling

How can learning this help you? While most people agree that English is a difficult language for spelling, and even though computers pick up many of the spelling errors on papers we type, it's still important to learn the main spelling rules. Often you need to write by hand, and even if you are using a computer, it doesn't pick up everything.

CHECK SPELLING ERRORS

ML 243 Student Activity: Introduction to Spelling

See how many of the following letters' 25 spelling errors you can find. Correct them. Several of the words are spelled correctly for other situations, so your spellchecker won't catch them. (1 point for every 5 errors with 25 in all) These misspelled words don't have to be in order; they just have to be written.

1. _____ 2. _____ 3. _____
4. _____ 5. _____ 6. _____
7. _____ 8. _____ 9. _____
10. _____ 11. _____ 12. _____
13. _____ 14. _____ 15. _____
16. _____ 17. _____ 18. _____
19. _____ 20. _____ 21. _____
22. _____ 23. _____ 24. _____
25. _____

Febuary 7, 2020

Deer Teecher,

Why did you give me a pour grade on my papur? I din't make that many errurs. I want two go too colledge, and now I mite not cuz of you're low grade four me. I here your just meen, an you tot us alot of wrong stuff! Pleese give me a hire grade, and I'll be quite when your talkin.

Yours truely,

A. Bad Speller

Mini Lesson 244: Spelling Rules and Patterns

How can learning this help you? By learning a few simple rules, you can become a better speller! Believe it or not, spelling can be fun as well as imminently important in any form of writing. Poor spelling causes the writer to lose credibility with the reader and sometimes implies that the writer is not, perhaps, well educated.

A FEW SIMPLE SPELLING RULES

Put *i* before *e*. This simple, well-known poem might help you remember.

Put *i* before *e* except after *c* or when sounded like *aye*, as in *neighbor* and *weigh*.

Exceptions to *i* before *e* include ei*ther, leisure, neither, seize, weird*.

An exception to *i* before *e* except after *c* is *financier*.

Nouns ending in *y*. When a suffix is added to a word ending in *y*, the *y* is usually changed to *i*.

Using *f* versus *ves* endings.

Example: *fs* is used in *chiefs, beliefs, roofs*; *ves* is used in *halves, selves, lives, knives, wolves*

ML 244 Student Activity: Spelling Rules and Patterns

Circle the correct spelling.

1. grumpyest/grumpiest

2. journies/journeys

3. leisure/liesure

4. neice/niece

5. knifes/knives

Mini Lesson 245: Misspelled Words Due to *Schwa*

How can learning this help you? Most of us have words and groups of words that we often misspell. Make a rough list of words you have trouble spelling. Spell them correctly, then refer to your list in the future.

RULES FOR *SCHWA*

Surprisingly, the *schwa* sound is one of the most common sounds in English. Unfortunately, it's probably the hardest sound to spell. It sounds like *oo* in *book*, but there are examples of the *schwa* sound being spelled by every vowel in the alphabet. It often occurs in an unstressed syllable.

ML 245 Student Activity: Misspelled Words Due to *Schwa*

The asterisk in these words represents the *schwa* sound. Please write the word in the blank.

1. el*ph*nt _____

2. ed*ble _____

3. f*tball _____

4. cart*r _____

5. palp*ble _____

NAME _____

Language Arts Mini Lessons

Mini Lesson 246: Identify the *Schwa (ise/ize)* Sound

How can learning this help you? Because the *schwa* sound can be spelled with every single vowel, it's the hardest sound for which to remember the spelling. The best thing you can do is memorize the letter(s) with each *schwa* sound.

SCHWA CAN BE CONFUSING

ML 246 Student Activity #A: Identify the Schwa (*ise/ize*) Sound

1. Find and underline 15 of the 18 *schwa* sounds in this very short story.

   Aunt Myrtle was quite a barber. During the county fair, she used her scissors to shorten a man's suspenders, cut some gum out of a squirrel's fur, and trim the edible parts of vegetables.

   Many words end with the *ise/ize* sound; *ize* is the more common spelling, and *ise* is a variation of it. Some of these words include *advertise, categorize, criticize, idolize,* and *philosophize.*

   Like the words with the *schwa* sound, the only way to learn the correct spelling of these is to memorize them. Make a list of your troublesome *ise/ize* words. Be sure to spell them correctly.

ML 246 Student Activity #B: Memorize Words with *ise/ize* Sound

As with words with the *schwa* sound, the only way to learn the *ise/ize* spelling is to memorize them.

1. With a partner make a list of ten *ise/ize* words. Be sure to spell them correctly.

1. _____   2. _____   3. _____

4. _____   5. _____   6. _____

7. _____   8. _____   9. _____

10. _____

NAME _____   Language Arts Mini Lessons

Mini Lesson 247: Spelling Review

How can learning this help you? Spelling words correctly is the way we have to communicate by writing. If you make lists of words that are troublesome for you to spell, and especially if you categorize them and occasionally review them, it can improve your spelling.

ML 247 Student Activity: Spelling Review

Answer the following questions.

1. Put *i* before e except after _____

2. If a singular noun that ends in *y* has a consonant before the *y*, does it become *ies* in its plural form?

   Example: party and baby _____

   _____

3. Do you keep or drop the final *e* before a suffix is added that begins with a vowel? Example: fade, strike _____

4. What is the name of the sound that sounds like *oo* in foot and can be spelled with any of the vowels?

   _____

5. Compare your answers with a partner's.

NAME _____   Language Arts Mini Lessons

Mini Lesson 248: Spelling Rules Review

How can learning this help you? This spelling review will help you remember the rules. Memorizing the rules will help you in your writing forever.

REVIEW

ML 248 Student Activity #A: Spelling Rules Review

Decide if the words in italics in the following sentences are misspelled. If they are, spell them correctly in the blank space. If you are unsure, study the preceding spelling principles.

1. Did you *receive* your *reciept*? _____, _____

2. The *ladies* took *there* *babys* to *partys* where they received wonderful toys. _____, _____, _____

3. My little brother made *too* knives in the *wolfs* den meeting at Cub Scouts. _____, _____

4. I *here* that you were *here* yesterday, *too*. _____, _____, _____

5. Jack wants to *by* *to* tickets to the show, *to*. He saw it last *Febuary*. _____ _____

6. *There* walking to *there* *care* over there. _____, _____. _____

7. Katrina *droped* her fork when she was *dineing* at the *Jensen's'* home. _____ _____, _____

8. My parents bought an old, *servicable* truck that *their* hopeful will hold up. _____, _____

9-10. Divide up your commonly misspelled words into groups of similar words. For instance, make a list of homonyms (*to, two, too*), words with the *schwa* sound (see below), and words that end in either *ise* or *ize*. Continue to add to your list as needed.

_____

_____

(CONTINUED NEXT PAGE)

ML 248 Student Activity #B: Spelling Rules Review

Make a list of at least ten words you have trouble spelling. Look up the correct spelling if you need to.

1. _____

2. _____

3. _____

4. _____

5. _____

6. _____

7. _____

8. _____

9. _____

10. _____

Get into a small group and compare the words you have trouble spelling with the others in your group. You may hear some words from other students that you want to add to your list.

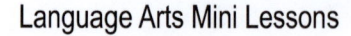

Mini Lesson 249: Reading Vocabulary / Context

How can learning this help you? This lesson is important because it helps with communication skills by developing a large, accurate vocabulary. When you learn to determine the meaning of an unknown, but needed word within the context of the words around it, then you have discovered its meaning without having to stop your reading and look up the word in a dictionary.

CONTEXT CLUES: THREE COMMON TYPES

If you don't know the meaning of a word or concept, try to find clues from the words and sentences that surround it. This is called the context, and you can usually get the overall meaning from it.

Definition: "A pencil is a writing utensil."

Example. "Teachers like Ms. Bonilla and Mr. Jensen help make our school great."

Synonym or Antonym: "Sagas are long stories passed on by ancient people."

ML 249 Student Activity: Reading Vocabulary / Context

1. What is the advantage of discovering the meaning of a word within its context? _____

2. What do you call the clues written close by an unknown word? _____

What are three common types of context clues?

3. _____

4. _____

5. _____

Mini Lesson 250: Using Context Clues

How can learning this help you? Using context clues is valuable because it helps you figure out the meaning of a word from the meanings of the words and phrases around it.

DETERMINE THE MEANING WITH CONTEXTUAL CLUES

ML 250 Student Activity: Using Context Clues

1. Choose a relatively unknown word for which you know the meaning.

   _____

   Write three sentences using that word. Have each sentence (2, 3, and 4) use one of the three types of context clues just listed.

   2. _____

   3. _____

   4. _____

5. Get into a small group and figure out the meanings of the unknown words in each other's sentences.

Mini Lesson 251: Prefixes

How can learning this help you? Have you heard the saying, "The proof of the taste is in the pudding?" It means that the proof of your comprehension of context clues or anything else is in how well you apply it. Learning these common prefixes can often help you figure out the meaning of unknown words.

WHAT CAN A PREFIX DO?

The word root carries the meaning.

The prefix doesn't change the spelling of the word root.

The suffix sometimes does change the spelling of the word root.

Examples of prefixes:

Prefix	Meaning	Example
bi-	two	bi + weekly
co-	together	co + author
de-	remove	de + plane
in-	not	in + secure
il-not	il	il + legal
mis-	incorrect	mis + place
pre-	before	pre + historic
re-	re-again	re + gain

ML 251 Student Activity: Prefixes

1. What part of the word carries the meaning? _____

2. Does a prefix or a suffix sometimes change the spelling of the word *root*? _____

3. What does *co* mean? _____

4. What does *in* mean? _____

5. What is a word (besides regain) that starts with *re*? _____

Mini Lesson 252: Prefixes and Suffixes

How can learning this help you? Keep interchanging different prefixes and suffixes. It's amazing how many different words you can create.

CREATING BY INTERCHANGING CAN END IN MANY DIFFERENT PREFIXES AND SUFFIXES!

Noun Suffixes	Meaning	Example
ance, ence	state of	correspond plus ence
ment	state of	govern plus ment
ness	state of	well plus ness
ist	one who or one that	art plus ist
Verb Suffixes	**Meaning**	**Example**
en	make or become	bright plus en
ise	make or cause to be	material plus ize
Adjective Suffixes	**Meaning**	**Example**
able, ible	capable of	flex plus ible
less	without	pain plus less
Adverb Suffixes	**Meaning**	**Example**
ly	in a certain way	careful plus ly

ML 252 Student Activity: Prefixes and Suffixes

1. Get into pairs.

2. Use the word root *port* and add different prefixes and suffixes to create 20 different words. You may use the same prefix with several different suffixes (re-*port*-er/ed/ing) and the same suffix with several different prefixes (-*port*-ing) to create your words.

1. _____ 2. _____ 3. _____ 4. _____ 5. _____

6. _____ 7. _____ 8. _____ 9. _____ 10. _____

11. _____ 12. _____ 13. _____ 14. _____ 15. _____

16. _____ 17. _____ 18. _____ 19. _____ 20. _____

Compare your list with other lists students created.

Mini Lesson 253: Suffixes

How can learning this help you? Suffixes added to the ending of words can be a letter or group of letters which change the original meaning of the word.

WHAT CAN A SUFFIX DO?

A suffix can be added to the end of a word root: catcher, rocked, portable, etc.

If a word ends with a silent *e*, drop it before adding a suffix that begins with a vowel.

>Example: wade plus *-ing* equals wading

Exceptions to these are when the suffixes start with the letters *a* and *o* and are used to keep the soft sound of the letters *c (suh)* and *g (juh)* in the word root.

>Example: serviceable and manageable.

If a word ends with a silent *e*, keep it when adding a suffix that begins with a consonant.

>Example: hope plus *-ful* equals hopeful

There are exceptions to these, such as argu*ment* (argue), tru*ly* (true), and whol*ly* (whole).

Double the final consonant before a suffix that begins with a vowel if you have both of the following conditions. The word ends in a single consonant and is preceded by a single vowel.

>Example: pat plus *-ed* equals patted
>Example: run plus *-ing* equals running)

The word either has only one syllable or its last syllable is accented.

>Example: prefer plus *-ing* equals preferring

Word Plus Suffix	Examples
vowel + *ys* = *ys*	toys, journeys, boys
consonant + *y* = *ies*	ladies, babies, parties
consonant + *y* = *ier, iest*	healthier, tinier, grumpiest, happiest

(CONTINUED NEXT PAGE)

ML 253 Student Activity: Suffixes

Circle the correct spelling.

1. proceeding   proceedeing

2. servicable   serviceable

3. truly   truely

4. spitful   spiteful

5. mapping   maping

Mini Lesson 254: Word Relationships

How can learning this help you? Knowing how to use synonyms, homonyms, antonyms, and word analogies helps you to get better control of your vocabulary, your writing, and your critical thinking.

SYNONYMS, HOMONYMS, ANTONYMS, AND WORD ANALOGIES

Synonyms are words that have about the same meaning as another word.

Example: *thin/slender*

Antonyms are words that mean about the opposite of another word.

Example: *thin/wide*

Homonyms are words that sound the same but have different meanings and often spellings.

Example: *hear/here; to/too/two*

Word Analogies can be the comparison of two unlike things. It can also be the relationship between pairs of words such as synonyms or antonyms.

Example: *thin* is to *wide* as *high* is to *low*. *Tall* is to *high* as *night* is to *dark*.

ML 254 Student Activity: Word Relationships

Tell what term each of the following definitions describes.

1. Words that mean about the opposite of another word. _____

2. Words that sound the same but have different meanings and often spellings. _____
_____

3. Words that have about the same meaning as another word. _____

What two things are in a word analogy?

4-5. What is the two-word term of this: "_____ is to _____ as _____ is to _____"

With a partner, create five examples of each of these.

Word Analogy

6. Synonyms _____

7. Antonyms _____

8. Homonyms _____

9. Word Analogies _____

10. Compare your words with another pair of students.

Chapter Thirteen: MLA Research Citations

Why is this chapter, important for you? You'll be called upon to write many research papers in high school, college, and potentially for your future occupation, so it's imperative that you know the importance of creating and using proper citations in your work.

A citation is the quoting and documenting of an authoritative source. Citing information from well-known sources gives your work credibility and helps prove your argument. The better you learn how to document research citations, the more credible your work will be, and the easier it will become for you. To protect your intellectual property and others, cite any idea, phrase, or quote that you did not create yourself.

Review: A citation is a quote or a reference to what someone else (usually an expert) said, wrote, or published. Citations are especially important in scholarly work because they protect you from either intentionally or unintentionally taking credit for work that is not your own.

The Lessons

Chapter Thirteen: MLA Research Citations	335
Mini Lesson 255: MLA	336
Mini Lesson 256: Why You Should Use Citations–MLA	337
Mini Lesson 257: Works Cited–MLA	338
Mini Lesson 258: Documentation for Works Cited–MLA	341
Mini Lesson 259: Plagiarism–MLA	342
Mini Lesson 260: Quotes–MLA	343
Mini Lesson 261: Ellipses–MLA	344
Mini Lesson 262: Citing Common Electronic Sources–MLA	345
Mini Lesson 263: End-of-Paper Citations–MLA	346

Mini Lesson 255: MLA

How can learning this help you? MLA and APA citation styles help you develop your academic writing. MLA is commonly used to document and cite papers in the field of language arts. Ironically, many groups, even within language arts, prefer APA because some find it easier to use than MLA. However, since MLA is still used the most in language arts works, it's still critical to have an understanding of this style.

MLA PRACTICES

As you prepare a research paper, you should study several sources on your topic and take accurate notes. This will help you gain a broad understanding of the topic, and it will help you decide on your direction and thesis statement.

Next, formulate an outline of what you want to say based on the conclusions you drew from your research. This way, you won't have to rely too much on paraphrasing and quoting. A good rule-of-thumb is to limit direct quotes to under ten percent of your paper.

Remember that you are the author of your paper, not the sources you're quoting. Research your topic, then write using your words and thoughts based upon your research.

Formatting Guidelines:

Double-space your entire paper.

Indent the first word of each paragraph.

ML 255 Check Understanding: MLA

1. Which citation style do students generally think is easier and more organized? _____

2. Does MLA require double-spaced or single-spaced lines? _____

3. Does MLA prefer that each new paragraph is indented or vertically double-spaced? _____

4. Should you first (A) write the paper or (B) research several sources on the topic? _____

5. You should not use direct quotes for over 10, 15, or 20 percent of the paper? _____

NAME _____   Language Arts Mini Lessons

Mini Lesson 256: Why You Should Use Citations–MLA

How can learning this help you? It is imperative to properly cite in MLA. The higher you go in education, the more research papers you will have to write. The following lessons will provide you with the information you need to correctly give credit to the sources you use in your papers using MLA (Modern Language Association).

WHY SHOULD YOU USE CITATIONS?

To let your readers know where you got your information.

To give proper credit for the words or ideas of others.

To gain credibility for your paper. It shows that you agree with other sources, who are probably experts.

IN-TEXT CITATIONS

An in-text citation comes at the end of a direct quote or some *paraphrased* information in the text. To write an in-text citation, type the last name of the author(s) and the year it was published. Enclose this information in parentheses before the period.

When using a *direct quote*, put the author's last name, the year it was written, and the page number from the source after the closing quotations and before the period.

VARIATIONS OF THE STANDARD IN-TEXT CITATIONS

If the author's name is listed as part of the immediate text, you don't need their name as part of the citation. Simply put the year this information was published. If it's a direct quote, include the page number in the citation.

> Example: "Your pre-writing is the most important portion of your writing" (Brown 105).
> Example: According to Richard H. Brown, "Your pre-writing is the most important portion of your writing" (105).

ML 256 Check Understanding: Why You Should Use Citations–MLA

1. What two things do you need in parentheses after you paraphrase information from a source?

   _____

2. What *third* thing do you need in parentheses after you directly quote a source? _____

3. How would you do the in-text citation for an author? _____

4. MLA stands for _____

5. APA stands for _____

NAME _____

Mini Lesson 257: Works Cited–MLA

How can learning this help you? A frustrating problem with citations is that different books give different answers, especially on author names. Sometimes different sections of the same book give contradictory statements. "This book will follow the official MLA Handbook (8th Edition), directions on page 21," "Begin the entry with the author's last name, followed by a comma and the rest of the name, as presented in the work." (MLA Handbook) If there is no author listed, use a shortened title and the page. (Example: Alcohol and Driving p. 126)

Author Citation Chart

Number of Authors	Name of Work Being Quoted	First and Last Names	Initials
1 Author	John G. Smith	Smith, John	Smith J. G.
1 Author No initials	John Smith	Smith, John	Smith, J.
2 Authors	John G. Smith	Smith John	Smith J. G.
3 Authors	Anita R. Lopez	Lopez, Anita	Lopez, A. R.
3 Plus Authors	John G. Smith, et al,	Smith, John G.	Smith J. G.
3 Plus Not First Author	, et al,	, et al,	, et al,

Remember that articles, conjunctions, and prepositions are not capitalized in a title.

HOW TO USE CITATIONS

One Author: Last name, First name. (Last name followed by the first and middle names such as Smith, John Andrew.)

Title of book. (Book. (with a period) or "Article." (with a period))

City: (with a colon) New York: (with a colon)

Publisher: Publication date, vol., p. or pp. 126 (with the demonstrated punctuation)

Example: Smith, Jonathan Andrew. The Classroom Bells Are Ringing. New York: Campbell and Carter Books, 2006, vol. 1, pp. 105-6.

Three or More Authors (first author separated by a comma and followed by et al., which indicates more than one author, then the page number):

Example: Clarke, et al, p. 126.

Two or Three Authors (separated by commas):

If there are two or three authors, list their names in the order they appear in the book.

Example: Smith, John Andrew, Anita Clayborne Dougal, and Robert Alvin Dubronsky.

If there is no author listed, use a shortened title and the page.

Example: Alcohol and Driving, p. 126.

(CONTINUED NEXT PAGE)

NAME _____   Language Arts Mini Lessons

ML 257 Check Understanding #A: Works Cited–MLA

Work on the following activities.

1. How would you write and punctuate the name John Smith in a Works Cited page? _____

2. How would you write and punctuate the name John G. Smith in a Works Cited page? _____

3. How would you write and punctuate the name for the second author, Anita R. Lopez, in a Works Cited page? _____

4. How would you write and punctuate the names for the second and third authors of a book in a Works Cited page? _____

5. What would you start an entry with when a source does not list an author? _____

ML 257 Check Understanding #B: Citations Most Books–MLA

Put these citations in the right order and correctly punctuate for the Works Cited page. Match the correct example from the top with the answers at the bottom.

Example:

Book: The Classroom Bells Are Ringing

Year Published: 2019

Authors: John G. Smith, Anita R. Lopez, and Robert A. Dubronsky.

_____

_____

ML 257 Check Understanding #C: Author Citation Chart

Answer the following questions with the correct information and punctuation. For help on the authors, refer to the Author Citation Chart.

1. First author: _____

2. Second author: _____

3. Multiple authors after the first one: _____

4. What words should not be capitalized in a title? _____

5. How do you punctuate the title of an article followed by a page number? _____

(CONTINUED NEXT PAGE)

ML 257 Check Understanding #D: Review

1. How much of the author's full name should you write at the end of a quote or paraphrase?
   _____

2. When using a direct quote, what else do you include at the end of the citation? _____

3. What punctuation marks should you use to enclose the source material? _____

4. How do you cite three or more authors in MLA style? _____

5. What does "et al" mean? _____

NAME _____   Language Arts Mini Lessons

Mini Lesson 258: Documentation for Works Cited–MLA

How can learning this help you? Documentation on the Works Cited page at the end of your paper may seem difficult and tedious. However, the more you study this now, the easier citing your sources will be later.

SOURCES

Sources in General:

Like all titles, capitalize the first word and all other words except prepositions, articles, and conjunctions.

Italicize (if typed) or underline (if handwritten) the title if it's a *long literary work* and put quotation marks around it if it is a *short literary work*.

Put a period after the title.

Source and Date:

Example: Publisher, Date.
Example: Penguin Books, 2006.

Sources without authors:

Example: Encyclopedia Title. Publisher, Year.
Example: Garrett, John H. and Thelma A. Wise, eds. Whisperings. Boston: Craighouse, 2019.
Example: Full name of an article should be the Title of Periodical Day Month Year: pages (Notice you don't put any punctuation after the periodical title.)

Interviews

Last name, First name of person interviewed. Personal Interview. Day Month Year.

ML 258 Check Understanding: Documentation for Works Cited–MLA

1. What punctuation after author's name? _____

2. What punctuation after author's last name? _____

3. What punctuation after title? _____

4. What punctuation after date? _____

5. What punctuation surrounds in-text citation? _____

Mini Lesson 259: Plagiarism–MLA

How can learning this help you? To avoid plagiarism, there are two places to give credit for other writers' information and thoughts that you choose to use in your paper: in-text—put within the paper right after you use the information—and in the Works Cited page at the end of the paper.

DON'T STEAL SOMEONE ELSE'S WORDS

To avoid plagiarism, give the original source credit for their work by using a standardized citation style like MLA or APA.

KEY POINTS:

Inform your readers where you got your information; with in-text citations, the author's last name and the page number(s), and a complete citation on the Works Cited page are required.

Give proper credit for the words or ideas of others.

Gain credibility for your paper, showing you agree with other sources' experts.

ML 259 Check Understanding: Plagiarism–MLA

Which two places do you give credit for the information sources in your paper?

1. _____

2. _____

What are two of the three reasons to give proper credit for someone else's words and ideas?

3. _____

4. _____

5. What is it called when someone claims that another person's writing is theirs? _____

Mini Lesson 260: Quotes–MLA

How can learning this help you? Direct quotations are the exact words from another work. Paraphrase your content as often as you can rather than directly quoting because paraphrasing allows you to use the material in the context of your paper.

WHEN QUOTING, USE THE EXACT WORDS OF THE WRITER

In some cases, you may be limited on the number of times you may use direct quotations. If you have too much quoted material in your paper you may be docked points.

HOW TO USE EXACT QUOTES

Start the quotation on a new line, with the entire quote. In-text quotes do not require quotation marks.

Indent ½ inch from the left margin.

The author's last name and publication date, or parenthetical citation should come after the closing quotation mark.

When quoting verse, keep the original line breaks and continue double-spacing throughout.

With *short quotations* (four typed lines or fewer of prose or three lines of verse), enclose it within double quotation marks.

Long quotations amounting to five or more lines are started on a new line. Indent the line ½ inch from the left margin and double-space. The citation, in parentheses, should come after the closing punctuation mark. Keep the original line spacing when quoting a poem or prose.

When quotations are more than four lines of prose or three lines of verse, create a free-standing block of text and do not use quotation marks. As with all long quotations, begin with a new line indented ½ inch from the left margin, and double-space paragraphs within the quotation.

ML 260 Check Understanding: Quotes–MLA

1. How many lines of text must there be in a long quote in MLA? _____

2. How do you punctuate long quotes in MLA? _____

3. If the long quote is multiple paragraphs, how do you punctuate each new paragraph? _____

4. How many lines can there be in a short quote? _____

5. How do you punctuate short quotes? _____

NAME _____

Mini Lesson 261: Ellipses–MLA

How can learning this help you? If you need to omit parts of a direct quotation, you should show you have omitted it by inserting ellipses where the omitted portion has been deleted. Ellipses in MLA are different from APA as there are three periods with a space before, between, and after them (. . .). If it is at the end of a sentence, add a final period with no space after the third period.

DIFFERENCES IN MLA ELLIPSES

The MLA ellipsis is space, period, space, period, space, period space (. . .) that is used to show that something has been omitted from the original quote.

At the end of a sentence, there is a fourth period directly after the last period of other punctuation.

Four ellipsis periods indicate an omission between two sentences with no space after the third period.

ML 261 Check Understanding: Ellipses–MLA

1. What is the proper way to format an ellipsis in MLA? _____

2. What is the purpose of using an ellipsis? _____

3. If an ellipsis is used at the end of a sentence, what further punctuation is required? _____

4. How many periods are in an ellipsis?? _____

5. Discuss the usage of ellipses with a partner.

Mini Lesson 262: Citing Common Electronic Sources–MLA

How can learning this help you? When citing an electronically accessed source, give enough information to the reader so they may be able to find the electronic source used.

MOST COMMON ELECTRONIC SOURCES

These are the five electronic parts of citations. They are listed in the order they should follow.

Author(s)

Title of article

Electronic address

Date of publication

Date you accessed the file

> Example: Author(s). "Title." Database or Journal Title, Edition, Volume, Publisher, Publication Date, Location (URL, pages, or DOI). Date of Access

ML 262 Check Understanding: Citing Common Electronic Sources–MLA

Write these five parts of a possible electronic source in the correct order. They are currently listed alphabetically.

Author(s)

Date of publication

Date you accessed the site

Electronic address

Title of article

1. _____

2. _____

3. _____

4. _____

5. _____

NAME _____

Mini Lesson 263: End-of-Paper Citations–MLA

How can learning this help you? If you learn and remember these general citation rules, they will help you for as long as you are writing papers, whether for school or work. These citations are purposely fictitious. They are also the same ones as in the APA chapter but are formatted for MLA here.

GENERAL RULES

Citations should be on your Works Cited page at the end of your research paper.

Start sources on a new page at the end of your paper and title it "Works Cited." Center this title in the middle and top of the page.

List each source alphabetically by the last name of the author(s). If a source does not have an author, use the first word of the title.

Double-space just like the rest of the paper.

Capitalize the first word in the title and all other words except articles, conjunctions, and prepositions.

For titles of long literary works like books and magazines, italicize if you're typing, and underline if you're writing by hand.

Short literary works' titles, such as articles and poems, should have quotation marks.

Use hanging indentation for each source; the first line of the source is flush with the left margin, and each other line is indented three spaces.

List multiple page numbers as pp. 225-50 (Note: MLA style omits the first sets of repeated digits, so omit the 2 from 250 in the citation: pp. 225-50).

If only one page of a print source is used, abbreviate with "p." before the page number (e.g., p.157).

If the excerpt spans multiple pages, use "pp" and use a hyphen within the span of pages.

ML 263 Check Understanding: End of Paper Citations–MLA

1. Do you start your end sources on a new page or at the end of your writing? _____

2. What do you title the page with your sources? _____

3. Do you single-space or double-space the source page and the rest of the paper? _____

4. Do you italicize, underline, or put quotes around the title of a long literary work that's typed?
   _____

5. How many spaces do you indent the lines after the first line of the source on an MLA Works Cited page? _____

Chapter Fourteen: APA Research Citations

Why is this chapter important for you? MLA procedures were taught in the previous chapter. This chapter will address APA Research Citations.

The Lessons

Chapter Fourteen: APA Research Citations 347
    Mini Lesson 264: Research and Citations–APA 348
    Mini Lesson 265: Pre-Writing–APA 349
    Mini Lesson 266: Elements Needed for a Title Page–APA 350
    Mini Lesson 267: Proper Format for a Manuscript–APA 351
    Mini Lesson 268: Outline–APA 352
    Mini Lesson 269: Case Rules in Titles–APA 353
    Mini Lesson 270: Author / Date Citations–APA 354
    Mini Lesson 271: Direct Short and Block Quotations–APA 355
    Mini Lesson 272: Reference List Entries–APA 357
    Mini Lesson 273: Reference Author Elements–APA 358
    Mini Lesson 274: Reference, Date, Title, and Source–APA 359
    Mini Lesson 275: Ellipses–APA 360

Mini Lesson 264: Research and Citations–APA

How can learning this help you? You will be required to write research papers in school. Many of you will be expected to research various topics and write research reports in your careers, so it is good to learn how to write them well. As you research topics, you should give credit for the expert information you have found in your research. To do this, write a citation, which tells your readers where you found some of your information. A citation means the quoting, paraphrasing, and documenting of some expert an authoritative source.

MLA and APA are probably the two most used citation methods. MLA stands for the Modern Language Association, and APA stands for the American Psychological Association

WHAT YOU MAY EXPECT TO LEARN FROM APA

- Title page
- Body
- In-text citations
- Short in-text quotes
- Long in-text quotes
- Reference list
- Printed citations
- Electronic citations

ML 264 Check Understanding: Researching and Citations–APA

List five of the things you expect to learn about regarding APA citations.

1. _____

2. _____

3. _____

4. _____

5. _____

Mini Lesson 265: Pre-Writing–APA

How can learning this help you? The elements of a well-written paper include structure, format, and organization. Manuscripts should have a properly formatted title page with the items below to qualify for a good evaluation in APA.

GENERAL GUIDELINES FOR APA FORMATTING

All APA text and citations should be double-spaced.

Margins should be 1" on the top, bottom, and sides.

Align the text to the left margin.

Indent the first line of each paragraph ½ inch.

Use a running header at the top left of the page with the title of your paper in all capital letters. The top right of the running header should include page numbers starting with 1 at the title page. Additionally, the running header should be ½" from the top of the page.

ML 265 Check Understanding: Pre-Writing–APA

1. Should the paper be single or double-spaced?

2. How large should you make the the top, bottom, and side margins?

3. Should the right margin be even or uneven?

4. How far do you indent the first line of each paragraph?

5. How far down from the top should the running header be?

NAME _____   Language Arts Mini Lessons

Mini Lesson 266: Elements Needed for a Title Page–APA

How can learning this help you? The first page an APA professional will see is the title page, and it *must* be correctly formatted.

TITLE PAGE FORM

                                                                                    Page Number

Page Number
Author(s)
Affiliation (school)
Course Name and Number
Instructor
Due Date

KEY POINTS

Page number flush right

Do not use a bold font.

   Example:

Title: The Big House

Author name format: Robert L. Brown

Affiliation: Mountain Ridge High School

Course name and number: LANG 20: Language Arts 10

Instructor: Jackie Peterson

Due date: April 4, 2021

   See also Publication Manual of the American Psychological Association pp. 30-31.

ML 266 Check Understanding: Elements Needed for a Title Page–APA

Put these title page items in the correct order.

Title Page Items	Order
Affiliation (school)	1. _____
Due date	2. _____
Student name	3. _____
Instructor	4. _____
Title	5. _____

NAME _____   Language Arts Mini Lessons

Mini Lesson 267: Proper Format for a Manuscript–APA

How can learning this help you? Learn the proper guidelines with APA now and their application will follow for every paper or manuscript you write in the future. The proper format can even determine whether or not a professional will choose to read it. Sloppily or carelessly formatted papers find the "round file" (the garbage can) more often than not.

ORDER OF PAGES: START EACH ON A NEW PAGE

Title page

Abstract

Text

References

Footnotes

Tables

Figures

Appendices

WHEN YOU BEGIN

Research first, then write.

Font choice: choose a common font so all readers can read it. Some well-used fonts are Times New Roman (12 point), Arial (10 point), Calibri (10 point), or Lucida Sans Unicode (11 point).

Line-spacing: Double-space the entire paper including the Title Page. Blank spaces before or after headings are not needed.

Alignment: left, "ragged," not justified; do not manually divide words or change hyphenation.

Paragraph indentation: indent every paragraph ½ inch; set your tab for ½ inch to be consistent. The exceptions to this rule include titles, author names, affiliations, instructors, dates, and tables.

APA has all pages numbered, including the title page, with the page number on the top right.

ML 267 Check Understanding: Proper Format for a Manuscript–APA

1. What should you do before you begin writing? _____

2. What are two examples of easy-to-read fonts? _____

3. Does APA prefer the writing to be single-spaced or double-spaced? _____

4. What is the proper indentation for a paragraph in APA? _____

5. Should you first (A) write the paper or (B) research several sources on the topic? _____

Mini Lesson 268: Outline–APA

How can learning this help you? Beginning with an outline ensures that your paper will flow logically and gives you a tool to keep your thoughts and research organized. Outlines can also help students generate a purposeful order to their arguments and can significantly aid in the writing process.

A GREAT OUTLINE IS THE BEGINNING OF A GREAT PAPER

There are several acceptable ways to create an outline.

- Traditional outline using Roman numerals
- A web
- Basic listing

In APA, there are five possible different heading levels. Headings identify the topic or purpose of the paper. Determine how long your paper needs to be based on your teacher's requirements or your desires. Well-formatted headings help guide your readers logically through the paper. Keep headings concise to lead the readers, not bore them. Having multiple levels is not a requirement. Use them when appropriate.

- Level One: Main ideas, making the point of that entire section of the paper
- Level Two: Subsections of level one, expanding on the section (have at least two)
- Level Three: Subsections of level two (have at least two)
- Level Four: Subsections of level three (have at least two)
- Level Five: Subsections of level four (have at least two)

ML 268 Check Understanding: Outline–APA

1. Why are two types of outlines? _____

2. What kinds of outlines are there? _____

3. Why should you use headings? _____

4. Should you ever have just one subsection of a level? _____

5. How many levels of headings are required? _____

Mini Lesson 269: Case Rules in Titles–APA

How can learning this help you? Case rules are easy to learn and easy to follow. Practice and consistency are the keys to making sure your headings and titles are correctly capitalized.

A WELL-WRITTEN PAPER USES UPPER AND LOWERCASE CORRECTLY IN TITLES AND SENTENCES

Major words in titles are capitalized: Proper nouns, pronouns, verbs, adjectives, adverbs, and all four-letter or more words

Minor words in titles are not capitalized: Short words (three letters or less) such as conjunctions, articles, and short prepositions

Capitalize the following in a research paper:
- Titles of tests, including sub-titles
- All headings
- Title of your paper
- Table titles
- Figure titles

Capitalize the following in a sentence:
- First word of a title
- First word of a heading
- First word of a subtitle
- First word after a colon or end punctuation
- Words followed by numbers or letters
- Proper nouns
- Titles of articles, books, reports, web pages, table column headings, entries, and notes

ML 269 Check Understanding: Case Rules in Titles–APA

1. What are major words? _____
2. What are minor words? _____

List three things that must be capitalized:

3. _____
4. _____
5. _____

NAME _____

Mini Lesson 270: Author / Date Citations–APA

How can learning this help you? There is one right way and there are many wrong ways to cite a source. Follow these guidelines to correctly cite APA. Whenever you quote or paraphrase material from another source, give credit to that source, both right after the quote or paraphrased material and on the reference list page at the end of the text.

IT'S ALL IN THE DETAILS: QUOTING SOURCES CORRECTLY IS IMPORTANT

IN-TEXT CITATIONS

Use in-text citations in the body of the paper, in tables, footnotes, and appendices.

Inform your readers where you got your information.

Give proper credit for the words or ideas of others.

Gain credibility for your paper by showing you agree with other sources who are probably experts.

Basics: Author, Date (if there is no date, indicate using *nd*), Title, Source

When used in the body of the paper, a parenthetical citation may be used in parentheses at the end of the sentence. The period for the sentence comes after the last parentheses.

Use commas before and after the year.

Use a semicolon to separate the source material from the citation.

> Example of an in-line citation:
> The project was led by Jonathan K. Taylor and Amita R. Dougal. They wrote, "Native Americans have perfected the craft of making silver jewelry for centuries. If we helped them with the marketing and let them focus on creating this jewelry, they would be much more successful."

NARRATIVE CITATIONS

When an author's name appears in the narrative text, the date should follow immediately in parentheses unless the date is a part of the narrative text, in which case no parentheses are needed.

ML 270 Check Understanding: Author/Date Citations–APA

1. Where are three places that in-text citations are needed? _____
_____

2. What do in-text citations provide for readers? _____

3. What does *nd* mean? _____

4. How do you set apart a date in a citation? _____

5. How do you create a narrative citation? _____

Mini Lesson 271: Direct Short and Block Quotations–APA

How can learning this help you? It is preferable to paraphrase information rather than use a direct quote. However, when direct quoting is necessary, proper punctuation should be used to make the information more understandable. There should be a clear distinction between the exact quotation and your original content.

BE PRECISE

Key Points for Direct Quotations:

- Cite author, year, and page number(s)
- Abbreviate page number with p.
- Abbreviate multiple page numbers with pp.
- Separate page numbers with an en dash (a hyphen is "-," en dash is a little bigger, "–," and an em dash is "—."
- For pages which are not continuous, use e.g., then p. or pp. and page number(s).

Key points for short quotations:

- Short quotations have fewer than forty words or four lines or less.
- Short quotations have four or fewer lines.
- Quotations are enclosed in double quotation marks.
- Always include a full citation in the same sentence, not after the sentence.

Key Points for Block Quotations (long quotations):

- Blockquotes are forty words or more.
- Blockquotes do not need quotation marks.
- Start a blockquote on a new line.
- Indent the whole block ½ inches.
- Double-space the entire quote.
- The citation should be in parentheses with no period after the ending parentheses.
- Do not include any extra space before or after the quote.

(CONTINUED NEXT PAGE)

Example of a blockquote:

> The teacher said that he would split the class into partners. They would then take the interview sheet he would give them and interview each other about the questions on the sheet. He said that they shouldn't tell the class anything too personal. Everyone should find out the answers to questions as if where have they lived other than in their current town, what is something they are especially good at, or what was a memorable experience—funny, scary, frustrating, etc.
>
> When it was their turn, both partners would come up to the front of the class, and they would tell the class about each other. Each time a person was finished telling about their partner, the class would choose one thing about that person that they wanted to remember about them and have a quiz on it the next day. After the teacher told the class about that, they were a little nervous, but also kind of excited.

ML 271 Check Understanding: Direct Short and Block Quotations–APA

1. How many lines are in a short quotation? _____

2. How many words are in a block quotation? _____

3. Are block quotations enclosed in quotation marks? _____

4. Are short quotations enclosed in quotation marks? _____

5. How much do you indent a block quotation? _____

Mini Lesson 272: Reference List Entries–APA

How can learning this help you? A reference list is usually included in a reference's appendix. There are specific rules for maintaining this list in the correct format. Reference lists cite all of the sources used in writing the paper. A bibliography is different, as it suggests sources for further reading and has notes relating to the source content.

Types of references:
- Textual works
- Data sets
- Software
- Tests
- Audiovisual media
- Online media

Four elements of a reference:
- Author
- Date
- Title
- Source

Punctuation of a reference:

Use a period after each reference item. Only refrain from using a period when it would affect a URL or other digital reference.

Commas may be used when there is more than one author or more than one issue, as well as when the page numbers are not sequential.

ML 272 Check Understanding: Reference, List Entries–APA

What are two types of references?

1. _____

2. _____

What are three elements of a complete reference? _____

3. _____

4. _____

5. _____

NAME _____   Language Arts Mini Lessons

Mini Lesson 273: Reference Author Elements–APA

How can learning this help you? Reference author elements refer directly to how author credentials and information are displayed. Precision in APA is critical and can make or break an APA entry.

DEFINITION, FORMAT, AND SPELLING

AUTHOR ESSENTIALS

The author(s), or groups, responsible for the work referenced are used to properly identify the source. This may be an individual or multiple people, a group institution, government agency, organization, or a combination of the above.

FORMAT

Surname first, comma, then initials

Use a comma to separate the first author from the second.

Use an & before the last author.

No comma is necessary between groups of authors.

Non-primary authors are mentioned using "with" (e.g. on a book cover)

ML 273 Check Understanding: Reference, Date, Title, and Source–APA

What are the five important formatting items for a proper author reference?

1. _____

2. _____

3. _____

4. _____

5. _____

Mini Lesson 274: Reference, Date, Title, and Source–APA

How can learning this help you? Reference dates, titles, and sources refer directly to how the date is displayed. Precision in APA is critical and can make the difference between crediting an author or plagiarism. Correct referencing also allows readers to find the cited work and read more on the subject.

A PROPERLY FORMATTED REFERENCE CONTAINS ONE OR MORE OF THE FOLLOWING

Date of Publication:
- Year only
- Year, month, day
- Year and month
- Range of dates

Title: Two Types:
- Stand-alone titles
- Part of a "greater whole" titles

Source Types:
- Periodicals
- Publications
- Databases and archives
- Social media application or company
- Websites and web pages (presented as a hyperlink with https://)

ML 274 Check Understanding: Reference, Date, Title, and Source–APA

What are two of the four types used to display dates needed for a proper reference?

1. _____
2. _____

What are the two types of titles?

3. _____
4. _____

What is one essential type of source needed for a proper reference?

5. _____

NAME _____

Mini Lesson 275: Ellipses–APA

How can learning this help you? If you need to omit parts of a direct quotation, you should show that you have omitted them by inserting periods where the omitted portion has been deleted. This type of punctuation is called an ellipsis. An ellipsis consists of three periods with a space before and after each one, plus a space after the last period (. . .).

OMITTING PART OF SENTENCES OR QUOTES

When the omitted words, phrases, etc. in the quote come at the end of a sentence which trails off, use an ellipsis (space, period, space, period, space, period) and then the proper end mark.

Example: The students in the gym were excited after the coach's pep talk when he said . . . .

When using an ellipsis in the middle of a sentence, simply use the space, period, space, period, space, period.

Example: The students . . . were excited after the coach's pep talk.

Use ellipses sparingly.

ML 275 Check Understanding: Ellipses–APA

1. What is the proper way to format an ellipsis in the middle of a quoted sentence in APA?

   _____

2. What is the purpose of using an ellipsis? _____

3. How many periods are in an ellipsis at the end of a sentence? _____

4. Can you overuse ellipses? _____

5. How do you end an ellipses at the end of a sentence? _____

Chapter Fifteen: SAT and ACT Tips

Why is this chapter important for you? This lessons will help you learn what to study in preparation for your SAT or ACT, and it shows what types of questions to expect on the test.

The Lessons

Chapter Fifteen: SAT and ACT Tips 361
    Mini Lesson 276: SAT/ACT 362
    Mini Lesson 277: Types of Reading Questions SAT/ACT 363
    Mini Lesson 278: Types of Writing Questions SAT/ACT 364
    Mini Lesson 279: Theme, Conventions, Audience, Organization 365
    Mini Lesson 280: Guess Questions to Pass the SAT/ACT 366
    Mini Lesson 281: Review Writing Materials to Pass SAT/ ACT 368
    Mini Lesson 282: SAT and ACT Essay Writing 369
    Mini Lesson 283: Pre-Writing Your Essay 371
    Mini Lesson 284: Write Your Rough Draft 373
    Mini Lesson 285: Revise Using the Writer's Checklist 374

Mini Lesson 276: SAT/ACT

How can learning this help you? Students can prepare to pass the SAT or ACT by having a rough idea of what types of questions will be on the test. It will help you know what to study and what not to.

HAVE A ROUGH IDEA OF THE TYPES OF QUESTIONS TO EXPECT

For the multiple-choice questions on reading and writing (and questions on science in the ACT), your teacher may give you practice passages to read and answer questions regarding them. Since half of the section on writing is creating an argumentative essay, causing many students to think this portion of the test is the hardest, your teacher may give you more guidance and practice to help prepare.

In the reading and writing multiple-choice sections, there will be passages of informational, functional, and literacy text. Read each passage, then answer questions. The actual writing portion of the test will provide a writing prompt and instructions on how to write an argumentative essay.

ML 276 Check Understanding: SAT/ACT

1. What do SAT and ACT lessons teach you? (a. or b.)_____

    a. What types of questions will be on the tests

    b. What questions will be on the tests

2. Which test has a science section?

    a. ACT,

    b. SAT

    c. Both _____

3-4. In the multiple-choice test, you will _____ a passage and _____ the questions.

5. For the writing portion of the test, what type of essay do you write?

    a. informative

    b. argumentative

    c. narrative. _____

Mini Lesson 277: Types of Reading Questions SAT/ACT

How can learning this help you? There are typically about ten reading strategies or terms followed by sample questions. Each test question will probably have four possible answers from which to choose.

THERE IS A STRATEGY FOR READING

ML 277 Check Understanding: Types of Reading Questions SAT/ACT

Match the correct strategy with the sample from above (details, inference, sequence, etc.).

1. Which statement is the best conclusion, based on the information presented?

   _____

2. What source provides the best information for this topic?

   _____

3. Why did this character most likely run into . . . ? _____

4. According to the article, what caused them to . . .? _____

5. What does this word mean in this sentence? _____

Mini Lesson 278: Types of Writing Questions SAT/ACT

How can learning this help you? Here are some sample writing questions. Just like the reading portion of the test, each question will probably have four possible answers from which to choose. Out of 30 questions, many will typically be from audience, organization, and purpose.

TYPES OF QUESTIONS ON CONVENTIONS

The types of conventions include usage, punctuation, capitalization, and spelling.

Example: "In sentence 9, the correct form of the verb is . . ."
Example: "Which correction is needed in the sentence above?"
Example: "Which is the correct way to write sentence 18?"
Example: "Which is the best way to combine sentences 3 and 4?"
Example: "How should sentence 6 be punctuated?"
Example: "Which of the following is an example of a sentence fragment?"

ML 278 Check Understanding: Types of Writing Questions SAT/ACT

Using the above examples as guides, create five questions like the ones you might find on the SAT and ACT.

1. _____

2. _____

3. _____

4. _____

5. _____

Mini Lesson 279: Theme, Conventions, Audience, Organization

How can learning this help you? Discover what types of questions to expect on the tests.

THEME, CONVENTIONS, AUDIENCE, ORGANIZATION, AND PURPOSE

    Example: What source provides the best information about . . .?
    Example: Through which company can a person order this publication?
    Example: Which research source specifically addresses this problem?
    Example: Which source would be most useful to add information to this text?

Theme (main Idea):
    Example: Which title best captures the theme of this text?
    Example: Which sentence does not support the focus of this text?

Conventions

Audience:
    Example: For which group of people was this text most likely written?

Organization:
    Example: Which of the following best describes the organization of this text?

Purpose:
    Example: The main purpose of this text is to . . ..

ML 279 Check Understanding: Theme, Conventions, Audience, Organiza-

Match the correct strategy with the following revised sample from "Sweden–a Great Country with a Great Language," using theme, conventions, audience, organization, and purpose.

Have you ever wondered what it would be like to live in Sweden? Many people picture Swedes as strong, hardy men with an ax over their shoulder, and the women in old-fashioned floor-length dresses, braided hair, carrying milk pails into simple log homes after milking the cow. Nothing could be further from the truth. Sweden has one of the highest standards of living in the world.

Nearly everything about Sweden seems modern. A high percentage have professional jobs like doctors and engineers, and 83% have a high school degree. Most live in tall, modern apartment buildings with all of the conveniences.

1. For which group of people was this text most likely written? _____

2. Which gender will comprise most of your readers? _____

3. What is the main idea of the passage? _____

4. Which of these theme possibilities is most likely the main idea of this passage? _____

5. Why is this question being asked? _____

Mini Lesson 280: Guess Questions to Pass the SAT/ACT

How can learning this help you? One of the best ways to prepare for tests is to guess what questions you would ask about a topic and then find the answers to those questions.

READING AND WRITING CATEGORIES FOR QUESTIONS

Audience	Drawing Conclusions	Purpose
Category	Inference	Sequence
Cause and Effect	Main Idea	Topic

"Points in Football"

American football is a violent, but sophisticated game. Perhaps nothing shows football's complexity more than its scoring system. For organization's sake, we'll go from the smallest to the largest amount of points you may earn. One point may be earned by kicking the ball through the goalposts right after scoring a touchdown.

Two points may be earned in three different ways. The least likely way is to score a touch-back, which means a player on the team with the ball is tackled behind their goal line or else the defensive team intercepts the ball or recovers a fumble behind the goal line. Two points may also be earned if a team runs or passes the ball into the end zone right after they have scored a touchdown.

Three points may be earned if the offensive team kicks a field goal, which means they kick the ball through the goalposts from where the team moved the ball.

Six points may be earned by running the ball into the end zone or throwing the ball to a player in the end zone.

If you can understand how teams receive these points, it will help you understand a little more of the game.

(CONTINUED NEXT PAGE)

ML 280 Check Understanding: Guess Questions to Pass the SAT/ACT

1. Work alone or with a partner.
2. Read the article "Points in Football."
3. Create ten questions based on this article and the SAT and ACT.

   1. _____
   2. _____
   3. _____
   4. _____
   5. _____
   6. _____
   7. _____
   8. _____
   9. _____
   10. _____

4. Trade questions with another person or group and answer each other's questions.
5. In addition to answering the other group's questions, evaluate how clear their questions are.

NAME _____   Language Arts Mini Lessons

Mini Lesson 281: Review Writing Materials to Pass SAT/ACT

How can learning this help you? The first step toward improving your abilities in taking the SAT and ACT is realizing what you need to study. Evaluate where you're strong and weak.

REALIZE WHAT YOU NEED TO STUDY

ML 281 Check Understanding: Review Writing Materials to Pass SAT/ACT

Evaluate what you need to study for the SAT and the ACT.

1. What study skills will help you personally the most? _____

2. What will help you the most in reading? _____

3. List the types of questions you personally need to study the most in reading.

_____

_____

_____

_____

4. What will help you the most in writing? _____

5. List the types of questions you personally need to study the most in writing.

_____

_____

_____

_____

Mini Lesson 282: SAT and ACT Essay Writing

How can learning this help you? Argumentative writing is the portion of the standardized tests on which students usually do the worst. Also, if your state requires a High School Exit Exam, you must pass this exam in order to graduate. The more you use the following principles, the better you will do on your essay.

THE THREE PARTS OF AN ESSAY

INTRODUCTION

Introduction: Catch the readers' attention, briefly explain the problem, and state your position in a thesis statement.

Thesis statement: Make your position clear on the problem you're addressing by creating a strong thesis statement. Remember that the thesis is the heart of argumentative writing. Clearly present it in the introduction since it is the touchstone for you, the writer, to keep returning to throughout the passage. It is the statement to be proved or maintained against objections.

Gain the reader's attention: Connect your readers to your topic with a story, quote, fact, etc. You can produce a powerful psychological impact for the reader(s) with a well-constructed introduction. Most readers come to the written text with their own opinions about the subject. You can help them change that.

Opposing viewpoint: Briefly acknowledge the opposing viewpoint(s). The reason the topic is controversial is that there are good and bad points to each side.

BODY

Body: This is where the points of your plan and its benefits appear. It is usually about 75 % of the paper's length. Acknowledge the opposition, then expand upon your thesis by explaining your plan and its benefits.

Points to be made: The body is usually composed of 3 to 5 points. Each point is like a mini-paper with a body of its own. Each point should be supported with logic and/or emotion.

CONCLUSION

Conclude: Make your final summary and appeal to your audience.

Restate your thesis: Tell why your plan is the most beneficial.

Emphasize your plan: Leaving your audience with some key fact or story to convince them to accept your point of view. Call to action: Request your audience's help and issue them a call to action.

(CONTINUED NEXT PAGE)

ML 282 Check Understanding: SAT and ACT Essay Writing

1. What is the heart of argumentative writing? _____

2. What is one of the parts of the introduction besides the thesis statement? _____

3. Approximately what percent of an essay's length should the body be? _____

4. How many points or reasons should a good essay typically have? 2-4, 3-5, 4-6, or 5-7? _____

5. What is one of the three things the book suggests to include in the conclusion? _____

NAME _____

Mini Lesson 283: Pre-Writing Your Essay

How can learning this help you? When writing your essay, you will be given a writing prompt about a controversial topic and asked to take a stand for or against the topic. Then you will write an argumentative essay about it.

WRITING PROMPTS

The person who grades your test won't care whether you are for or against the issue; they will only evaluate your paper on its quality. The more you think about possible controversial topics and how to develop a strong essay about them, the better you will probably do when writing your essay on the test.

The following is a sample writing prompt:

Imagine you attend school in an old building that needs to be torn down so that a new one can be built on the same property. The problem is deciding where you will go to school while your new school is being built.

Your school board says there are two options. One is to use the school building of a rival school during the late afternoon and evening. The other is to continue attending school in your old building while your new school is being built on your athletic fields, but you will have to forego football, baseball, and track competition for the years you are building the new school, then tearing down the old building and making new athletic fields where that building was.

ML 283 Check Understanding: Pre-Writing Your Essay

PRE-WRITING

Follow this form to create your essay's outline. Remember that this is where you do your major thinking and creating of ideas. Write just enough words for you to be able to remember what you mean. Don't write in complete sentences or worry about grammar here. Just get down your ideas.

WRITER'S CHECKLIST—FIRST PARTS

Ideas and organization

Focus on your audience and purpose for writing.

Develop and present a clear opinion about the topic in your thesis statement.

Support your opinion with ideas, explanations, and examples.

Present your ideas in the order that best supports your opinion.

(CONTINUED NEXT PAGE

NAME _____

FOR PLANNING PURPOSES AND DEVELOPING YOUR OUTLINE, USE THIS INFORMATION

1. Audience
2. Purpose

    Introduction

        a. Attention-getter

        b. Issue

        c. Opposing view: here or in the body

        d. Thesis statement

3. Body: your plan and benefits

    Point a

    Point b

    Point c

    Point d

    Point e

4. Benefits
5. Conclusion
6. Summarize thesis, plan, and benefits

        a. Final convincing fact or story

        b. Request for help with a call to action

Mini Lesson 284: Write Your Rough Draft

How can learning this help you? If you follow your outline and focus on your overall ideas, you may find that writing will become much easier. "Don't sweat the small stuff yet."

DON'T SWEAT THE SMALL STUFF . . . YET

Use your creativity to develop your ideas. Remember, drafting is a right-brained activity. Use the stream-of-consciousness method to draft. Let your overall ideas flow through your mind and onto the paper. Don't stop to worry about any conventions like grammar, spelling, punctuation, etc. yet.

ML 284 Student Activity: Write Your Rough Draft

_____
_____
_____
_____
_____
_____
_____
_____
_____
_____
_____
_____
_____
_____
_____
_____
_____
_____

NAME _____   Language Arts Mini Lessons

Mini Lesson 285: Revise Using the Writer's Checklist

How can learning this help you? The Writer's Checklist list is based on the Six Traits of Writing. Use it and see how much easier it is to revise your piece and how much better and more organized your work becomes.

WRITER'S CHECKLIST—REVISING YOUR ROUGH DRAFT WITH THE SIX TRAITS

Idea Development: Write specifically to your audience..

Organization: Break each topic into its own paragraph.

Voice: Strongly share your thoughts and opinions—you are the expert.

Word Choice: Use specific and accurate words, language that sounds natural.

Sentence Fluency: Use sentences that vary in structure and beginnings and make your sentences flow smoothly.

Conventions: Check correct grammar, capitalization, spelling, and punctuation; make sure others can read your handwriting>

ML 285 Student Activity: Revise Using the Writer's Checklist

1. What are three of the main parts of the Writer's Checklist? _____

_____

2. What should be the tone of your writing? _____

_____

3. In which of the steps in the Writer's Checklist listed do you think you do especially well?_____

_____

4. In which of the steps in the Writer's Checklist do you think you do especially poorly? _____

_____

5. Proofread each other's writing.

Chapter Sixteen: Speaking and Listening

Why are these mini lessons important for you? Communicating through speech is critical in every aspect of our lives. School leaders are placing more emphasis on improving our public speaking than ever before. That's because our society has moved from a manufacturing society to a thinking, discussing, and presenting society, whether it's at work or at home.

The Lessons

Chapter Sixteen: Speaking and Listening 375
    Mini Lesson 286: Speaking Principles 376
    Mini Lesson 287: Facial Expressions, Gestures, and Posture 377
    Mini Lesson 288: Speaking and Presenting Techniques 378
    Mini Lesson 289: Vocal Techniques 379
    Mini Lesson 290: Vocal Techniques with the Alphabet 380
    Mini Lesson 291: Pause for Effect 382
    Mini Lesson 292: Pausing and Eye Contact 383
    Mini Lesson 293: Physical Characteristics 384
    Mini Lesson 294: Voice and Physical Characteristics 385
    Mini Lesson 295: Mood 386
    Mini Lesson 296: Poise 387
    Mini Lesson 297: Involvement and Energy 388
    Mini Lesson 298: Imagery 389
    Mini Lesson 299: Presenting Literature Aloud 390
    Mini Lesson 300: Practice Voice and Character Placement 391
    Mini Lesson 301: Vary Posture, Character Placement, and Gestures 392
    Mini Lesson 302: PAIR Listening–Prior Understanding 393
    Mini Lesson 303: PAIR Listening–Anticipating 394
    Mini Lesson 304: PAIR Listening–Inputting 396
    Mini Lesson 305: PAIR Listening–Relating 396

Mini Lesson 286: Speaking Principles

How can learning this help you? The more you learn about speaking, listening, and presentation, the more confident you will become when having to present to a person, a group of people, even a large audience. This is also good to learn for those of you who do YouTube videos, webinars, podcasts, online workshops, etc. In-person or online presentations where speaking is involved are becoming more and more prevalent.

SPEAKING PUBLICLY CAN BE ENERGIZING!

Many of the exercises in this chapter tell you to quote the alphabet. The reason for this odd request is to give you something you can say without any effort while you work and focus on the various principles of speaking.

ML 286 Student Activity: Speaking Principles

1. Get with 3 or 4 students and say the alphabet together while looking around at each other.

2. At home imagine you are speaking before an audience. Say the alphabet as if you are speaking to that audience.

3. In class, get with 3 or 4 students and say the alphabet together in a boring way while looking around at each other. Now say it in a dynamic, enthusiastic way.

4. Present a nursery rhyme, part of a fairy tale, or something else you know, and look at your student group as your audience.

5. Be a respectful listener as the others recite their short story or nursery rhyme.

NAME _____   Language Arts Mini Lessons

Mini Lesson 287: Facial Expressions, Gestures, and Posture

How can learning this help you? You use many different methods of communication when speaking, including facial expressions, hand gestures, and even certain postures. For example, shifting from foot to foot conveys nervousness, while calm, relaxed shoulders indicate confidence.

HOW YOU LOOK AND USE BODY LANGUAGE ARE IMPORTANT

ML 287 Student Activity: Facial Expressions, Gestures, and Posture

Practice these physical characteristics (facial expressions, gestures, and posture) while reciting the alphabet. Remember to only use one hand at a time when gesturing.

Say alphabet	Expressions	Gestures	Posture
a, b, c, d, e, f, g	scared	Palm up	Lean slightly back
h, i, j, k, l, m, n, o, p	angry	Palm down	Lean slightly forward
q, r, s, t, u, v	scared	Palm up	Lean slightly back
w, x, y, and z	angry	Palm down	Lean slightly forward

1. Practice facial expressions and posture. (Worth 2 points)

2. Present a nursery rhyme, part of a fairy tale, or something else you know. Use two of the physical characteristics (facial expressions, gestures, or posture) as you present it. (Worth 3 points)

NAME _____

Mini Lesson 288: Speaking and Presenting Techniques

How can learning this help you? The more convincing your presentation is, the more influential your ideas will be, whether in an informal friends' discussion or a formal presentation or speech.

BE CONVINCING

The following points are simply ways to help you be more interesting and effective in your speaking and presenting. However, the key point is to stay natural and honest to yourself. If you use these principles without still being yourself, you will come across as phony and distrustful.

Go over these reading strategies as a class.

No.	Reading Strategy	Sample Question
1	Cause and effect	"According to the article, what caused them to . . .?": :
2	Details	"What forced these students to . . .?" "According to the directions, what is the correct way to use this product?"
3	Drawing conclusions	"Which statement is the best conclusion based on the information presented?"
4	Main Ideas	"What is the main idea of this passage?" "Why is the title of this passage appropriate?"
5	Inference	"Why did this character most likely run into . . .?"
6	Purpose	"What is the main purpose of this paragraph?"
7	Reference Skills (dictionary, encyclopedia, etc.)	"What source provides the best information for this topic?" "Which is the best reason to consider the information in this article reliable?"
8	Sequence	"Why are the directions numbered?" "Name the three things she did—in order."

ML 288 Student Activity: Speaking and Presenting Techniques

List five of the strategies most important to you.

1. _____

2. _____

3. _____

4. _____

5. _____

Mini Lesson 289: Vocal Techniques

How can learning this help you? These vocal techniques will help you be more interesting and effective when speaking.

CONFIDENTIAL TONE FOR IMPORTANT POINTS

Use a more intimate tone as if to suggest you are letting your audience in on an exciting secret. It's almost like a half-whisper, but make sure you don't let your volume drop so low that people can't hear you.

VOCAL VARIETY

There are three methods to help you add variety to your speech. Stay natural and honest.

Change your volume.

Change your speed.

Change your pitch between high and low.

ML 289 Student Activity: Vocal Techniques

1. The key point is to stay _____ and honest to yourself.

2. When you speak with a half-whisper, it's called a _____.

What are the three things you change to add vocal variety?

3. _____

4. _____

5. _____

Mini Lesson 290: Vocal Techniques with the Alphabet

How can learning this help you? The reason to use the alphabet is because we all *know* it, so it's easier to use something like it so we may focus on the speaking concepts the teacher wants us to learn.

SAY OR SING THE ALPHABET

Say or Sing the Alphabet	Volume
a, b, c, d, e, f, g	soft
h, i, j, k, l, m, n, o, p	loud
q, r, s, t, u, v	soft
w, x, y, and z	loud

1. Say or sing the alphabet aloud together.

2-3. When you do the alphabet this time, change from soft to loud, like the chart.

ML 290 Student Activity #A: Vocal Techniques with the Alphabet

Get with a partner and practice these techniques.

1. Share a supposed secret, a fairy tale, or even the alphabet. Use the confidential tone or half-whisper.

    to tell the first 20 to 30 seconds of a fairy tale.

2. Practice your vocal variety by saying the alphabet, pausing after g, p, v, and z, as shown below.

3. Using the alphabet change your speed between fast and slow.

4. Using the alphabet change your volume between soft and loud.

5. Using the alphabet change your pitch between high and low 4-5. Repeat the same thing.

(CONTINUED NEXT PAGE)

NAME _____   Language Arts Mini Lessons

ML 290 Student Activity #B: Vocal Techniques with the Alphabet

Follow the directions on this chart.

Say or Sing the Alphabet	Volume First Time	Speed Second Time	Pitch Third Time
a, b, c, d, e, f, g	Soft	Fast	High
h, i, j, k, l, m, n, o, p	Loud	Slow	Low
q, r, s, t, u, v	Soft	Slow	High
w, x, y, and z	Loud	Slow	Low

1. Say or sing the alphabet following the instructions in the chart.

2. Now change the volume and speed as you say the alphabet.

3.. Now change the speed and pitch.

4. Now change the volume and pitch.

5. Now change the volume, speed, and pitch.

NAME _____   Language Arts Mini Lessons

Mini Lesson 291: Pause for Effect

How can learning this help you? An effective pause screams with meaning. There are two major times to pause effectively.

EFFECTIVE PAUSES

Pause just before a keyword or phrase. This helps your audience pay attention to what you're about to say.

Pause just after a keyword or phrase. This helps your audience mentally digest what you have just said.

ML 291 Student Activity: Pausing for Effect

1. Follow these directions.

   Write the alphabet from a through g on the this line. _____

   Write h through p on the this line. _____

   Write q through v on the this line. _____

   Write w through z on the this line. _____

2. To practice pauses after key points, insert a backslash after the letters g, p, v, and z. That's at the end of each line.

3. Now, to practice pauses before key points, insert a back slash before the letters g, l, t, and x.

4. Say the alphabet with the pauses at each backslash.

5. Practice, then read or recite something that is about 20 seconds long. Use two of the three vocal variety methods (volume, speed, and pitch), and use pauses. Present this to a partner or sibling at home. You can use the sample nursery rhymes below to practice.

SAMPLE NURSERY RHYMES

Jack and Jill	Old Mother Hubbard
Little Jack Horner	Little Miss Muffet
Old King Cole	Twinkle, Twinkle Little Star
Old MacDonald Had a Farm	Row, Row, Row Your Boat
Wheels on the Bus	

Mini Lesson 292: Pausing and Eye Contact

How can learning this help you? The more you look at your audience, the more they feel included, so the more they want to listen to you and even agree with you on an argumentative piece.

EYE CONTACT

Look around at your audience as you speak to or with them.

Try to look around naturally, not in a pattern.

If it's too distracting to look at people, look *between* them. Then *you* won't be distracted, but your audience will feel as if you're *looking at them*.

ML 292 Student Activity: Pausing and Eye Contact

1. An effective pause _____ with meaning.

The two times to pause most effectively are:

2. _____

3. _____

4. The more you look at your audience, the more they feel _____.

5. If it's too distracting to look at people, look _____ them.

NAME _____

Mini Lesson 293: Physical Characteristics

How can learning this help you? If used correctly, physical characteristics can support and enrich your speaking. If used incorrectly, they can detract from it.

SUPPORT AND ENRICHMENT USED WELL CONVEYS YOUR MESSAGE BETTER

Facial expressions:

Try to support whatever emotion you're feeling with appropriate facial expressions. Remember to keep it honest and natural, though.

Gestures:

It's usually most effective to use only one hand at a time.

Make your gestures above the elbow.

Match your gesture to your emotion.

Palm up shows pleading and uncertainty.

Palm down shows power and certainty.

Use gestures for emphasis, not all the time.

Avoid repetitive gestures.

Posture:

Subtly match your posture to the emotion you're feeling.

Lean forward a little if you're giving a speech or presentation. It subconsciously makes your audience feel like you care about them and what you're telling them.

ML 293 Student Activity: Physical Characteristics

1. Try to support whatever emotion you're feeling with appropriate _____.

2. What do you do physically to make your audience feel like you're excited to be there? _____

3. When you gesture, is it more effective to raise your hand above or below the elbow? _____

4. Does "palm down" or "palm up" show more power and certainty? _____

5. Avoid _____ gestures.

Mini Lesson 294: Voice and Physical Characteristics

How can learning this help you? The more you learn to make a good delivery in your presentation, the more effective your presentation will be.

GOOD DELIVERY PRACTICE

Say the Alphabet	Speed	Volume	Pitch	Gestures
a, b, c, d, e, f, g	Fast	Soft	High	Palm Up
h, i, j, k, l, m, n, o, p	Slow	Loud	Low	Palm Down
q, r, s, t, u, v	Fast	Soft	High	Palm Up
w, x, y, and z	Slow	Loud	Low	Palm Down

ML 294 Student Activity #A: Voice and Physical Characteristics

1. Get with a partner and practice these techniques.

2. Share a supposed secret. Use your confidential tone or half-whisper.

3. Use the confidential tone to tell the first 20 to 30 seconds of a fairy tale.

4. To practice pauses after key points, insert a pause *after* the letters g, p, v, and z.

5. Now, to practice pauses before key points, insert a pause *before* the letters g, l, t, and x.

Say the Alphabet	Change Expressions	Change Gestures	Change Posture
a, b, c, d, e, f, g	scared	Palm Up	Lean Slightly Back
h, i, j, k, l, m, n, o, p	angry	Palm Down	Lean Slightly Forward
q, r, s, t, u, v	ccared	Palm Up	Lean Slightly Back
w, x, y, and z	angry	Palm Down	Lea Slightly Forward

ML 294 Student Activity #B: Voice and Physical Characteristics

1-5. Using the above chart, say the alphabet while changing the volume, speed, and pitch.

Mini Lesson 295: Mood

How can learning this help you? Mood means an overall feeling or state of mind. The more you can match your own mood to what your character is saying or presenting, the more convincing you will be when you speak.

CREATE A MOOD

Mood is the state of mind or feeling you're trying to create within the listeners of your presentation. It may be even more important in your reading than characterization. Mood sets the emotional context of the selection and is a combination of the presenter's poise, emotional involvement in the piece, and imagery of the scenes you're imagining in your presenting.

Voice: Your voice is usually the most important part of your mood in the presentation. That is partly because you can do so much to set the mood with your voice. Be loud and clear. Hit your consonants hard. At times, use a confidential tone, half-whisper as if you are telling us a special secret. Regularly change your voice's volume, speed, and pitch.

Character placement: Give each character a certain place to look when they are that character.

Emotional involvement: Remember a time you had similar emotions to the key emotions your main characters are feeling.

Sense imagery: If the place your characters are at is important to your presentation, decide on the most important one or two sense images in your selection and try to see, hear, touch, smell, or taste the key images you're describing.

Poise: Be confident in yourself. When you make a mistake, just remember that most other people will make mistakes, too. Your characters also make mistakes. Just keep on going with your presentation. You are performing or presenting this piece in a way that no one else has ever done.

ML 295 Student Activity: Mood

List five things you can do to create the mood for the presentation.

1. _____
2. _____
3. _____
4. _____
5. _____

Mini Lesson 296: Poise

How can learning this help you? Poise means the ability to confidently perform a task, whether things go smoothly or not. Be confident without being cocky. Keep your confidence when you make a mistake. Remember that you will probably make mistakes, but so will everyone else. Keep your poise.

POISE PRACTICE

ML 296 Student Activity: Poise

1. In a small group, say the alphabet while full of poise—confident, but not cocky.

2. Say the alphabet the same poised way, but purposely stumble over letters f, m, and r. Keep your

3. Say the alphabet in an overly dramatic way.

4. Practice the alphabet as if two very old characters were speaking.

5. Imagery practice: Get with a partner and describe a brief sense image—sight, sound, taste, etc.—to each other. It can be as simple as last night's dinner or this morning's breakfast.

Mini Lesson 297: Involvement and Energy

How can learning this help you? Let your mood and emotion match the emotion written into the text you're presenting. The more appropriate energy and involvement you have as the presenter, the more involved your listeners will be.

ROLE-PLAYING OR PRETEND

ML 297 Student Activity: Involvement and Energy

Split into pairs and act out these short scenes.

1. Pretend you are a guest on a children's TV show.

2. Pretend you are a television reporter.

3. Pretend you are a mortician at a mortuary.

4. Pretend you are a drill sergeant and a private.

5. Pretend you are a parent and a child.

NAME _____

Mini Lesson 298: Imagery

How can learning this help you? If you can imagine the images you're presenting in your text, it will help your audience to also imagine them.

IMAGINE YOU'RE PRESENTING THE ALPHABET WITH ANY OF THE IMAGES BELOW

Sense imagery (*see, hear, touch, smell, taste*)

Emotional imagery (*joy, sadness, anger, excitement, fear,* etc.)

ML 298 Student Activity: Imagery

1. Keep your confidence _____ you make a mistake.

2. Who will probably make mistakes? _____

3. Let your mood and emotion _____, the emotion written into the text you're presenting.

4. The more _____ you are as the presenter, the more involved your listeners will be.

5. If you imagine the images you're presenting in your passage, your audience will probably imagine them, too.

Try this in a group of 3 to 5 students.

Mini Lesson 299: Presenting Literature Aloud

How can learning this help you? Here are some ideas to help you when you present a passage of literature or portray a character.

IDEAS TO HELP YOU WHEN GIVING LITERARY PRESENTATIONS

Realism: The more realistic the story is, the more believable your interpretation should be with your voice, eyes, expressions, and gestures. As strange as it may seem, in comedy you should portray the character(s) as very serious—sometimes overly serious—which makes the ridiculousness of the comic situation even funnier. The reason for this is that if the situation seems humorous to the audience if you perform your character(s) as though things are very intense and important for you, it makes the situation—and your character(s)—seem even funnier.

Voice: A different voice for each character:

If your selection has multiple characters in it, suggest a different voice for each character. Again, the more realistic the literature is, the more believable each voice should be.

Character Placement: Look at a slightly different place (vertically and horizontally) for each character. Look at that same place each time that character speaks. It helps your audience keep the characters straight.

ML 299 Student Activity: Presenting Literature Aloud

1. The more realistic the story is, the more _____ your interpretation should be.

2. Why should you portray your character(s) especially intense in a comedy? _____

3. If your selection has multiple characters in it, suggest a different _____ for each character.

4. Why should you look at a slightly different place (vertically and horizontally) for each character?

   _____

5. Look at that same _____ each time that character speaks.

NAME _____   Language Arts Mini Lessons

Mini Lesson 300: Practice Voice and Character Placement

How can learning this help you? As you place each character in the same place, it makes it easier to tell which character is which.

PLACEMENT CAN HELP IN PRESENTATION

ML 300 Student Activity: Practice Voice and Character Placement

Say Alphabet	Character
a, b, c, d, e, f, g	Little Red
h, i, j, k, l, m, n, o, p	Wolf
q, r, s, t, u, v	Little Red
w, x, y, and z	Wolf

1. Choose two opposite characters like Little Red Riding Hood and the Big Bad Wolf, but use the alphabet again as though the letters are words that make sense to the two characters. Practice a different voice and character placement. Give each character an appropriate voice.

2. Look at a different place for each _____.

3. Looking at a different place is called _____.

4. Look at a slightly different place (vertically and horizontally) for each character. Look at that _____ place each time that character speaks. It helps your audience keep the characters straight.

5. Do this once in seriousness and once for comedy.

NAME _____

Mini Lesson 301: Vary Posture, Character Placement, and Gestures

How can learning this help you? If you have a slightly different voice and character placement for each character, it will help your audience keep track of the different characters, so they will be able to follow your story better.

VARY YOUR VOICE, POSTURE, CHARACTER PLACEMENT, AND GESTURES FOR DEFINITION

ML 301 Student Activity: Vary Posture, Character Placement, and Gestures

1. Divide into two circles with your desks.

2. Softly whisper to someone in each group something that is five to ten words long.

3. Have that person whisper what they heard to the person on their left.

4. That person then whispers it to the person on their left, and it continues around the circle.

5. When the last person hears the message, they tell the group what was heard.

Each group compares what was said first and last to see how close they were.

NAME _____ Language Arts Mini Lessons

Mini Lesson 302: PAIR Listening–Prior Understanding

How can learning this help you? What's your prior understanding of the topic?

LISTENING AND PRIOR UNDERSTANDING

Focus on yourself and what you already understand about this topic.

What's your own prior knowledge (if any) about the topic?

What's your own prior experience (if any) with the topic?

What's your prior attitude (if any) toward the topic?

What's your prior knowledge (if any) about the author?

MINI LESSONS 302- REFERENCE THIS ARTICLE "PEEKING AT THE CHRISTMAS TROMBONE."

ML 302 Student Activity: PAIR Listening–Prior Understanding

Answer what you can about these five questions regarding "Peeking at the Christmas Trombone."

1. What's your prior knowledge (if any) about the topic?

_____

2. What's your prior experience (if any) of the topic?

_____

3. What's your prior attitude (if any) toward the topic?

_____

4. What's your prior knowledge (if any) about the author?

_____

5. Is a trombone used more in a band or orchestra?

_____

Mini Lesson 303: PAIR Listening–Anticipating

How can learning this help you? What do you anticipate learning about the topic? After skimming through the title, introduction, and first part of this literature, what are your expectations? If this is expository (nonfiction), you may wish to skim through the beginning and ending of the passage, any bolded words and phrases, and any illustrations and their captions.

LISTENING AND ANTICIPATING

What are your predictions about the literature?

What questions do you want/need to find answers to in this literature?

How will you best find those answers?

ML 303 Student Activity: PAIR Listening–Anticipating

MINI LESSONS 303-   REFERENCE "PEEKING AT THE CHRISTMAS TROMBONE" ON PAGE 402.

After hearing the title and introduction, what are your expectations?

What are two predictions about the literature?

1. _____

2. _____

What two questions do you want/need to find answers to in this literature?

3. _____

4. _____

5. How will you best find those answers?

_____

_____

(CONTINUED NEXT PAGE)

Peeking at the Christmas Trombone

My family was quite musical, and in sixth grade, I started playing the trombone. I even played in the seventh-grade band. Boy, did I ever think I was a bigs hot? The problem was that I was using my dad's old beat-up trombone, and I was embarrassed.

Although I knew my parents were having a tough year financially that year, I was really hoping for a new trombone for Christmas. The week before Christmas I did my usual thing; pretended to be sick for a day. After everyone was gone, I systematically went through all of my parents' usual hiding places for Christmas gifts. Nothing. Then I happened to glance on the other side of my parents' bed, and there was an old beat-up trombone case with a broken handle. I was so disappointed that I nearly didn't even open the case. However, I finally did, and there, in a beautiful interior of blue velour, rested a gorgeous Bach Stradivarius trombone! (I had heard of Stradivarius violins, but I didn't know at the time that Bach Stradivarius trombones were supposed to be the best trombones in the world.)

I wept, and I even knelt down and prayed, giving thanks to God. It was the most wonderful present I had ever received, and it was my companion through high school and junior college, and years later my son played it until he was sixteen and bought his own trombone.

There was only one problem, and it was a big one; it was the hardest thing to act surprised on Christmas. I decided then and there to never peek into gifts again, and I never have. It ruins the surprise.

THERE WILL BE A QUIZ ON "PEEKING AT THE CHRISTMAS TROMBONE."

Mini Lesson 304: PAIR Listening–Inputting

How can learning this help you? What are you trying to input (comprehend from reading, listening, or viewing) this literature?

LISTENING AND INPUTTING

Check the correctness of your predictions.

Try to find the answers to your questions.

Pay special attention to headings, bolded words, topic sentences, etc.

Take notes.

Make inferences. (Make educated guesses from hints in the text.)

Look for text organization patterns. See if the text pattern is chronological, cause/cause effect, compare/contrast, description, problem/solution, question/answer.

Make connections. Connect your text with yourself, your learning, and your world.

Monitor your comprehension. Realize when you don't understand something or when you are distracted.

ML 304 Student Activity: PAIR Listening–Inputting

As you read/hear/view "Peeking at the Christmas Trombone," answer the following:

1. Check the correctness of your predictions.

2. Try to find the answers to your questions.

3. Take notes.

4. Look for text organization patterns. See if the text pattern is chronological, cause/effect, compare/contrast, description, problem/solution, question/answer, etc.

5. Make connections. Keep connecting your text with yourself, your learning, and your world.

NAME _____   Language Arts Mini Lessons

Mini Lesson 305: PAIR Listening–Relating

How can learning this help you? How can you relate this literature you have just read to your own life and learning?

LISTENING AND RELATING

General Comprehension Tips:

    Relate all of your new knowledge, opinions, and feelings to your prior understanding of the topic.

    Check the correctness of your predictions you wrote before reading.

    See if you found the answers to your questions you wrote before reading.

    Summarize what you just read.

    Find the main idea. Write it in a single sentence.

ML 305 Student Activity: PAIR Listening–Relating

1. Check the correctness of your predictions you wrote before reading.

2. See if you found the answers to your questions you wrote before reading.

3. Summarize what you just heard in 30 words or less.

_____

_____

_____

_____

4. Find the main idea. Write it in a single sentence.

_____

5. What lesson can you take from this reading and use in your own life and world?

_____

Chapter Seventeen: Citizenship

Why is this chapter important for you? Why include comments about citizenship in a language arts sourcebook? Citizenship is the key to our relationships between ourselves and other people, and it combines with self-discipline to help us develop and use our talents correctly.

The Lessons

Chapter Seventeen: Citizenship	398
Mini Lesson 306: Citizenship and Behavior	399
Mini Lesson 307: The Golden Rule	400
Mini Lesson 308: The Three R's	401
Mini Lesson 309: Combine the Golden Rule and Three R's	402
Mini Lesson 310: Participating in Groups	403
Mini Lesson 311: Outline a Fictitious Situation	404

Mini Lesson 306: Citizenship and Behavior

How can learning this help you? The better you treat your teachers and classmates, the better they are likely to treat you. However, it's also good to look ahead a few years. It is said that of all the employees who have been fired from their jobs, only 20% of them were fired because of their inability to do the work; 80% of them were fired because they couldn't get along with their fellow employees and/or supervisors. It's best to learn how to get along and contribute now before your job is on the line. Also, statistics show that almost 50 percent of all marriages end in divorce. The better we learn to use the following brief principles, the better we will probably get along with people, both now and in the future.

ML 306 Student Activity: Citizenship and Behavior

1. What is the key to our relationships between other people and ourselves? _____

2. What percent of people get fired because they can't get along with their bosses or co-workers? ____

3. What percent of marriages end in divorce? _____

4. The Golden Rule states, "Do unto others _____ you would have them do unto you."

5. That means that we should do the right things for the _____ reasons.

NAME _____   Language Arts Mini Lessons

Mini Lesson 307: The Golden Rule

How can learning this help you? Try to get along with others now and throughout your life. Choose the right and stay on the path of service and goodwill.

STAY ON THE PATH

Follow the Age-old Golden Rule

Do unto others as you would have them do unto you.

That means you should do the right things for the right reasons.

It's not, "Do unto others *before* they do (bad things) unto you."

It's not, "Do unto others *so* they do (good things) unto you."

It is, "Do unto others *as* you would have them do unto you."

You should do the right things for the right reasons.

Or follow this wise saying:

"Life isn't fair, but you must be."

John Huntsman Sr., billionaire businessman and philanthropist

ML 307 Student Activity: The Golden Rule

Write down five ways you will try to get along with others now and five ways you will try to get along with others as an adult. You may wish to base your ideas on The Golden Rule or some other way.

1. _____

2. _____

3. _____

4. _____

5. _____

Get into a group of 2 to 4 students and compare your answers. Feel free to change or add to your own answers as you listen to the other people in your group.

Mini Lesson 308: The Three R's

How can learning this help you? Learning and following the Three R's of Good Citizenship (respect, responsibility, and resourcefulness) will help you to not only get along with people but to become a responsible, successful citizen, whether tomorrow or twenty years from now. They are the fundamental points upon which people successfully function in life and society.

THESE PRINCIPLES WILL HELP YOU DEVELOP INTO A GOOD CITIZEN

Respect yourself, your teacher, and your classmates—both as people and as fellow learners. Respect their property as well. Let the teacher teach and allow the other students and yourself to have the opportunity to learn. Just as working within the structure of an athletic team is more important than individual athletic ability, working within the structure of a class is more important than individual academic ability. Respect for yourself, your teacher, and your fellow students is a big key to that.

Be responsible to learn what you are supposed to. You have probably heard the old adage, "You can lead a horse to water, but you can't make it drink" That certainly applies to your learning. Each person has a different amount of ability, whether it's in a classroom, a ball field, or a band room. It is up to you to use your ability to learn as much of the skills and knowledge as you personally are able to. You are the one who is responsible for you.

There is more to GPA than academic intelligence. Everyone has subjects, teachers, and assignments that are harder for them than for others. Those who do the best are those who are resourceful and responsible enough to keep trying with those subjects, teachers, and assignments that are hardest for them. Those who have the highest GPAs are those who in the future will most likely try hardest when parts of their jobs or their marriages become hard. They're the ones who will most likely be the most resourceful and responsible to find solutions to the future problems they encounter.

Be resourceful. Life is about solving the problems we encounter. Some claim that statistically, the best predictor of a person's success in life is their high school grade point average. Admittedly, there are numerous exceptions to this—both of those who have done much better and those who have done much worse than their GPA predicted. Also, this seems to favor those who do the best in academics; however, the world is also full of intelligent failures.

ML 308 Student Activity: The Three R's

What are the "Three R's of Good Citizenship?

1. _____ 2. _____

3. _____

4. Which is more important, the ability to work well with a team/group or individual ability? _____

5. What may be the best predictor of a person's success in life? _____

Mini Lesson 309: Combine the Golden Rule and Three R's

How can learning this help you? Take what you wrote about using The Golden Rule in the previous lesson and combine it with what you just learned about respect, responsibility, and resourcefulness to construct a plan for achieving your goals and getting along at home, at school, and with your friends this year.

CREATE A PLAN

ML 309 Student Activity: Combine the Golden Rule and Three R's

1. State what general type of work you may want to do for 40 years and what you need to do to prepare for it and get the job.

_____

_____

2. Construct a plan for achieving your goals.

_____

_____

3. Use The Golden Rule and the Three R's to describe the type of future relationships you want to have.

_____

_____

4-5. Write down at least two things that you think make a successful relationship and state how you will try to achieve them.

_____

_____

_____

_____

Mini Lesson 310: Participating in Groups

How can learning this help you? There are very few jobs in this world that require people to sit alone all day long without interacting. America has changed from a manufacturing society to an information and service society. That means we must learn to work in groups and collaborate with other people to solve problems and accomplish goals. Remember that much of your life will be spent contributing to a group effort, whether at work, in a marriage, or on some committee. The best rule is to follow The Golden Rule. Here are some simple ways to break that down.

WORKING WITH GROUPS CAN HELP YOUR WRITING

Respect other people and their ideas. Be positive.

Encourage quieter group members to participate. Like the saying, "Still water runs deep," some of the quietest people are often some of the most intelligent and creative.

In group work, participate appropriately.

Make sure you don't dominate the discussions. No one wants to hear someone go on without giving others their fair share of time.

Don't sit back and say nothing. If you don't have any ideas, it's your responsibility to get some to share. That's part of being resourceful.

Help keep your group on-task.

Carry your share of the workload.

Make sure you get your work done by the appropriate deadlines.

ML 310 Student Activity: Participating in Groups

Fill in the blanks for these keys to being a successful group member.

1. _____ other people and their ideas

2. Encourage quieter group members to _____.

3. Make sure you don't _____ the discussions.

4. Help keep your group on- _____.

5. Make sure you get your part of the work done by the appropriate _____.

Mini Lesson 311: Outline a Fictitious Situation

How can learning this help you? Role-playing a fictitious character can help us understand good and bad traits without offending anyone.

PRETEND AGAIN THROUGH ROLE-PLAYING

ML 311 Student Activity: Outline a Ficticious Situation

1. Based on the group (5 students) participation suggestions in Mini Lesson 310, create an outline of a fictitious situation about a classroom group of five students that is not functioning as it should. Include five characters, each with one of the following traits.

    Take charge _____

    Quiet, Intelligent _____

    Negative _____

    Self-centered _____

    Stick to topic _____

2. Make five slips of paper that have the above traits.

3. Each of the 5 people should pretend to have that trait in a skit.

4. After the skit, observers should discuss ways to resolve the problems in that group so that it can start functioning more effectively.

5. Discuss ways to resolve the problems in that group.

Appendix

Each separate chart or exercise refers to the chapter and Mini Lesson number in the book.

Chapter One: Study Skills

ML6: Reference Materials

NAME	URL
All Sides/Wikipedia	allsides.com
Google Scholar	scholar.google.com
History	history.com
Internet Archive	archive.org
Internet Public Library	pl.org

Mini Lesson 8: Media

Mini Lesson 10: Summary of Reference Skills

Call Numbers	Subjects	Focus
001-099	Generalities	Prequel to the Dewey Decimal System
100-199	Philosophy	Who am I?
200-299	Religion	Who made me?
300-399	Social Science	Who's the guy in the next cave?
400-499	Languages	How do I talk to that guy?
500-599	Natural Science	Let's talk about the world we see.
600-699	Applied Science	Now, let's make stuff out of what we see.
700-799	Arts and Recreation	Now, let's have some fun.
800-899	Literature	Let's tell our children how wonderful we are.
900-999	Geography and History	Let's tell our future children how wonderful we were.

Chapter Two: Speed Reading

Reference Book	Call Number	Title	Topic	Page
Encyclopedia				
Specialized Encyclopedia				
Atlas				
Almanac/Yearbook				
Dictionary				

Mini Lesson 14: Speed reading Practice Drills Part 1
Focus on one of these three principles.
Each time you do a speed reading drill:

- Pace. Use a pacer to force yourself to read quickly.
- Chunk. See groups of words, not just single words.
- Don't sub-vocalize. This is moving your tongue and/or lips as you read.

One-Minute Drill

This drill is meant to show you how fast you read for a short amount of time.

- Set a timer and read for one minute.
- Start at the top of a page.
- Read as quickly as you can until the timer goes off.

Reading Rate

Calculate your reading rate.

- Count the number of words in three normal lines. Example: 34 words.
- Divide those by three to get the average words per line (WPL). Example: 34 words divided by 3 lines equals 11 rounded.
- Count the number of lines you read. Example: 36 lines. Remember the number of lines in a complete page or column, then if you read more than that the next time, you don't have to count the lines in that page or column again.
- Multiply the WPL by the number of lines: 11 times 34 equals 374 words.
- Your reading rate is 374 words per minute (WPM).

Mini Lesson 15: Speed reading Practice Drills Part 2
Three-Minute Drill

- Set a timer and read for three minutes.
- Start at the top of a page.
- Read as quickly as you can until the timer goes off.
- Calculate your reading rate. Do this the same way as the One-Minute Drill.

- Count the number of words in 3 normal lines. Example: 32 words divided by 3 minutes equals 11 rounded.
- Count the number of lines you read: Example: 82 lines. If you read over one page or column, remember the number of lines on that complete page or column, then you won't have to re-count any complete pages.
- Multiply the WPL by the number of lines, or 11 times 82 equals 962 words.
- Divide by 3 to get your WPM or 962 divided by 3 equals 321 WPM.
- Discuss your experience doing the Three-Minute Drill with your partner.

Mini Lesson 16: Speed-Read an Entire Passage
Three-Times One-Minute Drill: First Reading Rate

- Set the timer for one minute.
- Start at the top of a page.
- Read as fast as you can until the timer goes off after one minute.
- Calculate your reading rate.
- Count the number of words in three typical lines: Example: 29 words.
- Divide 29 by 3 to get the average WPL. Example: 29 words divided by 3 equals 10 rounded.
- Count the number of lines you read. Example: 34 lines. If you read over one page or column, remember the number of lines on that complete page or column, then you won't have to re-count any complete pages.
- Multiply the number of WPL by the number of lines to get your WPM. Example: 10 times 34 equals 340 WPM.

Second Reading Rate

For the second timing, start at the same place you did the first time. See if you can read at least 50 percent farther than you did the first time.

- Set the timer for one minute.
- Read as fast as you can until the timer goes off.
- Calculate your WPM again.

Third Reading Rate

For the third and last time, start at the same place you did the first time. See if you can read at least 100 percent farther than you did the first time.

- Set the timer for one minute.
- Read as fast as you can until the timer goes off.
- Calculate your WPM.
- Discuss your speed reading experience in groups of 3 to 5 or else with the whole class.

Mini Lesson 20: Pushing the Limits of Speed reading
One last drill; see how fast you can go

- Set the timer so you can see how long it takes you to read the entire passage.

- Read the passage.
- When you finish the passage, write down the number of seconds, or minutes and seconds, it took you to read.
- Calculate your WPM by taking the total number of words in the passage by figuring the WPL, then words per page (WPP), then pages per passage (PPP).
- Suppose the passage you read is 2780 words long.
- Divide the total seconds into the total words you read in the passage. Carry the divider to the nearest hundredth.
- Suppose it took you 7 minutes and 40 seconds—or 60 seconds times 7 minutes equals 420 seconds. Add the 40 additional seconds to the 420 seconds, and it took you 460 total seconds.
- Divide 2780 words by those 460 seconds which equals 6.04.
- Multiply your answer by 60 (for 60 seconds) or 6.04 times 60 equals 363 WPM. You would have averaged 363 WPM while reading the whole passage.
- Get into a small group and discuss it.

Speed Reading Practice Chart

Date	Speed	Skill(s) Practiced Chunk, Pacer, Do Not-Sub-Vocalize	Text (Name)	Type of Text Narrative or Expository	Response

Chapter Three: Writing Process Pre-Writing

Mini Lesson 26: Creating a Narrative Outline

Fill this out to organize your narrative.

Protagonist. Start with the main character or protagonist. You must care about your protagonist. That will help you write about them so your readers will also care.

Triggering Event (upsetting incident). This sends the protagonist on a journey or a quest.

Obstacles. Throughout the journey, there will be obstacles. Readers, especially kids, like "and suddenly . . ." parts, or page-turners.

Choices. The protagonist will need to make crucial choices that will affect the outcome of his journey or quest.

Gains and Losses. The protagonist will acquire things like wisdom, and they will suffer disappointments.

Catastrophic Event. There will be a catastrophic event in which the outcome seems extremely important.

Change. When the protagonist arrives at home or to his destination, it has changed, as has the protagonist. Change is the central ingredient of each story.

Mini Lesson 26: More on Creating a Narrative Outline
Characters and Setting

Fill in the blanks below for an outline of one of your narrative topics. Write 20 words or less, and use incomplete sentences.

Characters

- Protagonist (hero)
- Antagonist (villain)
- Protagonist's most admirable trait

Setting

- Where it happens
- When it happens

Plot

- Beginning balance:
- Upsetting incident
- Rising action
- Climax
- Resolution (optional)

Mini Lesson 29: Creating a Web

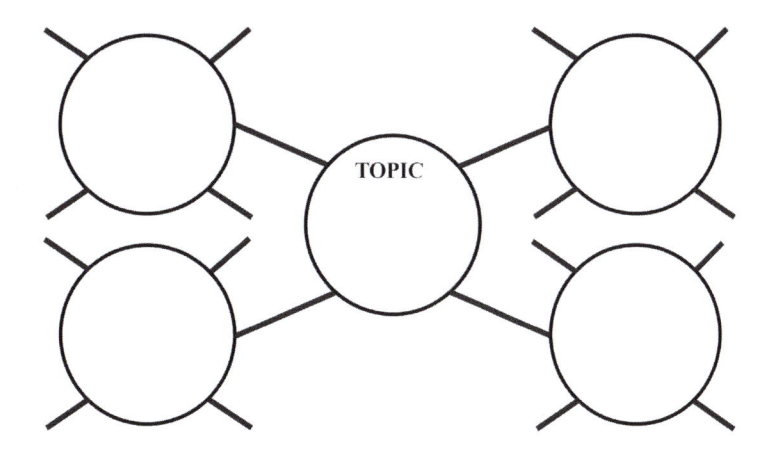

Mini Lesson 37: Proofreader Marks
Proofreader Marks Chart 1

Purpose	Symbol	Example
Insert a comma, semi-colon, or colon	/ , \: / ; \: / : \	Orlando Florida
Insert a hyphen or a dash	/ - \: / — \	one half
Insert parenthesis	( )	prior experience if any
Insert a period	/ . \	Dr
Insert a question mark or exclamation point	/ ? \: / ! \	Did you win
Insert a word	That a book.	That is a book.
Insert an apostrophe or quotation marks	/ ' \: / " \	Jills
Delete	noisy noisy	noisy
Replace	It's loud.	It is loud.
Transpose letters, words, and groups of words	Build the tall shed.	Build the shed tall.
Capitalize a letter	yellowstone	Yellowstone
Make a capital letter lowercase	Yellow bird	yellow bird
Close up space	horse shoe	horseshoe
Use italics	bumblebee	bumblebee

Proofreader Marks Chart 2

Operational Signs Symbol	Usage	Typographical Signs Symbol	Usage
⌒ (delete loop)	Delete	ital	Set in italic type
⌒ (close up)	Close up; delete space	rom	Set in Roman type
⌒ (delete and close up)	Delete and close up (use only when deleting a word)	bf	Set in boldface type
stet	Let it stand	lc	Set in lowercase
eq #	Make space between words equal; make lines between words	caps	Set in capital letters
∽	Trade consecutive words	sc	Set in small caps
ls	Letterspace	wf	Wrong font; change to correct font
¶	Begin new paragraph	X	Check type image; remove blemish
□	Indent type one em from left or right	∨	Insert here or make superscript
]	Move right	∧	Insert here or make subscript
			Punctuation Marks
[	Move left	∧	Insert comma
] [	Move center	∨' ∨'	Insert apostrophe or single quotation mark
⌐¬	Move up	∨" ∨"	Insert quotation marks
⌊⌋	Move down	○	Insert period
fl	Flush left	Set ?	Insert question mark
fr	Flush right	;/	Insert semicolon
=	Straighten type; align horizontally	:/	Insert colon
‖	Align vertically	=	Insert hyphen
tr	Transpose	M	Insert em dash
sp	Spell out	N	Insert en dash
#	Insert space	(|)	Insert parentheses

Chapter Four: The Six Traits of Writing

Mini Lesson 45: Six Traits of Writing

Trait 1: Idea Development
Trait 2: Organization
Trait 3: Voice
Trait 4: Word Choice
Trait 5: Sentence Fluency
Trait 6: Writing Conventions and Layout

Vicki Spandel's Method for Quick Evaluation

Ms. Spandel has been a leader in the Six Traits of Writing movement.

According to Ms. Spandel, you can efficiently evaluate a two-page paper in about three minutes by using this method.

Above Average = 4   Average = 3   Inadequate = 1

1. _____/5 Idea Development

   Is there a main idea?

   How is the quality of the details?

   How well is the paper supported/developed?

2. _____/5 Organization

   Is there a lead?

   Is there a road map?

   Is there an ending?

3. _____/5 Voice

   Would I read the paper aloud?

   Would the intended audience probably find it interesting?

4. _____/5 Word Choice

   How many strong words and phrases are there?

5. _____/5 Sentence Fluency

   How many different sentence beginnings are there?

6. _____/5 Conventions

Suggestions to improve the first four traits of a paper
Develop your idea

- Tell your readers something they don't know.
- Make sure your writing makes sense to others.
- Watch for differences between general and specific details.
- Study your topic from several different angles and points of view. That allows you to be knowledgeable (credible) about the topic and also gives you a broad background from which to choose, organize, and draw information.
- In an argumentative paper, choose an issue with a fairly strong counterargument that you feel you can refute.
- Eliminate redundant (unneeded, overused) information.
- Use questions to clarify and expand the main idea.

Organization

- Exposition: an introduction to the situation, as well as who the main characters are and how they got to be the way they are at the story's start.
- Beginning balance: life is bearable, but it foreshadows future trouble.
- Upsetting incident: life is no longer bearable. The protagonist (hero) tries to restore the beginning balance. The antagonist tries to permanently destroy it.
- Climax: the protagonist wins or loses.
- Resolution: tie up any loose ends. This is optional and only used part of the time.

Editing process; use the editing and proofreading symbols

- Read your piece concentrating on how well your paragraphs are developed.
- Study your piece for how complete your sentences are.
- Read your piece focusing on how much variety your sentence beginnings and lengths are.
- Read your piece again concentrating on your errors in grammar usage.
- Review your piece looking for punctuation errors.
- Study your piece concentrating on finding any spelling errors.
- Read your piece one last time focusing on your capitalization errors.

Proofreading process; use the editing and proofreading symbols

- Get into groups of three or four.
- Pass your paper to your left.
- Proofread the paper given to you according to the principles of revision. Purposely skip any editing problems you see.
- Pass the paper you just proofread for revision left again.
- Take the paper from the student on your right and proofread it according to the principles of editing.
- After each paper has been proofread for both revision and editing, take your own paperback and study the comments made. See which ones you agree with and which ones you don't.
- Thank the students who proofread your paper. Ask them to answer any questions you have.
- Even though you will undoubtedly disagree with some of their comments, don't discuss those with them unless you need clarification.

Expository or Argumentative Writing Outline

- Have a strong introduction.
- Catch the reader's interest.
- Write a thesis statement. This tells us your stand on the issue.
- Explain your points in the body of your essay. Give at least three points. Support each point with logic (reasoning, fact, or statistic) and/or emotion (story).
- Make a convincing conclusion.
- Restate your points.
- Give a final convincing fact or story.
- In an argumentative essay, request your readers to help make your plan work.
- Follow either the Informative or Argumentative Outline form in the Appendix.

Introduction

- Choose an entertainer or athlete and tell us why they are so great.
- Catch our interest:
- Thesis statement:

Body

- Explain your points; first point:; second point; third point

Conclusion

- Summarize final point; call to action for argumentative; purpose of the introduction; purpose of the conclusion

NARRATIVE OR STORY WRITING OUTLINE

- Remember there must be two parties trying to beat each other in the story.
- Choose your protagonist (hero) and antagonist (villain).
- Give the protagonist at least one admirable quality (courage, honesty, strength, wisdom, loyalty, beauty, etc.) that the reader can respect about them.
- Show the quality; don't just tell about it.
- Remember, the more the reader admires the protagonist, the more they care about them. The more they care about the protagonist, the more they care about what happens to them. The more they care about what happens to the protagonist, the more they care about the story.

Characters and Setting
Characters

- Protagonist (hero)
- Antagonist (villain)
- Protagonist's most admirable trait

Setting

- Where it happens
- When it happens

Plot

- Beginning balance
- Upsetting incident
- Rising action
- Climax
- Resolution (optional)

Narrative Six Trait Standards

1. Idea Development

- Choosing the Idea
- Have I shown the narrator's and/or the protagonist's involvement in the story?
- Is it as original and interesting as I can make it to my audience?
- Developing the idea
- Is the story focused? Does it stick to the main storyline?
- Have I added all the important details needed without adding unnecessary ones?
- Have I made it believable for the type of narrative writing I'm using?

2. Organization

- What? Have I covered the what (plot) parts clearly?
- What is the exposition? Things move from bearable to unbearable.
- What is the rising action? The struggle between restoring the beginning balance and destroying it.
- What is the climax? (The point when either the protagonist or antagonist wins.) Have I made it important to the protagonist to win this and restore the beginning balance?
- What is the change in the protagonist?
- What is the resolution? (Are all of the loose ends tied up and resolved?)
- Have I covered the other necessary parts of the Five W's plus How clearly?

    1. How does this happen?
    2. When does this happen?
    3. Where does this happen?
    4. Why does this happen?

3. Voice

- Who? How well have I created the protagonist (hero)? The more the readers care about the protagonist and their friends, the more they care about what happens in the story.
- Have I made it clear who the protagonist (hero) is?
- Have I clearly shown what their most admirable trait is? (Like honest, brave, etc.)
- Have I clearly shown the protagonist's feelings and thoughts?

    Example: "Terrified, I slowly turned and looked behind me."
    Example: "She decided that the only way to get Dan's attention was to . . ."

- Have I followed the advice of "show, don't tell?" Have I just come out and said, "Luke was brave," or have I shown the readers he was brave by describing something he did or said, or by telling what someone else said about him.
- Have I shown how the protagonist changes or grows during the story?
- Have I made it clear who/what the antagonist (villain) is?
- Have I adequately shown the antagonist's needs/desires?
- Have I developed a strong rising action between the protagonist and antagonist that is important for each of them to win?

4. Word Choice

- Have I shown key parts, not just described them?
  Good: Jared took a bite of the juicy peach.
  Better: As Jared bit deeply into the ripe peach, he felt its sweet, rich juice run down his throat.
- Imagery
  Have I helped my readers imagine what I've written? Does my imagery develop the characters, further the plot, and/or create the feelings and responses I desire?
- Sense Imagery (see, hear, feel, taste, touch)
- Emotional Imagery (joy, fear, sadness, anger, excitement, etc.)
  Strong, specific words; use strong, specific words (especially verbs and nouns)

5. Sentence Fluency

- Sentence Variety
    Example: The old man sat down. The bench creaked beneath his weight. The bench was also old.
- Sentences vary in length
- Sentences read smoothly when read aloud

6. Writing Conventions

- Correct grammar usage
- Punctuation correct
- Spelling or punctuation errors

Chapter Ten: PAIR Reading Comprehension

PAIR Comprehension Forms: Expository Writing

Prior Understanding

- What's my prior knowledge about the topic?
- What's my own prior experience (if any) with the topic?
- What's my prior knowledge (if any) about the author?

Anticipating

- After skimming through the first (title, first paragraph, bold words, illustrations, and last paragraph) of this literature, what are my expectations?
- What are my predictions about what I'll learn?
- What questions do I want/need to find answers to in this literature?

Inputting

- What am I inputting (learning from reading, listening, or viewing) from this literature?
- Who is this about?
- When does this happen? (Year, season, time of day, etc.)
- Where does this happen?
- What happens? (Main Idea)
- How does this happen? (Details)

Relating

- Why does this happen?
- What (if anything) would I do differently, if I could change something?
- What (if anything) is the theme, or author's message about life and/or people?
- What can I relate to my own life and learning from this literature?

PAIR COMPREHENSION FORM: NARRATIVE—IMAGERY

Sense imagery that you want your readers to observe: hear, touch, smell, taste

Emotional imagery that you want your protagonist to feel in your story: happiness, excitement, fear, anxiety, anger, other

REP Process (Revising-Editing-Proofreading Process)

Revising Process: give suggestions of how to improve the first four traits of a paper

- Here are some examples of what to revise, according to the first four traits.
- Check your overall idea and content, as well as its development.
- Make sure your organization is showcasing your idea and content.
- Evaluate your piece for how strong your voice (your opinions, thoughts, and feelings) is.
- Re-read your piece, concentrating on strong, specific words and imagery. Especially assess your verbs. Use active, specific ones.
- Check variety in sentence beginnings and lengths.

Editing Process: use the editing, or proofreading, symbols

- Read your piece concentrating on how well your paragraphs are developed.
- Study your piece for how complete your sentences are.
- Read your piece focusing on how much variety your sentence beginnings and lengths are.
- Read your piece again concentrating on your errors in grammar usage.
- Review your piece looking for punctuation errors.
- Study your piece concentrating on finding any spelling errors.
- Read your piece one last time focusing on your capitalization errors.

Proofreading process: use the editing, or proofreading, symbols

- Get into groups of three or four. Pass your paper to your left.
- Proofread the paper given to you according to the principles of revision. Purposely skip any editing problems you see.
- Pass the paper you just proofread for revision left again.
- Take the paper from the student on your right and proofread it according to the principles of editing.
- After each paper has been proofread for both revision and editing, take your own paperback and study the comments made. See which ones you agree with and which ones you don't.
- Thank the students who proofread your paper. Ask them to answer any questions you have.
- Even though you will undoubtedly disagree with some of their comments, don't discuss those with them unless you need clarification.

Chapter Eleven: Contest Writing

Mini Lesson 111: Write an Essay Outline

Essay Outline

- If you learn to craft your essay around an outline like this example below, your writing will be more organized and clear.

Introduction

- Catch the reader's interest.
- Thesis statement: include a measurable objective in your thesis statement. This is the heart of the essay. Keep referring back to it.
- Briefly acknowledge counterarguments.
- Minimize the counterarguments

Body: explain your points

- First point
- Second point
- Third point

Conclusion: convince the reader

- Summarize
- Final statement
- Call to action for an argumentative essay

Works Cited

Brinnin, John Malcolm. Elements of Literature. Holt, Rinehart, Winston, Course Two, p. 341.

Davis, Donald. Telling Your Own Stories. August House Publishers, Inc. 1993.

Gallagher, Kelly. Write Like This. Stenhouse Publishers. 2011. p. 12.

Graves. Donald. Creator of The Writing Process. p. 70.

Lake, Suzan. Utah Teachers of English and Language Arts Conference (UTELA). Salt Lake City, Utah.1997.

Lowry, Lois. Writers' Conference in Salt Lake City, Utah. 2003.

MLA Handbook. 8th ed., The Modern Language Association of America. 1977.

Publication Manual of the American Psychological Association. 7th ed., The American Psychological Association. 2020.

Spandel, Vicki. Six Traits of Writing. Workshop for Nebo School District. Springville, Utah. 2000.

Surrell, Jason. Screenplay by Disney. Disney Editions. p. 204.

Table of Contents for HTML

For Educators: *How to Use This* **Book**	*iii*
About the *Author*	*iv*
Acknowledgments	*v*
Chapter One: *Study Skills*	*1*
Mini Lesson *1: Note-Taking*	*2*
Mini Lesson *2: Verbal and Non-Verbal Signs*	*3*
Mini Lesson *3: Textbooks and Other Study Material*	*4*
Mini Lesson *4: Test-Taking*	*5*
Mini Lesson *5: Lowering Test Anxiety*	*6*
Mini Lesson *6: Library Reference Skills*	*7*
Mini Lesson *7: Reference Materials*	*8*
Mini Lesson *8: Media*	*9*
Mini Lesson *9: Media Reference Skills*	*10*
Mini Lesson *10: Summary of Reference Skills*	*11*
Chapter Two: *Speed Reading*	*12*
Mini Lesson *11: Speed Reading*	*13*
Mini Lesson *12: Speed Reading Skills*	*14*
Mini Lesson *13: Practice Speed Reading*	*15*
Mini Lesson *14: Speed Reading Drills Part 1*	*16*
Mini Lesson *15: Speed Reading Drills Part 2*	*17*
Mini Lesson *16: Speed Read an Entire Passage*	*18*
Mini Lesson *17: Pushing the Limits Speed Reading*	*20*
Mini Lesson *18: Pacing*	*21*
Mini Lesson *19: Chunking*	*22*
Mini Lesson *20: Conquering Sub-Vocalization*	*23*
Chapter Three: *Writing Process / Pre-Writing*	*24*
Mini Lesson *21: Writing Process / Pre-Writing*	*25*
Mini Lesson *22: Interesting Your Readers*	*26*
Mini Lesson *23: Brainstorming for Nonfiction Sources*	*27*
Mini Lesson *24: Brainstorming for Narrative Sources*	*28*
Mini Lesson *25: Nonfiction or Expository Outline*	*29*
Mini Lesson *26: Narrative Outline*	*30*
Mini Lesson *27: Narrative Outline / Characters and Setting*	*32*
Mini Lesson *28: Narrative Outline / Plot*	*33*
Mini Lesson *29: Creating a Web*	*34*
Mini Lesson *30: Drafting / Stream-of-Consciousness*	*35*
Mini Lesson *31: Point of View / Person*	*36*
Mini Lesson *32: Preparing to Draft Your Narrative*	*37*
Mini Lesson *33: Draft Your Narrative*	*38*
Mini Lesson *34: Revise a Draft*	*39*
Mini Lesson *35: Revise Your Own Writing*	*41*
Mini Lesson *36: Do Not Edit Yet*	*42*
Mini Lesson *37: Revise, But Don't Edit*	*43*
Mini Lesson *38: Prepare to Edit*	*45*
Mini Lesson *39: Edit*	*46*
Mini Lesson *40: Proofreading*	*47*
Mini Lesson *41: What Proofreaders Do*	*48*
Mini Lesson *42: Proofreading Symbols*	*50*
Mini Lesson *43: Analyzing Your Proofreading*	*51*
Mini Lesson *44: Practice!*	*52*
Chapter Four: *Six Traits of Writing*	*53*
Mini Lesson *45: Six Traits of Writing*	*54*
Mini Lesson *46: Trait 1 Idea Development*	*55*
Mini Lesson *47: Choose an Idea to Develop*	*56*

Mini Lesson 48: Creating Ideas for Narrative Writing ... 57
Mini Lesson 49: Improving Idea Development ... 58
Mini Lesson 50: Trait 2 Organization / Expository Writing ... 59
Mini Lesson 51: Trait 2 Organization / Narrative Writing ... 60
Mini Lesson 52: Improve Organization ... 61
Mini Lesson 53: Write and Compare ... 62
Mini Lesson 54: Rough Outline ... 63
Mini Lesson 55: Trait 3 Voice and Enthusiasm ... 64
Mini Lesson 56: Trait 3 Voice / Improvement Suggestions ... 65
Mini Lesson 57: Voice in Expository Writing ... 66
Mini Lesson 58: Voice in Argumentative Writing ... 67
Mini Lesson 59: Voice in Narrative Writing ... 68
Mini Lesson 60: Voice in a Story ... 69
Mini Lesson 61: Write a Description ... 72
Mini Lesson 62: Write a Short Fairy Tale ... 73
Mini Lesson 63: Word Choice Using Accurate and Vivid Words ... 74
Mini Lesson 64: Show, Don't Tell ... 76
Mini Lesson 65: Improve Voice and Imagery ... 77
Mini Lesson 66: Expository and Argumentative Word Choice ... 78
Mini Lesson 67: Narrative Word Choice ... 79
Mini Lesson 68: Trait 5 Sentence Fluency ... 80
Mini Lesson 69: Improve Sentence Fluency ... 81
Mini Lesson 70: Sentence Length ... 82
Mini Lesson 71: Trait 6 Writing Conventions ... 83
Chapter Five: Modes and Genres ... 84
Mini Lesson 72: Modes and Genres ... 86
Mini Lesson 73: Experience with Modes and Genres ... 87
Mini Lesson 74: The Descriptive Mode ... 88
Mini Lesson 75: The Importance of Description ... 89
Mini Lesson 76: Creating Description ... 90
Mini Lesson 77: Prose ... 91
Mini Lesson 78: Imagery in Poetry ... 92
Mini Lesson 79: Describing / Images ... 94
Mini Lesson 80: Create a Free Verse Poem ... 96
Mini Lesson 81: Expository Mode ... 97
Mini Lesson 82: Expository / Functional Genre ... 98
Mini Lesson 83: Expository / Informational Genres ... 100
Mini Lesson 84: Argumentative Mode ... 101
Mini Lesson 85: Argumentative Mode Genres ... 102
Mini Lesson 86: Essay Outline ... 103
Mini Lesson 87: Three Parts of an Essay ... 104
Mini Lesson 88: Create an Essay Draft ... 105
Mini Lesson 89: See All Sides of an Issue ... 106
Mini Lesson 90: Narrative Mode ... 107
Mini Lesson 91: Genres in the Narrative Mode ... 108
Mini Lesson 92: Drama ... 109
Mini Lesson 93: Fantasy ... 110
Mini Lesson 94: Folklore ... 111
Mini Lesson 95: Horror ... 112
Mini Lesson 96: Mystery ... 113
Mini Lesson 97: Personal Narrative ... 114
Mini Lesson 98: Poetry ... 115
Mini Lesson 99: Poetry Terms ... 117
Mini Lesson 100: Science Fiction ... 118
Mini Lesson 101: Young Adult Literature ... 119
Mini Lesson 102: Reviewing Narrative Writing Genres ... 120
Mini Lesson 103: Business Mode ... 121
Mini Lesson 104: Block Business Letter Format ... 122
Mini Lesson 105: Business Email Format ... 124
Mini Lesson 106: Friendly Letter Format ... 125
Chapter Six: Contest Writing ... 126
Mini Lesson 107: Why Enter a Contest? ... 128

Mini Lesson *108: Writing Process for a Contest* *129*
Mini Lesson *109: Pre-Writing Introduction* *131*
Mini Lesson *110: Three Main Categories of Contests* *132*
Mini Lesson *111: Essay Outline* *133*
Mini Lesson *112: Trait 1 Ideas* *135*
Mini Lesson *113: Trait 2–Organization / Outline* *136*
Mini Lesson *114: Trait 2 Organization / Plot* *139*
Mini Lesson *115: Poetry Organization* *143*
Mini Lesson *116: Rough Draft* *145*
Mini Lesson *117: Stream-of-Consciousness Writing* *146*
Mini Lesson *118: Rough Draft Review* *147*
Mini Lesson *119: Trait 3 Voice* *148*
Mini Lesson *120: Revising Overall Content* *151*
Mini Lesson *121: Trait 4 Word Choice* *153*
Mini Lesson *122: Editing Paragraphs and Sentences* *156*
Mini Lesson *123: Editing Usage and Punctuation* *158*
Mini Lesson *124: Editing Spelling and Capitalization* *159*
Mini Lesson *125: Editing Rhyme and Rhythm* *160*
Mini Lesson *126: Proofreading* *161*
Mini Lesson *127: Proofreading Each Other's Papers* *162*
Mini Lesson *128: Proofreading Ideas and Organization* *163*
Mini Lesson *129: Proofreading–Voice and Word Choice* *164*
Mini Lesson *130: Proofreading Paragraphs and Sentences* *166*
Mini Lesson *131: Proofreading Usage and Punctuation* *167*
Mini Lesson *132: Proofreading Spelling and Capitalization* *168*
Mini Lesson *133: Trait 5 Sentence Fluency* *169*
Mini Lesson *134: Proofreading Rhyme and Rhythm* *171*
Mini Lesson *135: Word Choice in Poetry* *172*
Mini Lesson *136 Some of the Best Writing Contests* *173*
Chapter Seven: *From Phrases to Paragraphs* *174*
Mini Lesson *137: Sentences and the Sentence Backbone* *176*
Mini Lesson *138: Practice Using the Sentence Backbone* *179*
Mini Lesson *139: Phrases and Clauses* *180*
Mini Lesson *140: Prepositional Phrases* *181*
Mini Lesson *141: Identifying Prepositional Phrases* *183*
Mini Lesson *142: Creating Prepositional Phrases* *184*
Mini Lesson *143: Prepositional Phrases* *185*
Mini Lesson *144: Verbal Phrases* *186*
Mini Lesson *145: Understanding Clauses* *188*
Mini Lesson *146: Dependent Clauses with Commas* *190*
Mini Lesson *147: FANBOYS Conjunctions* *191*
Mini Lesson *148: Types of Complements* *192*
Mini Lesson *149: Reviewing Sentence Parts* *194*
Mini Lesson *150: Practice Sentence Parts* *196*
Mini Lesson *151: Sentences with Errors* *197*
Mini Lesson *152: Sentence Fragments* *198*
Mini Lesson *153: Run-On Sentences* *199*
Mini Lesson *154: Types of Sentences* *200*
Mini Lesson *155: Complex Sentences* *201*
Mini Lesson *156: Compound Sentences* *202*
Mini Lesson *157: Sentence Combining* *203*
Mini Lesson *158: Review Different Sentence Types* *204*
Mini Lesson *159: Subject/Verb Agreement* *206*
Mini Lesson *160: Paragraphs* *208*
Mini Lesson *161: Topic Sentences in Paragraphs* *209*
Mini Lesson *162: Practice Paragraphs* *210*
Mini Lesson *163: Supporting Sentences in Paragraphs* *211*
Mini Lesson *164: Paragraph Principles* *212*
Mini Lesson *165: Sentences in Paragraphs* *213*
Mini Lesson *166: Summary Review for Paragraphs* *214*
Mini Lesson *167: Dialogue Paragraphs* *216*
Mini Lesson *168: Punctuation in Dialogue Paragraphs* *217*

Mini Lesson *169: Focus on Layout* 219
Mini Lesson *170: Improve Your Writing and Layout* 220
Chapter Eight: *Parts of Speech* 221
Mini Lesson *171: Identifying Parts of Speech* 222
Mini Lesson *172: Using Parts of Speech in Sentences*.. 223
Mini Lesson *173: Nouns*... 224
Mini Lesson *174: Pronouns* 226
Mini Lesson *175: Pronoun Contractions*... 228
Mini Lesson *176: Indefinite Pronouns*... 229
Mini Lesson *177: Plural Indefinite Pronouns* 230
Mini Lesson *178: Vague Indefinite Pronouns* 231
Mini Lesson *179: Proper Adjectives*.. 232
Mini Lesson *180: Verbs and Auxiliary Verbs* 233
Mini Lesson *181: Verb Tenses*... 235
Mini Lesson *182: Adverbs*.. 237
Mini Lesson *183: Adverbs and Adverb Contractions*... 238
Mini Lesson *184: Conjunctive Adverbs*.. 240
Mini Lesson *185: Adjectives and Adverbs* 241
Mini Lesson *186: Synonyms and Substitutes for* **Said**.. 242
Mini Lesson *187: Prepositions*... 243
Mini Lesson *188: Preposition or Adverb* 245
Mini Lesson *189: Coordinating and Correlative Conjunctions*.. 246
Mini Lesson *190: Interjections*... 248
Mini Lesson *191: Identifying the Parts of Speech* 249
Mini Lesson *192: Review the Parts of Speech* 250
Mini Lesson *193: Review Pronouns, Nouns, Adjectives, Interjections*... 251
Mini Lesson *194: Review Verbs, Adverbs, Prepositions, Conjunctions*... 252
Chapter Nine: *Writing Mechanics*.. 253
Mini Lesson *195: Capitalization*... 254
Mini Lesson *196: Capitalizing Titles* 255
Mini Lesson *197: Do Not Capitalize* 256
Mini Lesson *198: Practice Capitalization*... 257
Mini Lesson *199: Punctuation Introduction*.. 258
Mini Lesson *200: Commas* 259
Mini Lesson *201: Practice with Commas* 261
Mini Lesson *202: Comma Splices* 262
Mini Lesson *203: Semicolons*.. 264
Mini Lesson *204: Colons*... 266
Mini Lesson *205: End Marks*.. 267
Mini Lesson *206: Apostrophes–Singular, Plural, or Possessive* 268
Mini Lesson *207: Apostrophes/Contractions vs Possessive Pronouns* 270
Mini Lesson *208: Dashes, Commas, and Parentheses* 271
Mini Lesson *209: Hyphens*... 272
Mini Lesson *210: Quotation Marks in Dialogue* 273
Mini Lesson *211: Quotation Marks / Underlining / Italics* 274
Mini Lesson *212: Commas and Periods Review*.. 275
Mini Lesson *213: Punctuation Review*.. 276
Mini Lesson *214: Making Errors on Purpose*.. 277
Chapter Ten: *Literary Elements*... 278
Mini Lesson *215: Characterization*.. 279
Mini Lesson *216: Conflict*.. 280
Mini Lesson *217: Plot Exposition*.. 281
Mini Lesson *218: Plot Rising Action* 282
Mini Lesson *219: Plot Crises*... 283
Mini Lesson *220: Plot Climax and Resolution* 284
Mini Lesson *221: Dialogue and Point of View* 285
Mini Lesson *222: Setting and Imagery*.. 287
Mini Lesson *223: Finding Story Elements* 288
Chapter Eleven: *PAIR and KWL Compared*... 293
Mini Lesson *224: Compare PAIR with KWL* 294
Mini Lesson *225: PAIR Prior Understanding / General Comprehension* 295
Mini Lesson *226: PAIR Anticipating / General Comprehension* 296

Mini Lesson *227: Inputting / General Comprehension* 298
Mini Lesson *228: Relating / General Comprehension* 299
Mini Lesson *229: Prior Understanding in Expository Text* 300
Mini Lesson *230: Anticipating in Expository Text* 302
Mini Lesson *231: Inputting in Expository Text* 303
Mini Lesson *232: Relating in Expository Text* 304
Mini Lesson *233: Prior Understanding in Argumentative Text* 305
Mini Lesson *234: Anticipating in Argumentative Text* 307
Mini Lesson *235: Inputting in Argumentative Text* 308
Mini Lesson *236: Relating in Argumentative Text* 309
Mini Lesson *237: Prior Understanding in Narrative Text* 310
Mini Lesson *238: Anticipating in Narrative Text* 312
Mini Lesson *239: Inputting in Narrative Text* 313
Mini Lesson *240: Relating in Narrative Text* 315
Mini Lesson *241: Comprehension Application* 316
Mini Lesson *242: Text Organization Patterns* 317
Chapter Twelve: *Expanding Your Vocabulary* 320
Mini Lesson *243: Introduction to Spelling* 321
Mini Lesson *244: Spelling Rules and Patterns* 322
Mini Lesson *245: Misspelled Words Due to* **Schwa** 323
Mini Lesson *246: Identify the* **Schwa (ise/ize)** *Sound* 324
Mini Lesson *247: Spelling Review* 325
Mini Lesson *248: Spelling Rules Review* 326
Mini Lesson *249: Reading Vocabulary / Context* 328
Mini Lesson *250: Using Context Clues* 329
Mini Lesson *251: Prefixes* 330
Mini Lesson *252: Prefixes and Suffixes* 331
Mini Lesson *253: Suffixes* 332
Mini Lesson *254: Word Relationships* 334
Chapter Thirteen: *MLA Research Citations* 335
Mini Lesson *255: MLA* 336
Mini Lesson *256: Why You Should Use Citations–MLA* 337
Mini Lesson *257: Works Cited–MLA* 338
Mini Lesson *258: Documentation for Works Cited–MLA* 341
Mini Lesson *259: Plagiarism–MLA* 342
Mini Lesson *260: Quotes–MLA* 343
Mini Lesson *261: Ellipses–MLA* 344
Mini Lesson *262: Citing Common Electronic Sources–MLA* 345
Mini Lesson *263: End-of-Paper Citations–MLA* 346
Chapter Fourteen: *APA Research Citations* 347
Mini Lesson *264: Research and Citations–APA* 348
Mini Lesson *265: Pre-Writing–APA* 349
Mini Lesson *266: Elements Needed for a Title Page–APA* 350
Mini Lesson *267: Proper Format for a Manuscript–APA* 351
Mini Lesson *268: Outline–APA* 352
Mini Lesson *269: Case Rules in Titles–APA* 353
Mini Lesson *270: Author / Date Citations–APA* 354
Mini Lesson *271: Direct Short and Block Quotations–APA* 355
Mini Lesson *272: Reference List Entries–APA* 357
Mini Lesson *273: Reference Author Elements–APA* 358
Mini Lesson *274: Reference, Date, Title, and Source–APA* 359
Mini Lesson *275: Ellipses–APA* 360
Chapter Fifteen: *SAT and ACT Tips* 361
Mini Lesson *276: SAT/ACT* 362
Mini Lesson *277: Types of Reading Questions SAT/ACT* 363
Mini Lesson *278: Types of Writing Questions SAT/ACT* 364
Mini Lesson *279: Theme, Conventions, Audience, Organization* 365
Mini Lesson *280: Guess Questions to Pass the SAT/ACT* 366
Mini Lesson *281: Review Writing Materials to Pass SAT/ ACT* 368
Mini Lesson *282: SAT and ACT Essay Writing* 369
Mini Lesson *283: Pre-Writing Your Essay* 371
Mini Lesson *284: Write Your Rough Draft* 373

Mini Lesson 285: *Revise Using the Writer's Checklist* 374
Chapter Sixteen: *Speaking and Listening* 375
Mini Lesson 286: *Speaking Principles* 376
Mini Lesson 287: *Facial Expressions, Gestures, and Posture* 377
Mini Lesson 288: *Speaking and Presenting Techniques* 378
Mini Lesson 289: *Vocal Techniques* 379
Mini Lesson 290: *Vocal Techniques with the Alphabet* 380
Mini Lesson 291: *Pause for Effect* 382
Mini Lesson 292: *Pausing and Eye Contact* 383
Mini Lesson 293: *Physical Characteristics* 384
Mini Lesson 294: *Voice and Physical Characteristics* 385
Mini Lesson 295: *Mood* 386
Mini Lesson 296: *Poise* 387
Mini Lesson 297: *Involvement and Energy* 388
Mini Lesson 298: *Imagery* 389
Mini Lesson 299: *Presenting Literature Aloud* 390
Mini Lesson 300: *Practice Voice and Character Placement* 391
Mini Lesson 301: *Vary Posture, Character Placement, and Gestures* 392
Mini Lesson 302: *PAIR Listening–Prior Understanding* 393
Mini Lesson 303: *PAIR Listening–Anticipating* 394
Mini Lesson 304: *PAIR Listening–Inputting* 396
Mini Lesson 305: *PAIR Listening–Relating* 397
Chapter Seventeen: *Citizenship* 398
Mini Lesson 306: *Citizenship and Behavior* 399
Mini Lesson 307: *The Golden Rule* 400
Mini Lesson 308: *The Three R's* 401
Mini Lesson 309: *Combine the Golden Rule and Three R's* 402
Mini Lesson 310: *Participating in Groups* 403
Mini Lesson 311: *Outline a Fictitious Situation* 404
Appendix 405
Works Cited 420
Table of *Contents for HTML* 421